B

D1598814

WALKING GEORGE

WALKING GEORGE

THE LIFE OF GEORGE JOHN BETO
AND THE RISE OF THE MODERN
TEXAS PRISON SYSTEM

DAVID M. HORTON AND
GEORGE R. NIELSEN

Number 5 in the North Texas Crime and Criminal Justice Series

University of North Texas Press
Denton, Texas

10 9 8 7 6 5 4 3 2 1

Permissions:
University of North Texas Press
P.O. Box 311336
Denton, TX 76203-1336

The paper used in this book meets the minimum requirements of the American
National Standard for Permanence of Paper for Printed Library Materials,
z39.48.1984. Binding materials have been chosen for durability.

Library of Congress Cataloging-in-Publication Data

Horton, David M.
   Walking George: the life of George John Beto and the rise of the modern Texas
prison system / David M. Horton and George R. Nielsen.
      p. cm. — (North Texas crime and criminal justice series ; no. 5)
Includes bibliographical references and index.
   ISBN-10: 1-57441-199-3 (cloth : alk. paper)
   ISBN-13: 978-1-57441-199-7 (cloth : alk. paper)
   1. Beto, George John, 1916-1991. 2. Texas. Dept. of Corrections—Officials and
employees—Biography. 3. Prisons—Texas—Officials and employees—Biography.
4. Prison administration—Texas—History. 5. College teachers—Texas—Biography.
I. Nielsen, George R. II. Title. III. Title. III.
Series.
HV9468.H77 2005
365'.92—dc22

                              2005008454

Walking George is Number 5 in the North Texas Crime and Criminal Justice Series

Text design by Eric Sawyer of Rose Design

This book is for Marilynn Beto
and her children, Dan, Lynn, Mark, and Beth

Contents

List of Illustrations

Frontispiece: George J. Beto

Begin after page 58

1. Louis Henry Beto
2. Margaret Beto
3. George J. Beto in a soldier's uniform
4. George J. Beto at Concordia College, Milwaukee
5. George J. Beto the "Deerslayer"
6. George J. Beto, President of Concordia College, Austin
7. Beto family in Austin
8. Cartoon from *The Concordia Record*
9. O. B. Ellis
10. H. H. Coffield
11. Governor Price Daniel, George J. Beto, and former Governor Allan Shivers
12. George J. Beto in 1959
13. George J. Beto's installation as President of Concordia Theological Seminary
14. Map of Texas Department of Corrections
15. George J. Beto, Governor John B. Connally, and H. H. Coffield
16. George J. Beto talking to inmates
17. Members of the Texas Board of Corrections
18. George J. Beto in a wheelchair
19. George J. Beto "walking the units"
20. Max Rogers, Jack Kyle, H. H. "Tubby" Sandel, and George J. Beto
21. George J. Beto and Arleigh B. Templeton
22. George J. Beto in front of the Walls Unit
23. Governor Preston Smith, Lieutenant Governor Ben Barnes, former Governor Allan Shivers, H. H. Coffield, and George J. Beto
24. George J. Beto, Marilynn Beto, and Governor Preston Smith
25. George J. Beto with trademark Stetson hat
26. George J. Beto, Distinguished Professor in the College of Criminal Justice
27. The George J. Beto Criminal Justice Center

Acknowledgments

George Beto was a big man who cast a long shadow. It is, therefore, not inconceivable that two mortals were needed to write his biography. George Nielsen, one of the authors, grew up in Thorndale, Texas, a small town about an hour's drive from Austin. His family, typical of many during the Depression and war years, was not poor, but disposable income was scarce and reserved for necessities. Having a bicycle of his own, for example, was not a high priority. Nielsen met George Beto for the first time after a church service at which Beto had been the guest preacher. Nielsen's father, who was the teacher and organist, introduced him to Beto, and in the course of exchanging pleasantries Beto learned of the youngster's plight of not owning a bike. Beto informed him that Concordia students often returned home at the end of the school year leaving bikes on the campus that were no longer in working order, but could be repaired. Beto told young Nielsen he would get him one. Several months later, after hope had been extinguished, a panel truck from Concordia arrived at Thorndale to pick up some food for the students, and true to Beto's word, it dropped off a bicycle. With the help of a brother and a parts catalog, the bike was soon operational and George Nielsen had wheels. In 1946, the bike went with him when, at the age of fourteen, he entered Concordia and Beto became a polestar in his life.

Thirty years later, in 1976, David Horton met Beto shortly after Horton's arrival in Huntsville, Texas, where he planned to study for a doctorate in criminal justice at Sam Houston State University's Institute of Contemporary Corrections and the Behavioral Sciences (now the George J. Beto Criminal Justice Center). While he was in the Institute's library, assessing the range and depth of the collection on historical criminology and penology, he was distracted by someone who had entered. Out of the corner of his eye he caught a glimpse of a six-foot four-inch man dressed in a suit and tie who exuded a commanding presence. Without any doubt it was "Walking George" whose image and reputation was common lore in the world of corrections. Horton had read that Beto possessed more than just a passing familiarity with the dead languages, and that he was known to occasionally toss out a Latin phrase or two in his conversations. Horton, himself, had studied Latin in high school and for six of his undergraduate semesters at Washington State University, so he decided to introduce himself to Beto with the classic greeting that was used in the days of the Caesars. Beto had just taken a book from the shelf when Horton boldly said, *"Salve, magister!"* ("Greetings, professor!"). Beto spun around, stared hard at him for a moment in silence, and then with a sly and bemused grin, responded in his deep voice, *"Salve, discipulus!"* ("Greetings, student!").

In 1998, after having been awarded a research sabbatical by St. Edward's University, Horton began collecting materials and conducting interviews on his own, until 2002, when Nielsen joined forces with him to co-author the study. One author is acquainted with the Lutheran teachings and traditions that were a formative element of Beto's life; the other is a scholar of historical criminology and penology who is familiar with Beto's contributions to the theory and practice of criminal justice. However, just as Beto did not separate his two lives, the authors did not divide their work into two distinct segments, but each encroached on the other's spheres in order to integrate both aspects of Beto's life into a single, unified study.

This biography was not written to honor the man although his life was one of service that fully deserves to be honored. It was written to be instructive, a purpose of which Beto, as a life-long educator, would have approved. Part of his life took place in the context of dramatic growth and change in the Lutheran Church from the time of the Great Depression to the Vietnam War. Because Beto was part of this era and participated in the church's educational system in which he built and preached boldly, his biography is informative on that topic. In a similar manner, his life was intertwined in a dynamic period of the Texas Prison System as it emerged from a time in which the treatment of prisoners bordered on the inhumane to a time when it was one of the most enlightened systems in the free world. Then as a reprise, after being director of the Texas Department of Corrections, he repeated this feat when he expanded his focus from solely on corrections to the young, burgeoning academic discipline of criminal justice and helped to develop a premier program for the international community.

Although he was ordained and retained his name on the clergy roster, Beto rarely preached a sermon for a church service during the last twenty-eight years of his life. He did however, speak at funerals, frequently selecting I Corinthians 4:2 as his text: "It is required in stewards that a man be faithful." A recurrent theme at these events, whether at the graveside of a civil servant or of a servant of the church, was the concept of a faithful servant, the faithful servant, of either church or state, who contributed to uplifting humanity. Yet in each of these instances he could as well have been speaking of his own faithfulness, for that is what his life was, and in that sense his biography also is exemplary and instructive. He was "a horse that stayed hitched."

This study could not have been written without the assistance of many people, and we would like to thank those who helped make it possible. We are genuinely indebted to the family of George Beto, without whose encouragement, support, generosity, and patience this study would not have been possible. George's wife Marilynn and their children, Dan, Mark, and Beth O'Donnell all heartily endorsed the study, and they shared freely of their time, personal family papers, and photographs.

Many of George Beto's former students, friends, and colleagues took time from their busy schedules to grant us personal interviews, speak on the telephone, and send letters and electronic mail that were especially helpful. We owe an enormous debt of gratitude to Rev. Paul Bohot, Dr. Roddy Braun, Dr. Richard Dinda, Waldo Huneke, Dr. Richard Jungkuntz, Dr. Heino Kadai, Rev. James Linderman, Dr. Ray Martens, Rev. Paul Nelson, Dr. Milton Riemer, Margaret E. Scholtz, Henry Sorrel, Curtis Taylor, Fred Viehweg, Charles Wukasch, Dr. David Zersen, and Dr. Ted Zoch.

Deserving a special note of gratitude for their assistance are:

George Beto's brother, Dr. Louis Beto

W. J. "Jim" Estelle, Jr., Director of the Texas Department of
Corrections, 1972–1983

Jack Kyle, former Texas Department of Corrections Warden

Donald Weisenhorn, retired Sam Houston State University Professor of Criminal Justice whose index to the Beto Archives
in the Newton Gresham Library (SHSU), was an invaluable
research tool.

We received valuable research assistance from:

Carol Barrett, Associate Director, Ex-Students' Association,
University of Texas at Austin

Dr. Marty Duchow, Registrar, Concordia University, Mequon,
Wisconsin

Norman W. Holmes, Director of Library Services, Concordia
University, Austin, Texas

Rev. Mark Loest, Assistant Director, Concordia Historical
Institute, St. Louis, Missouri

Linda Lyons, Registrar's Office, University of Texas at Austin

Cheryl S. Patton, Newton Gresham Library, Sam Houston
State University, Huntsville, Texas

and the staffs of the Legislative Reference Library and the
Texas State Archives, Austin, Texas.

Matthew Bunce, Martin Eifert, Dr. Robert Temple Munday, Jen-
nifer L. Petersen, Stephanie Bess Turner, Donald Weisenhorn, and
Stacey Woodall read various versions of the manuscript and provided us with valuable editorial comments and feedback. Undergraduate student research assistants Katherine E. Rich and Ashley L.
Leal gave valuable assistance in many ways, large and small, which
they always rendered in a punctual, efficient, and cheerful manner. A
special note of thanks is due to Donovan Petersen for his sharp mind
and critical eye. Finally, recognition must be given to Karen DeVin-
ney, managing editor of the University of North Texas Press, for her
contributions toward preparing the manuscript for publication.

Chapter 1

THE EARLY YEARS: HYSHAM, MONTANA; NEW ROCKFORD, NORTH DAKOTA; AND LENA, ILLINOIS (1916–1939)

"I love this country," proclaimed George Beto in a 1981 speech. "My grandparents came from the ghettos of Prague, from virtual peonage in East Germany, and from the submarginal farms of the Netherlands. . . . In spite of handicaps—ignorance of the language and culture of this land—they were able to carve out for themselves respectable places on the economic, social, religious, and political horizons of this country."[1]

The East German ancestor he referred to was his grandfather, John Beto, from the province of Pomerania. Pomerania, located on the flat and sandy coastal plain south of the Baltic Sea, went unblessed of fertile soil or mineral wealth. Originally the inhabitants of Pomerania had been Slavic, but in 1772 the area had come under the control of neighboring Prussia, and by the time that John Beto was born, it had been thoroughly Germanized. Although sought after by the Germanic invaders in earlier times, it was not highly regarded as a region vital to German power, nor were its citizens held in high esteem. Otto von Bismarck, the architect of German unification, attempting to underscore the complete insignificance of southeastern Europe, once said that the Balkan area "was not worth the bones of a single Pomeranian grenadier."

The family surname is derived from the town of Bütow (Bytów in Polish), which is situated fifty miles west-southwest of Danzig

(Gdansk). Detailed information about John Beto is limited, but he migrated in the late 1860s, thereby missing the American Civil War, and yet soon enough to avoid becoming cannon fodder for Bismarck's ambitions of a united Germany.

Although John Beto arrived in America without wealth, he soon acquired a combination general store and saloon located in northern Cook County, Illinois, approximately fifteen miles northwest of Chicago's Loop. His property, almost four acres in size, was situated on the southwest corner of what is now the intersection of Dempster Street and Milwaukee Avenue in the town of Niles. In the midst of a large German community and located along a plank road leading to Chicago, John's business thrived, and he provided his family with a comfortable life.

John Beto married Catherine "Kate" Hudna on October 8, 1873. Kate, born on April 30, 1853, in "the ghettos of Prague," then the capital of Bohemia and now of the Czech Republic, immigrated to the United States with her brother when she was eighteen. She arrived in Chicago shortly before the great fire of October 8–9, 1871, which she witnessed in all its horror. Kate had been forced to flee her hotel room in her nightgown in order to escape the flames and was one of 100,000 Chicagoans left homeless.

Both John and Kate were known not only for their outgoing personalities, but also as prominent citizens of the community. After John died in 1909, Kate continued to operate the business with the help of her children until 1926, when she sold it along with the home, and bought a new home in Park Ridge, Illinois. Kate lived as a widow for another twenty-four years and died on March 31, 1933. Both John and Kate are buried in Park Ridge, Illinois.

John and Kate had ten children, four of whom died in infancy. The one child who plays an important role in this story is Louis Henry, born on June 26, 1889, at the family home and business. Few records of Louis' early years are preserved, but clearly documented is his ardent love for golf. In addition to abutting a main artery to Chicago, his home stood within three miles of the Glenview Golf Club. As he came of age Louis not only caddied and learned the game of golf itself, but he excelled in it and won several tournaments in his teenage years.

Louis received his elementary education in the local public and Lutheran parochial schools of Maine Township, and in 1904, at the age of fourteen, he enrolled in Northwestern College, in Watertown, Wisconsin. Northwestern College, a Lutheran institution affiliated with the Wisconsin Synod,[2] was a preparatory school for seminary studies. Patterned after the German *Gymnasium*, it stressed a classical education with a heavy emphasis on languages. Although in Germany study at the *Gymnasium* led directly to the university, in America the four years of secondary education were followed by two years of study on the collegiate level. In 1911 Louis Beto entered Concordia Seminary, in St. Louis, a Lutheran institution affiliated with the Missouri Synod, which at that time was the stronghold of conservative Lutheranism and Lutheran education in the United States. At some point during the course of his study at Concordia Seminary, Louis met Margaret Witsma at a church function and the couple later became engaged to be married. In keeping with the practice endorsed by the seminary, the two postponed their wedding until Louis graduated.[3]

Margaret Witsma was the daughter of George Witsma, Sr., and Wilhelmina Mencken Witsma. George Witsma, Sr., was born on a "submarginal farm in the Netherlands" on July 23, 1845. While still in his teens near the end of the Civil War, he immigrated by himself to the United States. He arrived penniless, unable to speak or read English, and possessed only the equivalent of a rudimentary third-grade education.

Shortly after landing in America, he made his way to St. Louis, Missouri, where he found shelter in a boardinghouse for men near the Union Pacific Train Station. Witsma initially worked as a salesman in Barr's Department Store, a landmark St. Louis haberdashery. But before long, Witsma went into real estate and participated in St. Louis' post-Civil War real estate boom, and as the city prospered and grew, so did Witsma. He married Wilhelmina Mencken, George Beto's only native-born American grandparent. The union produced two children, George, Jr., born August 11, 1894, and

Margaret, the future spouse of Louis Beto, who was born on May 26, 1896.[4]

Ministry of Louis Beto

After three years of study, Louis graduated from Concordia Seminary in June 1914 and was assigned to a small parish in Hysham, Montana.[5] Following his ordination on August 23, Louis made his way overland by train to his parish. The small congregation, composed of German, German-Russian, and Scandinavian immigrants, was not a self-sustaining congregation, but a mission station or mission congregation. A mission congregation, either because of its small size, or because of the poverty of the people, found itself unable to bear the total costs of maintaining a parish. Instead, the church denomination subsidized the mission congregation for whatever amount was necessary. The amount of the subsidy at the time when Pastor Beto traveled west was invariably minimal, and for all practical purposes these Lutheran ministers could well have taken the oath of poverty. Louis knew from the beginning what he was getting himself into but it was an opportunity to minister to the people and to gain experience. Hysham was not necessarily an abiding city.

Hysham began as a refueling and water stop on the Northern Pacific Railroad for trains running on the line from Seattle to Kansas City. Even though the rainfall in the southeastern part of Montana was inadequate for traditional farming methods, the development of dry-farming plus the availability of large tracts of cheap or free land from the railroads or the government, made settlement a reality. Its location on the Yellowstone River also contributed to the growth of the small agricultural town. When Louis arrived in the late summer of 1914 the town, with a population of about one hundred, consisted only of one general store, a post office, a one-room schoolhouse, and about twenty houses. The subsidized mission congregation did not even own a church building so Louis preached to his congregation in the homes of his parishioners or, on occasion, in Hysham's single-room red brick schoolhouse. After obtaining a residence and getting acquainted,

Louis returned to St. Louis to marry Margaret Witsma on November 17, 1914. She was eighteen years old, and the culture shock for the young couple from urban homes must have been immense.[6]

Even though Louis' ministry in Montana was to the Lutheran immigrant farmers in the Hysham vicinity, his parish soon expanded to an area of about two hundred square miles, and included a number of isolated, far-flung pockets of Lutheran farmers and Crow Indians. On a horse named Teddy, Louis faithfully rode a circuit every week that took him through seven mission stations, with such picturesque names as Pease Bottom and Froze-to-Death Creek.

While Louis made the rounds on his weekly preaching circuit, Margaret entertained herself as best she could by playing solitaire and, weather permitting, taking long walks. Away from her family and friends, she was homesick in the little frontier town, and this feeling of isolation was heightened during the extended periods that Louis was away riding the circuit. She cried frequently, and often went down to the Northern Pacific Railroad Depot and stood on the platform as the express train from Seattle to Kansas City sped by, wishing she were on it.[7]

On the bitterly cold Sunday night of January 19, 1916, fourteen months after their marriage, Margaret, with the help of a midwife, gave birth to their first child. Louis had left the previous week on his preaching circuit and returned to find both his wife and a baby boy well and resting at home. The child was baptized George John Beto. The family history preserved in the oral tradition suggests that George very nearly died in his first year from diphtheria, a virulent disease of the upper respiratory system.[8]

Because Pastor Beto had been ordained and installed into a parish, he was eligible for a "call" from any congregation in the Synod. And in 1916 he received a call from a dual subsidized mission parish of New Rockford and Melville, North Dakota, which was searching for a pastor. New Rockford, the location of the parsonage, was a small community in the east-central part of the state. The New Rockford congregation had been established in 1901, and consisted mainly of German Russian immigrants. Although the New Rockford congregation was considered a subsidized mission station unable to financially support a Lutheran minister on its own, the poor, but devout, parishioners cooperatively had constructed a permanent house of worship in 1903. The Betos arrived in New Rockford on December 10, 1916, five weeks before young George's first birthday.[9]

Louis, for the first time, had his own church and pulpit from which to preach. He also rode a small circuit on the Fort Totten Indian Reservation once a week, where he ministered to the Sioux and Chippewa Indians. These treks, while no doubt brutal in winter, were certainly less demanding of his time than those in Montana and allowed him to be home more frequently with his wife and child. His work in the parish was also rewarded, because within three years after his arrival in New Rockford, Louis had succeeded in elevating the congregation from the status of a subsidized mission station to a fully independent and self-supporting church.

In the summer of 1919, Pastor Beto received yet another call. This one came from a larger congregation in Lena, Illinois. The congregation had lost its pastor, and after the lay leaders collected names of pastors for their call list, they sent Pastor Beto the call. Beto, however, decided to remain in New Rockford and returned the call. The Lena Lutherans then sent the call a second time with the plea that "This field is very much in need of a shepherd," and if it remained vacant too long, many members would drift into another congregation.[10] Then, judging his ministry to be needed more in Lena than in New Rockford, Beto once again moved his wife and child farther east, arriving in Lena on December 21, 1919, almost three years to the day after arriving in New Rockford. His circuit riding days were now behind him; Louis occupied the pulpit at St. John's Lutheran Church on Lena Street for the next thirty-one years until his death in 1950.

Located in the gently rolling hill country in northwestern Illinois seven miles south of the Wisconsin border and 125 miles west of Chicago, Lena was home for George Beto during his formative years. When the Beto family arrived, Lena was the hub of a prosperous and progressive farming community with a population of about 1,000 residents. It prided itself on paved streets and sidewalks lit with electric lamps, a hospital, a public library, and a telephone service. The tidy, picturesque town also had an opera house where local talent as well as traveling stage companies performed and where silent movies were shown to the accompaniment of a pianist. On Main Street, in the center of Lena, stood a large, gazebo-like covered bandstand. The bandstand was a popular venue for the people of Lena, especially during the pleasant and balmy summer evenings when musical performances were held free of charge.[11]

St. John's Lutheran Church had been established in 1889, and by 1919 the attendance at the Sunday worship services was approximately one hundred.[12] The established and financially independent church was capable of providing its pastor and his family with a comfortable and secure middle-class standard of living. When the Betos first arrived they lived for two years in a house provided for them by the congregation until a spacious parsonage was built next to the church for their permanent residence. The parsonage built for the Beto family still stands, and the old church, now replaced by a larger place of worship, houses an insurance company.

Louis' contribution to the Lena community extended beyond his work in the congregation. From the time of his arrival, Louis quickly immersed himself in the civic life of the community and began organizing and promoting activities that enriched the condition and quality of life of the people of Lena. With a particular interest in young people, Louis was instrumental in establishing the first high school football team in Lena, and later, during the Depression years, when times were hard, he organized citywide softball leagues for their diversion. Additionally, he was an active sponsor and advisor to the Young People's Society, an interdenominational group dedicated to promoting good citizenship as well as the benefits of education and the dignity of work. Groups of twenty-five to thirty teenagers regularly held their meetings in the basement of St. John's Church, and Louis frequently organized outings for them to the not-too-distant Black Hawk Monument on the Rock River where they would socialize, roast wieners, play games, and sing.

Louis's passion for golf, acquired during his teenage years in Chicago, had lain dormant since his seminary years. Playing golf on the western plains was unrealistic, but once Louis returned to Illinois he could fondly hope that his five-year hiatus from the links was over. Lena, however, did not have a golf course, and the few courses scattered about northwestern Illinois made it possible, but not convenient, for Louis to begin playing again. The only solution was to construct a course in Lena. Within eight years of his arrival in Lena, Louis and four other men had raised the money to start a golf club. They purchased a forty-acre farm located a short distance north of town and in June 1928 the Lena Golf Club was incorporated under the laws of the state of Illinois. With the help of the other charter members, Louis supervised the conversion of the farm into a nine-hole golf course, with bent greens, clean fairways, and beautiful water hazards.[13]

Louis, with his active participation in civic affairs, was not the typical Lutheran pastor. Pastors in general, although they performed the same ecclesiastical functions, varied the focus of their ministry. One pastor, for example, might concentrate almost exclusively on his flock, teaching Bible classes, visiting the sick and bedridden, or counseling individuals. Another may be more scholarly, reading theological studies, attending conferences, and even writing articles for publication. Louis Beto illustrated a third focus by spending his discretionary time in civic affairs. Years later, when George entered the ministry, he emulated his father's civic-mindedness, but not the passion for golf. The thread of civic involvement can be seen flowing from father to son. Like his father's, George's ministry included service to the community.

Margaret and the Beto Home

And neither was Margaret, the pastor's wife, idle. Still in her early twenties when they moved to Lena, she had matured into a tall woman with a friendly, outgoing, and pleasant personality. She participated fully in the life of the church and frequently accompanied her husband as he paid his annual visits to members of the congregation. When her son George preached her funeral sermon, he observed that in spite of her "loyalty and fierce faithfulness to the Lutheran Church she possessed an ecumenical spirit, and attended all churches and participated in the activities of all denominations." Like her husband, she enjoyed Lena's social groups and belonged to many women's clubs and was an avid card player. And along with all those activities, she gave birth to three more children: Walter in 1920, Louis, Jr., in 1922, and Dorcas in 1924.[14]

The poverty and hardship that Margaret experienced during her five years in Hysham and New Rockford impressed upon her a sense of thrift and frugality, which she practiced for the rest of her life. She seasonally canned fruit and vegetables. Instead of buying new schoolbooks Margaret purchased used ones for her children. Before the beginning of the new school year she and her children sat around the kitchen table where they used homemade paste and denim cut from old overalls to recover and patch the old books, thereby making them serviceable for another year. Diapers for all the babies, handkerchiefs, and kitchen towels were cut, bleached, and sown by Margaret from Godshaw Sugar sacks, and the boys' pants were patched with sections cut from Russell's Best flour sacks. Years later George exaggerated to his children that when he was a child he went about Lena with pants patched in the rear that read "Russell's Best!"[15]

Home life at the parsonage in Lena was pleasant and intimate. The center of family life was the dinner table. Noon and evening meals, taken in congregate, always began and ended with prayers. Discussions were lively and animated, and the variety of topics included schoolwork, social activities, summer jobs, current events, and, of course, how everyone fared in the latest round at the golf course. Both Margaret and Louis used the dinner table talk to encourage the children to improve themselves through education, and to take advantage of the opportunities that were presented to them.[16]

George Beto's Youth in Lena

George's boyhood years may well have been in the decade of the Roaring Twenties, and Lena may have been only 125 miles from

Chicago, but life in Lena moved at its own pace. It was undisturbed by the crime, speakeasies, and vagaries of life in the big city. Children in small-town America lived carefree lives that were generally free from the distractions of contemporary youth. George belonged to the Boy Scouts and as a young child routinely attended YMCA camps. About a mile and a half outside of Lena was a beautiful hilly area known as "The Rocks." There a creek emptied into a large pond, where in summer George met his friends to swim, socialize, and picnic. In the winter months he joined his companions to ski and sled down the gently sloping hillsides.[17]

George's primary education was acquired during the years 1922–1930, when he attended the Lena public schools from the first through the ninth grade. George was a good student, attentive to his studies, and from a very early age was a voracious reader, a trait which he exhibited his entire life. Indeed, so great was his love of reading that his mother Margaret could easily get young George to obey by merely threatening not to take him to the library to check out more books.[18]

And not surprisingly, he was devoutly religious. In 1926, while in the fifth grade at Lena Elementary School, the teacher gave ten-year old George an assignment to write an essay titled "My Future Occupation." This is what he wrote:

> I would like to be a minister when I grow up. To prepare for this occupation I would like to go to North Western [sic] University and then to Concordia Seminary. I would like to be a preacher because my father is a preacher and my mother once said that God had given father and mother four children and all lived past infancy and she wanted one of us children to be a preacher. But my main reason is to save souls for the Great God that reigns over us. I would like to have a mission post as my father did. I would like to have my mission post in Canada, Alaska, South America, or the Western United States.[19]

As a teenager in Lena, George and his boyhood friends were frequent inhabitants of Ansel Duth's pool hall on Main Street in downtown Lena. Typical of American pool halls during the period of Prohibition, no brewed or spirituous liquors were served at

Ansel Duth's establishment. In addition to pool tables, there were card tables and slot machines, and customers could purchase tobacco products, newspapers, soda water, candy, and snacks. Ansel's pool hall was also a popular retreat for farmers, tradesmen, employees of the Illinois Central Railroad, and retirees. Two wooden church pews placed on the sidewalk in front of the pool hall provided seating for the men who gathered in the evenings to socialize. George and his friends joined the customers and were readily tolerated by the older men. Ansel charged George and his friends five cents to play a game of pool. The winner received a voucher from Ansel for five cents worth of merchandise or tokens to play the slot machines. Some of the boys cashed in their windfall for cigarettes, which they sold to their fathers for cash, but George kept his cigarette winnings for his own personal use.[20]

If it is true, as George Beto later maintained, that God made the country, man made the city, and the devil made the small town, he certainly helped Lena live up to its billing. It was at this time that George developed an appetite and a flair for two penchants that he excelled at and immensely enjoyed during all of his adult life. The first of these was poker playing. Even as a young boy George was very fond of playing poker, a skill that he no doubt first learned at Ansel's. George played not only at Ansel's, where he learned much from the skilled and experienced older men, but George and his peers met and played poker in an old abandoned house. The house was on a farm owned by the parents of one of George's friends, and the boys, after receiving permission, remodeled the place to serve as a card parlor and club house. On Sunday afternoons, while his parents visited with parishioners, George often invited his friends to play poker in the basement of the church.[21]

The second penchant was for practical joking. George was fondly described by a childhood friend as "a very energetic lad who seemed to seek out mischief and play pranks on unsuspecting people."[22] One of several reported in the family archives is a joke Beto played on the men from Ansel's pool hall. One morning George came running into Ansel's and breathlessly announced to all present that a fight between two well-known and colorful Lena characters was about to commence in an alley behind the barbershop across the street. Everyone except George quickly rushed out of the pool hall, ran across Main Street, and burst through the front door of the barbershop and out its back door, which opened onto the alley. Even the barber and his customers, some still lathered-up and only half shaved, followed the excited men from Ansel's out into the alley to witness the affair. No one was in the alley. There was no fight![23]

Halloween provided the setting for more pranks. George and his friends did not miss the ritual tipping over of outhouses, a traditional prank that was part of the rite of passage for most rural youths.[24] More creative, however, was the escapade when these same boys hoisted a farm wagon to the roof of the Lena High School building. They disassembled the wagon and hauled it on a rope piece-by-piece to the roof of the high school where it was reassembled. George's brother Louis remembers that this prank left George with an injured arm, and that for a period of time after the incident he wore either a cast or a sling.[25]

While George had a mischievous and playful side to him, he also was a dependable and hard worker who earned his own spending money. The value of hard work and the dignity associated with it were indelibly impressed upon George, and by his early teenage years he had acquired a reputation in Lena as a reliable lad who was not afraid of labor. During the school year George rose early in the morning to assist Ansel Duth pick up the bundles of newspapers at Illinois Central Railroad depot, where the *Chicago Tribune* and *Herald Examiner* newspapers lay on a gravel driveway. They loaded the bundled newspapers onto a two-wheeled wooden handcart and took them to the pool hall, to be assembled and put out for sale.[26]

George always had a summer job during his teenage years. He could have worked with his brothers Louis and Walter at the Lena Golf Club, but George chose instead to work as a hired hand on the various farms in the Lena area. During the summer months he earned $1.25 a day digging drainage ditches, tending to the needs of farm animals, helping with the harvests, and generally assisting his employers with the never-ending chores of a working farm. The manual labor that George performed was hot, dirty, and physically demanding, and certainly more arduous and less glamorous than working at the golf course. It is quite possible that during this period George acquired his life-long love of riding horses, tending livestock, and working the land.[27]

Whether shooting pool or enjoying a concert at the gazebo, George experienced no unreasonable restrictions from the Lena citizens. It was an open, democratic society where people could come and go, children could attend school, and pranks were tolerated. It was a homogenous community and people were treated equally. Later in life George learned that not everywhere in the United States did such a situation exist, and that racial segregation forged a society different from that of his childhood. His Lena experiences helped mold his world view and influenced his responses to events that confronted him as an adult.

George Beto's Formal Education

By 1929 George had decided on a career as a minister of the Lutheran faith. He remarked to one of his childhood friends that he thought he was the one chosen to be the minister in the family; he believed his brother Walter was not minister material and Louis was too young, so it was up to George to follow in his father's footsteps.[28] When George decided to leave the Lena public school system and prepare himself academically for the Lutheran ministry he moved from a secular educational environment into a religious one.

At the time that George arrived at his conclusion, the Lutheran Church Missouri Synod's system of pastoral education consisted of a number of regional residential schools that combined the four years of secondary classes with the first two years of college. Upon graduation, the typical young man entered Concordia Seminary in St. Louis where he studied for two years, served a year of vicarage in a Lutheran parish or institution, and then returned for a final year of study.

Instead of enrolling at Northwestern College, the school his father had attended and which he had mentioned in his grade school essay, George decided upon one of the regional schools, Concordia College, in Milwaukee, Wisconsin. Not only was it relatively close to home, but family tradition maintains that George was swayed to this choice by a traveling book salesman, who also happened to be the son of a Lutheran minister. The salesman was unfamiliar with Lena, so George escorted him about town. The salesman himself had gone to Concordia College in Milwaukee, and described in very favorable terms for George all the attributes of the town and the school. After listening to the salesman's description George returned home and announced his desire to go to Milwaukee.[29] He already had completed the first year of the Lena high school, so his decision not only meant leaving his friends and classmates, it meant leaving, at the tender age of fourteen, his protecting family and a comfortable home. He arrived in Milwaukee in September 1930, the second year of the Great Depression.

Located on seven and one-half acres in the heart of a residential area of west Milwaukee, Concordia College, founded in 1881, was a preparatory school supported entirely by the Missouri Synod. The curriculum was rigorous by any high school or junior college standards today and maintained a heavy emphasis on languages. In addition to six years of Latin, three years of Greek and German, and two years of Hebrew, students were also required to take religion, history, math, and science.[30]

When George arrived at Concordia, he was one of about 250 students who were housed in three dormitories. Nearly all of his fellow students were looking to the Lutheran ministry as their life's work. Concordia College initially turned out to be a great disappointment for George. After attending classes for just a few weeks he became disillusioned with the school. For the first time in his life George was away from his loving, close-knit family and his circle of friends he had known since childhood. Additionally, the curriculum at Concordia College was extremely rigorous and the expectations of student performance were certainly much greater than what one would ordinarily expect to encounter in the public schools of the period. When he came home for his first visit he announced to his father that he was through with the preparatory school and did not want to go back to Milwaukee. He argued that he was not at all happy with the food and that he preferred life at home in Lena. Furthermore, he told his father that he felt the traveling salesman had misrepresented the preparatory school to him by embellishing its virtues. Louis was not at all convinced by his son's change of heart and mind, and he abruptly and very firmly told George, "You started up there and you are going to finish up there." George dutifully returned to Milwaukee and his studies at Concordia College, and completed the academic year. But his discontent remained and during the summer, as he worked on the farms around Lena, he brooded about his future and dreaded his return to the Milwaukee school.[31]

The fall months of 1931 at Concordia College turned out to be something of a Donnybrook for George, a crisis not so much of faith as it was of character and capability. In a letter George wrote in the early fall of 1931 to his beloved uncle, mentor, and confidant, George Witsma, Jr., George openly complained about the great amount of hard work he had to do, and he questioned whether or not he was capable of such rigorous academic demands. He also questioned whether he could live up to the expectations the Lutheran Church had of its ministers. His "Dutch uncle" lived up to his title and responded to George in a letter that undoubtedly had a profound impact on fifteen-year-old George, and served to steer him onto a course that forever changed his life:

Dear George: Your letter to me is largely a discussion of the difficulties you are encountering, and you remark at one place that if the work is as hard as this next year you doubt whether you will return. I will have no quarrel with you if you discontinue your studies for the Lutheran ministry, but I certainly cannot compliment you on your desire to quit because the work is hard. If you wish to, give up your studies for the ministry, but do not lower yourself in your own opinion, and in mine, by an admission that it is because you consider the work too hard. If you will compare the work you have to do now with the work you will be called upon to do later in life, you will realize what a very easy task you have now. If you fail now in these years to cultivate such a desire and capacity for hard work and perseverance, you may rest assured it will become increasingly difficult to cultivate as you grow older. If you quit because the work it too hard you will have lowered your own morale, and you will surely quit other tasks later in life for the same reason.[32]

George took this advice to heart. He applied himself to the study of Latin and Greek and eventually graduated with honors (*summa cum honore*). Years later George reminisced about the time he spent in Milwaukee and the great lesson of life he learned there: "I disliked every day I was there. The discipline there was Spartan in character and the course of study was extremely rigorous. But it taught me a lesson that has been valuable to me—to do the things I don't like to do. As I look back I am thankful that my father did not heed my requests to take me out of the school."[33]

Even though the nine months of the school year may have been tortuous ones, his three months of summer were back home with his parents and friends. There George's life returned to normal, the food was more to his taste, and he was back to his old shenanigans. During the summer months of 1931 George and his friends perpetrated a good number of pranks, so that when the boys departed for their respective schools their absence was readily noticed by the people of Lena. The evidence for this is found buried in the archives of the *Lena Weekly Star* newspaper, whose editor wrote as follows:

> It appears that one of our young men attending college took some exception to an article published some time ago relative to the prank- lessness and quietness of our town since the boys returned to college. We will say that the student in question has made good use of his time while attending college; this evidenced by the vocabulary he uses in typing the letter, unless he had one of Daniel Webster's book of words handy and scanned the pages to get the proper word and phrases for the letter. Following is the letter, and we hope the writer, who signs himself as G. J. B., Secretary, Indolent Student League of the Occi- dent, will pardon us when we say that it is our heartfelt wish that it neither cast a blemish on nor serve to lacerate the otherwise spotless integrity of the gentleman concerned.[34]

G. J. B. of course is George John Beto! This is what George, who styled himself the Secretary of the Indolent Student League of the Occident, wrote in response to the editor of the *Lena Weekly Star*:

> Dear Sir: In perusing the columns of your most fascinating and interesting periodical, I chanced upon an article that seemed to me a blemish on and a laceration of the spotless integrity of the gentlemen concerned. It seems that you permitted an article to be sent to press which stated that the young gentlemen of our fair village who are improving their minds and intellects at institutions of higher learning were perpetrators of several practical jokes and pranks during the summer recess. That you, a journalist of the first order, a past master at the art, should have so bold an effrontery as to allow such calumny to pass before the ocular organs of the hoi polloi, caused my colleagues and me great concern. And since our escutcheon must remain unsullied, it is only right that we demand an exculpation and exoneration. Hoping that the necessary measures will be taken, I remain G. J. B., Secretary of the Indolent Student League of the Occident.[35]

By the following summer of 1932, George had saved enough money to purchase his first automobile, a black 1915 Model T Ford that sported a bright brass radiator. He bought the well-maintained Tin Lizzie for $15.00 from one of the farmers for whom he worked. Even though more than fifteen years old, the Model T served him well.[36]

At this time George's physical appearance matched his mental powers. He was reaching his height of six-feet four-inches and the summers of agricultural labor had hardened his muscles. His physical dimensions also gave him confidence. He was physically fit, able, and handsome. Later in Texas his characteristic slouch while sitting and his fiddling with the glasses were deceptive. When he stood up and crowned his head with his gray Stetson, there was an unmistakable presence of physical strength.

With his successful completion of the program of study at Concordia College, George was well prepared to begin his seminary years. His choice of seminary was his father's alma mater, Concordia

Seminary in St. Louis. However, since the days of Louis Beto, the seminary had been moved to a seventy-one acre campus in suburban Clayton, and there new and elegant buildings served a student population of around 500. The fourteen-member faculty provided a three-year course of study in theology, which was designed expressly to prepare young men for the Lutheran ministry. In keeping with the policy of Concordia College, no charge was assessed for tuition and lodging; students only paid for their board.

It was at Concordia Seminary that George came of age and passed from his teenage years into young adulthood, entering in September 1935 at age nineteen. By George's own admission, the time he spent at Concordia Seminary studying for the Lutheran ministry were the most relaxed and untroubled years of his life. This is how George described his years at the seminary:

> My stay at Concordia Seminary embraced the years 1935–37 and 1938–39. Those years at St. Louis were the most carefree of my life. The seminary physical plant was impressive; living accommodations were commodious; academic demands were extremely moderate; the food was more than adequate; and companions were congenial. Generally, I found my fellow seminarians congenial companions. The camaraderie of the institution was one of its greatest assets. Manifestly, some were stuffy, pietistic, and old beyond their years. However, in that relatively large conglomerate of humanity, they could be avoided. My closest friends were Kurt Voss, Hartwig Schwehn, and Kurt Biel. All of us were sons of pastors. . . .
>
> When I came to St. Louis, only three faculty members had earned doctorates from reputable institutions. In later years, as I reflected on the instruction I received, I came to appreciate belatedly their approach to learning. They were less dogmatic and more empirical in their evaluation of problems.
>
> I attended morning chapel services faithfully during the three years in St. Louis. The services were simple: a hymn, an address by an ungowned professor, a prayer, a closing verse, and a blessing. The singing in morning chapel was powerful and thrilling. To hear over four hundred male voices join in singing the great hymns of Christendom could be spine-tingling. . . .

The seminary had few rules: no card playing; engagement [to be married] was prohibited; no liquor on campus; no cheating, etc. No special effort to search out violators of the rules was made. However, when violators were detected punishment was summary, and expulsion was not unheard of. . . .

The years at St. Louis were halcyon. If I had them to live again, I wouldn't change them. However, as I reflect on those days, I resent the efforts of my teachers to bind my conscience in areas which today—as a result of experience and study—I know they were wrong.[37]

George's courteous and friendly demeanor earned him the friendship and respect not only of fellow students, but also of many of the faculty as well. His peers chose him for positions where leadership qualities were required. While at the St. Louis seminary he served as alumni editor of the school newspaper (the *Alma Mater*), business manager of the Missionary Society, program chairman for the university "Smoker" (an annual event featuring an evening of dining, discussion, and good cheer), and an elective position on the student council. In addition to his studies and his extracurricular activity, George spent a lot of time with his uncle, George Witsma, Jr., the man who years earlier had come to George's aid with sage advice during his troubled second year at the preparatory school in Wisconsin. Witsma regularly picked George up at the seminary on Friday afternoons and brought him to his home for the weekend. While at the house George and his uncle, who had also attended a Lutheran boys' preparatory school in his youth, frequently sat in the living room and argued religion for hours, often comparing their translations of scripture from Greek and Hebrew into English.[38] By this time the Model T was long gone, but Witsma regularly lent George the family car so he and his friends would have transportation for their Saturday evening outings.

While most seminarians accepted a vicarage assignment to a parish after the second year at the seminary, George chose instead to finish a bachelor's degree at Valparaiso University, in Valparaiso, Indiana. Located in the northwest corner of Indiana, the Valparaiso Male and Female College had been founded in 1859, and by the end of the nineteenth century the institution had acquired the reputation as the "poor man's Harvard." In 1925 the Lutheran church purchased it with the goal of providing the best possible liberal arts education in an atmosphere that reflected Christian precepts and ideals. When George arrived in 1937, Valparaiso had fifty-two faculty members and an enrollment of 511 students.[39] To help pay expenses, Beto mopped the floors of the dining room. In May 1938 George received his bachelor of arts degree in history. Then in the fall, he returned to the seminary to complete his theological studies and in June 1939 graduated with the centennial class of the seminary. His graduation took place, incidentally, on the twenty-fifth anniversary of his father's graduation from the same institution.

The Depression and widespread unemployment, however, continued unabated, and only a few congregations were submitting requests for graduates. Hoping for better times, George returned home to Lena where he lived with his parents in the parsonage and frequently occupied the pulpit in his father's church as well as others in the area. But George's wait for an assignment grew tedious. In a letter George wrote to friends in early July 1939 he expressed his growing frustration and waxed pessimistic about his uncertain future:

I have been preaching every Sunday. Two weeks ago the congregation at Freeport had the rare privilege of hearing my oratorical finesse in the German tongue. After I had finished one of the pious souls approached me and said, "You are a little bit more at home in the English, aren't you?" I feebly answered yes and wondered in what way I was to understand that statement. Last Sunday I was free. That freedom coupled with my growing boredom prompted me to go to Chicago where I visited a couple of friends, saw the Arlington Classic at the race track, and had a very enjoyable date with a girl. I returned home to continued boredom. Every time I go up town some silly soul asks me if I have a place as of yet. The somnolent sectarians here in town fail to realize that in the Lutheran Church you cannot just go before a church council, lay your qualifications on the line, and demand a position.[40]

By the end of the month his anxiety had grown, and perhaps his hope for a quick position was beginning to wane. George expressed the routine of his daily life as follows:

> At 9 in the morning I arise, partake of a light breakfast, read the Chicago Tribune, smoke a couple of Camels lifted from my father's desk, and then help my youngest brother Louis mow one of the several lawns for which he has the contract. Then I eat dinner, after which I repair to the divan where I sleep for an hour. A gnawing appetite for a smoke usually awakens me in time to walk leisurely uptown to fetch the afternoon mail, where daily I continue to look in vain for an envelope with Greek letters on it from the synod. Then I return home where I read for a couple of hours. Finally I eat supper, go uptown for an hour or so, come home, read until one or two in the morning, go to sleep, get up, and do it all over again. The net result of this is that I am slowly going mad. If something does not happen soon I shall be ready for commitment to the State Hospital for the Insane at East Moline.[41]

Unbeknownst to George, on July 28 the president of a small Lutheran preparatory school in central Texas submitted to the dean of the Concordia Seminary in St. Louis an "Application for Supply," thus setting in motion the placement process whereby seminarians received their first position. Henry Studtmann, President of Concordia College in Austin, Texas, was seeking a person to fill an entry-level teaching position. Studtmann was looking for a generalist, someone who could teach a wide variety of courses on the secondary level including United States History, English, Algebra, Economics, and Civics, and someone who would also "live in the college dormitory and therefore also supervise the study period and have at least part charge of the evening devotions." Additionally, the new faculty member would have "opportunities to preach in the local church and in other congregations of Texas."[42]

No sooner had John Fritz, Dean of Concordia Seminary, received the request from President Studtmann, than he wrote a letter dated August 2 to George, asking him, "Will you be the man to go to Austin?" George accepted immediately and enthusiastically, and in a letter dated August 11, Studtmann officially welcomed George to the faculty as an assistant instructor. In less than four weeks George was on his way to Texas.[43]

News of George's imminent departure spread through Lena quickly, and the *Lena Weekly Star* reported that "George Beto, popular young Lena man, will soon start as an assistant instructor in Texas." This set off a round of dinner parties and socials that lasted three weeks. Perhaps the most memorable of these occurred the week before George was to depart for Texas. On Tuesday evening, August 22, the entire congregation of St. John's Lutheran Church assembled in secret in the church's basement in order that they might surprise George with a going-away party. An unsuspecting George was completely flabbergasted by the large number of old friends and acquaintances gathered in his honor: a most fitting and proper way to honor an erstwhile prankster! As a token of the congregation's love and esteem, they presented George with a substantial purse to help him get started. The following Monday morning, August 28, 1939, George left by train for Austin, where he arrived two days later. He had one week to get settled in and to prepare his lessons before school opened on Wednesday, September 6.

Even though Beto left the Midwest for Texas, he did not shed his Midwestern mentality, the Midwestern accent, or its social values. Later, in Texas, he displayed the trappings of his adopted state such as the Stetson hat and the spur tie clasp with GJB in the center, and, on occasion, his cowboy boots, but his character had been formed. He played the role of a quintessential Texan, and the Texans accepted him, but the Midwest had left its imprint.[44]

Chapter 2

CONCORDIA LUTHERAN COLLEGE, AUSTIN, TEXAS (1939–1959)

Concordia College, Beto's initial place of employment, had been founded thirteen years earlier, in October 1926, and like other preparatory schools of the synod, was modeled after the German *Gymnasium*. It differed, however, from the other synodical schools in that the Austin school was a college in name only and was limited to four years of secondary schooling. The school had been located on twenty acres in the northeastern part of Austin in proximity to the University of Texas. Henry Studtmann, the first president, had guided the school through its formative years and continued to do so during the Depression of the 1930s. The school was governed by a Board of Control, representatives of the synod who worked without compensation.[1]

When Beto first set foot on the Concordia campus he saw "a couple of buildings in a sea of Johnson grass, infested with rattlesnakes and scorpions." The larger of the two buildings, Kilian Hall, was named in honor of the Wendish pastor who had been instrumental in giving the Missouri Synod a foothold in Texas.[2] Located on the first floor of the building were the kitchen, dining hall, an auditorium for chapel services, and a small apartment that Beto occupied. In the center of the first floor were the classrooms. The residential rooms for the students occupied the second story. The second, a smaller building in the shape of a cube, provided space for a lounge with a radio and a music room on the upper level, and a science laboratory and a small exercise room with a basketball hoop on the lower level. A short distance from the student buildings were two residences, constructed of stucco in Spanish style: one occupied by the president of the school and the other by a professor.

The faculty, matching the small student body, was few in number. In general there were three types of instructors. Several professors were clergymen who had calls, and with that tenure. They maintained the continuity of the school and served in both administration and the classroom. President Studtmann, for example, taught the religion courses. A second group was composed of part-time teachers who were hired as needed. One of these, Mrs. Lillian Bedichek, wife of the noted writer Roy Bedichek, taught Spanish for many years. And there were always one or two young men, often seminary vicars, who were hired for a year or two to teach some courses, live in the dormitory, and supervise the students. This was the group that included Beto, except in his case he had already graduated from the seminary. The most likely career route for him was to serve a year or two and then go into a parish.

In spite of the Johnson grass and the rattlesnakes, Beto was delighted with Texas and with Concordia. Shortly after Beto arrived in Austin he wrote to his friends about his initial impressions: "I arrived in Austin on the thirtieth of August. Upon arriving at the college I was pleasantly surprised. Exclusive of the Prof's houses the college consists of two buildings, both built in the mission style and modern in every respect. Everybody on the faculty except President Studtmann has an M.A. The faculty consists of President Studtmann and three professors."[3]

The daily rhythm of life for the approximately thirty-five students enrolled at Concordia College in the fall of 1939 was highly structured. Students were awakened at 6:00 AM and ate breakfast in the dining hall between 6:30 and 6:45. They then returned to their rooms to arrange them and prepare for the day. After attending chapel service from 7:30 to 8:00, students went to their morning classes until noon, when lunch was served. Afternoon classes were scheduled from 1:00 to 3:00 PM. From 3:00 until dinner at 6:00

students were free to study, socialize, or participate in intramural or interscholastic athletics. After dinner the students had a mandatory study period until the evening chapel service at 9:00 PM. After chapel there was an hour before bed check, and lights out. Classes were scheduled Tuesday through Saturday, with Sunday and Monday free.[4]

Beto as Teacher and Housemaster

Beto's schedule for his first three years was strenuous. He was in the classroom nineteen hours a week teaching courses on U.S. History, World History, Algebra, Civics, Economics, and Religion.[5] The students immediately took to Beto. His teaching style was energetic, animated, and colorful; he paced the room, never sitting behind a desk. Later, when he acquired eyeglasses, he would take them off while lecturing and use them to point at a student or jab them into the air to drive home some bit of wisdom.[6] No matter what subject he taught, humor and good will were standard fare. When asking a question, he might add, "The first person to answer this question wins an all expense, one week trip to Dime Box."[7] He also was given to frequently quoting colorful Latin or biblical phrases, so if his question went unanswered or he was disappointed with the classroom performance of a student he would signal his frustration and displeasure with the question "Is there is no balm in Gilead?" meaning there is nothing, short of a miracle, that could help this class.[8] He rarely, if ever, lectured from prepared notes, a remarkable talent because he was assigned to teach courses outside his specialties of history and religion.

Beto used the classroom to a greater advantage than did most teachers. He spent whatever amount of time was necessary to cover the assignment for that day. But if he finished the lesson before the hour was concluded, which was usually the case, he used the remaining time for questions, comments, and observations from his students on any topic.[9] Questions from the boys covered a wide range of concerns, including the impending war in Europe, contemporary national and state issues, morality and behavior, what it means to be a man, and sex. When questions of theology came up in these informal discussions Beto addressed their concerns not from the point of view of a textbook, but in terms of the practical application of Lutheran doctrine. In this context Beto did not teach the boys as much as he fathered them, and they accepted this and respected him for it. He had an uncanny ability to perceive the personal development needs of his students, and he used his classes to work on those kinds of needs and problems.[10] His students recall that often the insights and knowledge they gained from his classes had nothing to do with the topic of the course.[11] Beto thoroughly enjoyed what he was doing:

> Do I like to teach? Absolutely! World History and U.S. History are really a pleasure to teach. In World History there is ample opportunity to discuss everything under the sun. I really throw the bull in that course. By bull I mean to say that I give the boys access to that vast cargo of learning I have taken on during the course of years. My Freshman Algebra course is more pleasant than I thought it would be. The class is composed entirely of lumina and as a result I derive a certain amount of pleasure in teaching them. My appellations for the members of my various classes vary. Sometimes I call them gentlemen, then again boys, and occasionally I prefix the name of an individual with the noble title of brother. As yet I have had no difficulties with discipline in the classroom.[12]

The personal touch, moreover, stimulated students to study the text and to read books he suggested. Many of the students came from rural areas and from small towns. Simply living in Austin was enriching, and for some the heated bathroom with showers and flush toilets was a luxury. There was an emphasis on a classical education as well as on expanding the horizons. Soon Beto was taking students on field trips to the county jail and to courts. He rented films for a free movie night and included such classics as *How Green was My Valley* and *Mutiny on the Bounty*." The Latin professor, Gotthold "Pappy" Viehweg, initiated a music appreciation hour on Monday nights during which he played recordings such as Bach's *B Minor Mass*. Attendance was mandatory and for many the music went unappreciated, but interest revived when he brought in his lovely daughter to sing some German *Lieder* by Schubert and Schumann. And Mrs. Bedichek's husband, the director of the Texas Interscholastic League, provided tickets for the tournaments and contests.

Even though the primary purpose of the school was to prepare church workers either for the pastoral ministry or as teachers in the Lutheran parochial schools, Concordia also admitted general students, or non-church work students, who lived either in the dormitory or commuted. Some of the students, from any of the three classifications, originated from cities such as Houston and New Orleans. To them the rules and restrictions, and not the urban setting, provided the culture shock. These students were a mixed blessing, providing a bit more sophistication for the campus, but at times initiating activities that were deemed undesired by those responsible for enforcing the rules.[13]

Beto also had charge of the dormitory, a position that carried the title of housemaster. Like clockwork he woke the boys at 6:00 AM after he had already eaten his breakfast and read the newspaper.[14] He also made the rounds during the evening study period to see that everyone was at their desks engaged in homework. Later, there was another round for bed check. Transoms above the doors simplified the night rounds in that they revealed any telltale light in the room. It was also Beto's habit to walk the corridors of Kilian Hall at any hour of the day or night, ostensibly to check on the welfare of the students, but also to insure that no student had slipped off campus without permission. One never knew when he would show up. Sometimes he appeared silently and suddenly at the open door of the dormitory room where he would then peer in to see that all was well before continuing his stroll down the hall to the next room; at other times he stopped to sit and talk with the boys, trading stories and learning about their hometown, their home life, and their perspective on the world.[15]

Throughout his years at Concordia, Beto gained an intimate knowledge of each student. He knew his hometown, the pastor of the congregation, and generally the parents. When greeting students he included comments about their place of origin such as "Martin from Fayette County" or addressed them by a nickname he gave them. The nicknames were usually based on ethnic origin, a descriptive adjective, or a surname, such as "The renegade Dane," "*Schimpfer*" (German for someone who complained frequently), or "Fritz" for someone whose surname was Ebert (also the name of the president of the Weimar Republic). The students referred to him as "King George," but called him "Dean Beto" or "'Prof' Beto."

The daily routine of prowling the halls of the dormitory looking after the physical, intellectual, and spiritual welfare of his charges quickly earned him legendary status among the boys at the school. As word of this activity spread he enjoyed the respect and confidence of the parents who sent their sons to Concordia.[16] When Beto first arrived in 1939, discipline had deteriorated. President Studtmann, a small and gentle person, had aged and was losing control of the student body.[17] Typical schoolboy antics such as smoking, sneaking out after bed check, failing to attend chapel, being noisy in the dormitory, being late to class, and cursing had to some extent gone unchecked by Studtmann. Beto quickly changed that, and in the course of doing so he earned the respectful fear of the boys for his adeptness at catching rule violators and the swiftness with which he disciplined them. However, the nature of the punishments he imposed were not seen by the students as draconian. When Beto caught students in violation of one of the rules he did not make a big fuss about it, but simply chose one of several punishments he routinely employed: a verbal reprimand, deprivation of privileges by restricting the student to campus, or requiring a certain number of hours of labor (*Strafarbeit*) on campus washing windows, helping the groundskeeper, or mopping floors.[18]

In reality, Beto was quite understanding of the foibles and foolishness of the young boys under his charge; after all, Beto had been something of a hellion himself in his youth. Perhaps because of this he was not overly harsh in his discipline. Instead, there was a firm but gentle aspect to his correction, "a manly and masculine piety that students responded to."[19] Beto called it "benevolent discipline."[20]

In a letter to friends shortly after his arrival at Concordia Beto recalled his experience with dorm supervision and discipline:

In addition to my teaching duties I keep order in the dormitory. I am as much fitted for that job as for piloting an airplane. I make my rounds at night (11 o'clock). About 15 minutes after I go downstairs some wit throws a [metal] waste paper basket down the length of the hall. Now that does not bother me, since in my day I was not averse to a little fun myself. I also hold chapel every night. I don't mind that as it gives me practice in extemporaneous speaking. In connection with chapel I'd like to point out another example which shows that my hell-raising days are not far enough behind me to make me a good martinet. My organist failed to show up, and I was fool enough to ask "Is there anyone here who is able to play the piano?" You can guess the answer I received. Everybody started calling the name of some goof who couldn't play a note. I thought it was so good I laughed myself. A really first class disciplinarian wouldn't do that![21]

Despite his initial concerns about his ability to supervise the boys, by the beginning of the 1940 spring semester Beto was convinced he had found his calling in life, and was troubled about the prospect of leaving Concordia and Austin when his temporary two-year appointment expired: "I certainly enjoy teaching these boys. I dread to think of the day when I will have to leave. I feel I am cut out for this type of work, so naturally the thought of doing something else one year and one-half hence does not exactly thrill me. And besides, I like this mild Texas climate a lot better than the cold late winters of Northern Illinois."[22]

Graduate Education

Perhaps realizing within the first month of his arrival at Concordia that he wanted to stay, in October 1939 Beto took the first step toward a master's degree by writing to the admissions office at the University of Texas and asking for an evaluation of his transcripts.[23] He did not begin graduate study immediately because out-of-state tuition was more than he could afford. So he waited a year, gained residency status, and then took courses in the 1940 summer session.[24] At that time the university did not charge tuition for summer school courses, so Beto made up for lost time, without spending a cent, by registering for a full load. With Concordia closed for the summer break, and without family responsibilities, his ambitious plan was not unreasonable. To his seminary friends he wrote, "During the summer session here you can carry fourteen hours. You only need thirty-six for a master's degree."[25] He repeated his schedule the next summer, and then, in the summer of 1942, while he was writing his thesis, he took several math classes, including a class on mathematics of investment. He eventually completed his thesis, a seventy-five page study entitled "The Marburg Colloquy of 1529: A Textual Study," in the summer of 1943. The graduate committee appointed to oversee his work approved it and he received his Master of Arts degree in History on February 29, 1944.[26] In later years journalists often inaccurately reported that Beto's degree was in Medieval History. He did take one course in that historical period, but his history courses ranged from American History to Indian History, and his thesis topic would be classified as Reformation History.

His transcripts from the University of Texas clearly show that Beto used virtually all of his elective hours to take courses offered by the Department of Sociology. For the first time he was formally exposed to a broad range of social issues, including criminology, public welfare, and race relations.[27] He selected the criminology class, which may well have been the spark that ignited his later pursuits, because it met at 7 AM, a convenient hour for him. Yet that fire, if indeed it existed, took time to smolder, because he continued to think in terms of religious education, and once the masters degree was finished he started his doctoral courses in Educational Administration. Instead of following his summer school pattern, he took most of his doctoral courses during the year beginning in 1944 and continuing until he received his doctorate in 1955. The title of his dissertation was "Arguments Found in the Literature for the Continued Existence of the Protestant Church-Related Liberal Arts College."

Surprisingly, one of his doctoral electives was a seminar in physical and health education. Never known for any interest in athletics, he applied himself enough to earn an "A" in the course.[28]

To meet his foreign language requirement he chose Latin, one of his favorite languages. Doctoral language examinations generally were paper and pencil affairs administered to groups of students at scheduled intervals. Beto was the only one who chose Latin, so his examination was scheduled to be taken in the office of the chairman of the Department of Classical Languages. When Beto arrived to take what he thought would be a written examination, he learned that the professor had not prepared one. Instead the exam would be oral. After an hour of conversation the department chairman congratulated Beto for not only passing the examination, but also his good command of the language. Beto had not studied the language since his seminary days.[29]

Additional Service and Tenure

In addition to his teaching responsibilities, dormitory supervision, and work on his advanced degrees, Beto was involved in a number of other activities. During his first two years at Concordia Beto directed the athletics program, taught Bible classes, and, curious as it may be, produced and directed a promotional film for the school. The physical, mental, and emotional energy needed to sustain such a variety of activities would have exhausted lesser men.

Concordia had found it difficult to gain name recognition among the Lutherans in Texas, a prerequisite for raising money for the improvement of the physical facilities of the campus. In 1940 Beto convinced the Board of Control that a movie would be a good way not only to raise money for the institution but also to increase its student enrollment.[30] The Board of Control assented to the request, and with a donated sixteen millimeter camera Beto began filming with a view to highlighting the school's physical plant, student life, and campus activities.[31] Beto and his movie camera became such a common sight on campus that one student wrote "It seems as though crawling into an air raid shelter is the only way to escape Dean Beto and his movie camera these days. He is determined to finish that Technicolor Concordia film in time for use next spring, and it looks like he will." The film was completed and ready for circulation around the state "to interested congregations, organizations, and individuals" by late fall 1943.[32] Because costs associated with having a sound track for the film were prohibitive, Beto wrote the script for the film, which was intended to be read by Concordia faculty who would accompany the film when it was shown around the state. The tire shortage and gas rationing caused by the war, however, made it impossible for any faculty member to accompany the showing of the film, so the script was not heard.[33]

By January 1941 Beto's two-year temporary instructorship had only six months remaining before it expired. Recognizing Beto's value to the institution, the Board of Control in January 1941 asked the Board for Higher Education (BHE), the Missouri Synod's administrative agency for its educational system, to grant Concordia Austin a special favor; the Board beseeched the BHE to "let us keep Mr. Beto for another year."[34] The Board concurred, and Beto's temporary instructorship was extended, thereby delaying for at least one more year the fears he initially expressed in 1939. Then the Board of Control implemented the process of establishing a permanent position, and sent a resolution to the synodical convention, which met in June 1941, for authorization to establish a professorship in science.[35]

Eventually the synodical procedure was completed and Concordia's Board of Control, on March 25, 1942, issued him a call to a permanent faculty position as Professor of Science and Mathematics, effective September 1942.[36] At approximately the same time Beto received a call to a parish in Amarillo, so he had a choice between a career in an educational institution or in the parish ministry. Beto readily accepted the call from Concordia and returned the call to Amarillo. In September Beto became the fourth professor on the Austin faculty.

A conflict, however, remained between the old synodical rules and the new realities. All tenured professors had previously held parish positions and then were called to the educational institution. And because they had initially served in a congregation, they had been ordained. In Beto's case he had never served a congregation nor had he been ordained. Finding enough suitable faculty members from ordained clergy who were "apt to teach" and also willing to leave the parish was not easy. So when an ideal person like Beto was identified, exceptions needed to be made. But a call to Concordia was not a call to a congregation and did not fulfill the prerequisite for ordination. The solution was to make him an assistant pastor at a local congregation with minimal duties and then ordain him into the ministry.

In keeping with this acceptable bending of the rules, Beto was ordained in 1944 at St. Paul's Lutheran Church, the Lutheran church nearest to the campus. For years Concordia students had walked the one and one-half mile distance to 16th and Red River every Sunday to attend church services. (That location is currently part of the University of Texas campus now occupied by the Erwin Center.) As "assistant pastor" Beto was not responsible for any of the heavy responsibilities assigned to the pastor, such as administering communion, visiting the sick, or burying the dead, unless of course one of the parishioners happened to inconveniently die while the pastor was away. But at the same time Assistant Pastor Beto received no compensation.[37] Generally the assistant pastor would preach if the pastor were going to be out of town or on vacation. Given his many responsibilities at the college, it is not surprising that Beto did not frequently occupy the pulpit at St. Paul; he preached perhaps three or four Sundays a year at St. Paul and taught Bible classes. But when Beto did preach in Austin it became something of an event, and many people who might not otherwise regularly attend Sunday worship service showed up. Beto generally preached on a text from one of the Pauline epistles. Because he did not like long, rambling sermons, Beto's preaching style was concise and direct; he pointed out to the congregation what the Bible said, provided an explanation of what the passage meant, and applied it to a Christian's life.[38]

Marriage and Family

In 1939 Beto first met Marilynn Knippa at St. Paul Lutheran Church in Austin. Marilynn, a native Austinite, was one of seven children reared in a religious home. The Knippa family was an established and well-known family in Austin where they owned and operated several self-serve grocery stores that went by the name "Kash-Karry."[39]

Marilynn was still in high school when they first met, and Beto briefly dated two of her older sisters. Two years later, after graduation, he called Marilynn for a date. Marilynn recalls being so surprised she asked Beto if he didn't have the wrong sister. He responded "No, I was just biding time waiting for you to grow up," to which Marilynn responded "Well then, in that case I feel like your third choice!" On their first date in the fall of 1941 they went to a movie theater, where at some point during the film Marilynn recalls that Beto whispered to her, "To what do you attribute your unparalleled feminine pulchritude?" Being a young and sheltered teenager, Marilynn was unaccustomed to hearing such remarks, and was naturally somewhat taken aback by the young, tall, and handsome professor from Concordia. Beto must indeed have been smitten by Marilynn, because on their third date he proposed marriage. Despite the fact that Marilynn was attracted to Beto, and found him intelligent and fun to be with, she rejected his marriage proposal. But Beto was not to be deterred. In December 1942 he proposed again, this time successfully, and plans were set in motion to wed in the early spring. Marilynn recalls that "That did not give me much time to sew my wedding dress, so I worked on it in the evenings at home because I worked at Kash-Karry during the day. George would phone me every evening after his chapel service with the students and ask how my sewing was coming along."[40] They were married in her parents' home on the evening of March 5, 1943. The Rev. Martin Koehneke, Marilynn's brother-in-law and a classmate of Beto's at Concordia Seminary in St. Louis, read the double ring rites. The young couple established their first home in a small cottage five blocks from Concordia College. Marilynn was twenty years of age and Beto was twenty-seven.[41]

In the next eight years four children would be born: Dan in 1944, Lynn in 1946, Mark in 1948, and Beth in 1952.[42] Beto was a good father and enjoyed hugging and playing with his young children. As they grew older Beto kidded and teased his children in a loving way, and they responded in equal measure. Like his father before him, Beto was not the disciplinarian in the family; Marilynn was. With the exception of the first few years of their marriage, Beto was not home enough to discipline the children, and Marilynn had to be, in effect, both parents. He was often out of town on business, and on Sundays he often preached at Lutheran Mission Festivals all around Texas.[43]

But despite the long days Beto spent at the campus and the many weekends he was away from his family, everyone survived. Marilynn later summed up the early years of their marriage: "Since there are no perfect people, there cannot be any perfect marriages. At times ours definitely was not perfect. We had some rough times. I remember telling George once that anyone who is head of a college or institution should be a single person because he has little time for the family. I wondered if his job didn't come before his family."[44]

Gathering Food and Raising Funds

In addition to providing for his own family, Beto became directly involved with the sustenance of the students. Because Concordia was a boarding school providing three meals a day to growing teenagers, food acquisition was a significant part of the budget. Beto took a system, initiated in 1929 with the founding of the school, and brought it to new levels. Under this system a college vehicle was sent to Lutheran congregations or individuals to collect food for the college pantry. The system lasted well into the late 1950s and provided everything from ham and eggs to pickles and preserves. Individual farmers or ladies groups gathered and prepared the foods and notified the college of its availability.[45]

One student remembers fondly the variety of donated food that made its way to the school kitchen:

> Beto was one of the best scroungers I ever encountered. He knew someone somewhere in the east who had an apple orchard, and every year we would receive cases of apple butter. A lot of army surplus butter as well as powdered milk and powdered eggs ended up on our dining hall. How and from whom he got the stuff is a mystery. Often

it was venison from one of his fellow Kiwanis Club members. Beto also had an arrangement with the state wildlife people. Whenever the state game wardens seized the carcass of a deer killed illegally they would deliver it to campus.[46]

At some point in the early 1940s Beto took up deer hunting. It is quite possible that he was introduced to the sport by Albert Schultz of Eola, who was elected to the Board of Control in 1947. Situated near Eden, a small town south of San Angelo in West Texas, the Shultz Ranch covered 10,000 acres. The Shultz family heritage was German Lutheran, and it had grown wealthy not from ranching, but rather from the many natural gas wells that dotted the ranch. Beto ostensibly went to hunt deer on the Schultz ranch for relaxation, but the invariable result of his trips to West Texas was venison for his students.[47]

Several stories about how Beto actually acquired the venison circulated for decades among the student body, and subsequently became part of campus lore. One story was that Beto was really not all that adept at stalking his prey. The students were privy to the fact that in the farmyard outside the Shultz ranch house was a sixty-foot wooden trough filled with corn to attract deer. It was rumored on campus that in the morning Beto, while still dressed in his pajamas, simply looked out the window of his bedroom at the ranch and shot deer as they were feeding in the trough. Another campus legend held that Beto had the ranch-hands tie up a deer, making it all but impossible for his bullet to miss its mark. The proof of this, according to the legend, was evident on the necks of the deer Beto brought back to campus: they all had rope burns![48] So well known was this story on campus that it was memorialized in cartoon form, and appeared many times over the years in *The Record*, one of the school's student newspapers. Insecure men of lesser character would have taken umbrage at the lampooning of their manly hunting skills, and would maybe even try to quash such talk. Beto, however, took no offense because he knew the students intended none, and he secretly found the stories amusing.

In 1945 the fortunes of Beto's career at Concordia brightened. Because of his energy and proven ability to get things done, Beto was appointed business manager of the school on July 25, with his duties to begin on August 1. As business manager, he was responsible for making all purchases and sales for the school, and for "contracting and administering all funds used for [those] purposes."[49] Beto had become, in essence, Concordia's chief financial officer. As a result of his new appointment he was freed from his responsibility as housemaster, and Carl Heilman, the new English instructor, took the position.[50] Beto, nevertheless, continued to check rooms in the dormitory, albeit with less regularity and frequency.

Beto's appointment as business manager came at an auspicious time for the college. Since the founding of the college in 1926, no new buildings had been constructed on campus, and Kilian Hall was becoming intolerably overcrowded. Beto understood that if the college was going to prosper in the postwar years and accommodate the influx of new students that had been predicted, money would have to be raised to improve the physical facilities.[51] With his appointment as business manager, Beto began his fund-raising activities for the college, an endeavor that would over the coming years make him legendary among Texas Lutherans for being able to separate people from their money.

Concordia's major source of revenue was funding from the Missouri Synod and distributed by the administrative agency, the Board for Higher Education. Each fiscal year the BHE provided an amount for the operation of the school. The synod also owned the land and buildings, which it permitted Concordia to use without cost. In order to obtain funding for a new building, the school's Board of Control presented a resolution, with appropriate documentation, to the triennial convention of the synod. During the Beto years, the synod granted $120,000 for a classroom building (Kramer Hall), $200,000 for a kitchen, dining hall, and infirmary (Texas Hall), $135,000 for renovation of Kilian Hall, $150,000 for a men's dormitory (Behnken Hall), and $58,000 for the addition to the library.

But the generosity of the synod did not meet every need of the school, and Beto turned to Texas Lutherans for additional support. It was said among his contemporaries that Beto knew where every dollar was among the Lutherans in Texas and he began to "shell

the woods" with greater intensity. Beto also knew the Texas Lutherans were not easily separated from their money, even if it was for
the worthy cause of Lutheran education. He characterized his
prospective donors as "tighter than the bark on a tree," and said
that "they would hum in a high wind."[52] To be successful in raising
money for Concordia, Beto realized he would have to charm them
out of their money, and for this reason he trusted no one but himself with the important task of raising funds for the school's development. In this vein, Beto was fond of saying that the reason he
went himself instead of sending someone else was that "people
liked to talk to the organ grinder and not his monkey."[53]

Beto frequently disappeared from campus for two or three days
at a time, sometimes inviting a student to accompany him who was
from the area where he was going to solicit donations.[54] The student served the purpose of drawing a connection between the
locale Beto was visiting and Concordia College in Austin. The key
to Beto's ability to raise money was that he knew how to talk
plainly to the rural Lutherans who had disposable financial
resources. When he visited potential donors at their churches and
in their homes he could easily converse with them about cattle
ranching, farming, the weather, and religion. By the late 1940s and
early 1950s everyone Beto visited knew he was there to ask for
funds for the school. Nonetheless, as his reputation increased over
the years, the Lutherans he visited around the state were honored
that he would come calling on them, and wealthy Lutheran farmers
and ranchers obliged him as best they could.[55]

A typical trip was reported in the student newspaper. Beto left
Austin on November 22, 1947, for Menard and the ranch of Frank
Wilkinson. On the following Sunday morning he preached at the
10:00 AM church services in Eden and the 11:30 services in
Menard. The parishoners presented him with $1,000 for the gym-
nasium. Sunday night he was back at the Wilkinson ranch and left
the next day with the money and a nine-point buck.[56]

Beto's ability to raise funds in Texas enabled the school to
accelerate its growth. From 1937 to 1944 the college had received
a yearly average of $567 from donors; in 1945, with Beto in charge
of fund-raising, the college took in $2,787 and by 1956 the figure

had risen to $6,445.[57] In addition to raising money for the operating budget, he focused on buildings. The third building on the campus was the gymnasium, which was built with $35,000 from Texas and $25,000 from the synod. The fourth was the Hirshi Library built for $80,000 from a single donor.[58] And the chapel was made possible with a grant for $60,000 from "a pious and aged Texas couple." The most ambitious project was raising $216,000 from Texas Lutherans for Studtmann Hall, a dormitory for women. In 1959, the year he accepted the call to Springfield, Beto was in the middle of constructing the men's dormitory, having secured a gift of $100,000 to supplement the synodical grant. So successful was Beto in his fund-raising activities that he was instrumental in securing the money to construct seven buildings on the Concordia campus between 1945 and 1957. Beto, feeling answerable to the people who gave money, felt obligated to make sure their money was spent wisely. In order to report to his donors that Concordia was getting its money's worth from their donated funds, he personally supervised the construction of building projects; if there was excavation or construction going on, he walked the building sites daily and kept abreast of the construction progress by communicating directly with the project foreman.[59]

In addition to his responsibilities as a husband and father, business manager, teacher (since becoming business manager he taught only three courses), and fund-raiser, Beto, in 1945, accepted an appointment from the University of Texas to teach naval history in the Naval Reserve Officer Training Program for two semesters. The position paid $900,[60] and the money was no doubt a boon to his growing family. He undertook the job even though he had not the slightest knowledge about naval history! In 1949 Beto mused to a reporter about his two semesters teaching at the University of Texas: "I told the class at the first period that I didn't know anything about naval history and neither did they, so I'll act as an umpire between you and the book. We got along alright, but I became a little perturbed two weeks after I had started teaching the course when I read a book by Barzun [titled] *A Teacher in America,* containing the statement that any fool can teach naval history."[61]

Concordia Presidency

Beto had been business manager for only three years before he assumed the presidency of Concordia. In November 1948 he was elected by the school's Board of Control to replace Henry Studtmann, who had retired the previous August after twenty-three years as president. Beto was installed as Concordia's second president on Sunday, January 16, 1949, at St. Paul Lutheran Church, just three days before his thirty-third birthday. His parents came to Austin for the occasion, and his father presided over the rite of installation at the evening worship service. A large audience filled the church, and included Lutherans from around Texas as well as his non-Lutheran friends.[62] The new position also entailed a change of residence. The family left its first home a few blocks from campus and occupied the campus home designated as the president's residence.

As president, Beto delegated very little authority, and made all the important decisions. Consequently, the faculty as well as the Board of Control lost influence. They continued to meet as they always had, of course, but in reality it was a perfunctory exercise and a pro forma gesture. Beto did not believe in long meetings, so faculty meetings and those of the Board of Control were brief and to the point. He was viewed as being smart enough, and so frequently right in his decision making, that the faculty and the Board of Control simply accepted his decisions as the best way to do things. Beto unquestionably had the complete trust of the Board of Control, which gave him what he wanted. Furthermore, when the opportunity presented itself, Beto made sure that people whom he trusted and worked well with were appointed to fill vacancies on the board. So complete was his control that Beto's stepping stone to the presidency, the position of business manager, became superfluous during the tenure of his presidency. One business manager who served under Beto recalled that "when Beto became president, being the business manager did not mean a thing. Beto made all the decisions. My responsibility as business manager was merely to write the checks and debit the amount against a particular account for the stack of bills I received from him every week."[63]

Beto's twenty years at Concordia Austin can roughly be divided into two halves. It was not so much a matter of one part being a teacher and the other being a president as it was between the school being exclusively a secondary school and the school including a junior college. His approach and philosophy during the years from his arrival in 1939 to 1951, the year when Concordia added the two years of college, were very much the same. The student body remained small, the buildings matched the student body, and the educational offerings were limited. But with the addition of the junior college, buildings, staff, faculty, and courses all needed expansion. Beto's style continued to remain hands-on, but it was impossible to do it with the intimacy he had used during the high school years. He delegated more authority, especially in dormitory supervision. Already in 1949, with the completion of the Hirshi Library, he moved his office from Kilian Hall to a wing of the library. When he was not out of town, he spent more time in his office and worked with a secretary. He arrived at the office early in the morning and impressed everyone by responding to each item of mail within twenty-four hours. His goal was to handle each piece of correspondence only once.[64] Access to him remained easy because he placed his desk in the anteroom facing the open door while the secretary occupied the adjoining office. Casual conversation was not encouraged and once an issue had been settled, Beto did not initiate small talk. Either the guest raised a second issue or there was an uncomfortable silence and an awkward exit. But the changes in administrative style were to be expected and Beto changed his style so logically that it was almost imperceptible.

Although the dream of a junior college was present at Concordia's foundation, the formal request for synodical support was not made until 1947. The convention, however, referred the resolution that proposed adding the first year of college in 1948 to the BHE for study. Three years later, in 1950, the convention approved, but Beto asked for a delay until the next year to coincide with the completion of a classroom building.[65] Another factor in the decision was a sizeable number of gifted students in the 1951 high school graduating class. This group of young men was the first to spend six years on the Austin campus, and a bond of fellowship developed between Beto and these students.

During the second half of his administration from 1951, when the school had become a junior college, to 1959, when he relinquished his position, the high school enrollment declined and the greater maturity of the college students set the tone on campus. In 1956 the numbers were almost equal, with seventy-three students in high school and sixty-eight in college. By 1959 the high school numbered only sixty-six and the college had grown to one hundred and fifteen. Also, during his second ten years, Beto faced the challenge of changing the school to include racial minorities and making it coeducational. Without official instructions from St. Louis, or for that matter, without consultation with anyone, Beto racially integrated the Concordia campus in 1953 by enrolling the first African American.[66]

Racial Integration

Beto may properly be counted among those brave Texans who led the way in championing racial equality and desegregating education in the state. He was no stranger to the racial animus that permeated Southern culture, and by 1950 he began to make his position on racial equality unequivocally clear. Sometime during the late 1940s Beto received a summons to report for jury duty, and subsequently served as a juror in a criminal trial where a black man was the defendant. After the conclusion of the trial Beto unabashedly expressed to the students in one of his classes at Concordia his doubts about the fundamental fairness one could expect in a criminal trial in Texas where the defendant was black. He underscored his concern by telling the class that while he and most of the jurors were deliberating in good faith and honestly trying to reach a fair and just decision, one of the jurors kept muttering, "That nigger's guilty."[67] In another instance, when asked by a newspaper reporter from the *Austin American Statesman* in 1950 about his views on racial desegregation, Beto responded: "They [African Americans] pay taxes, they fight wars, they are citizens, and they should receive equal opportunity for higher education."[68]

The answer was given in response to a racial desegregation case that originated in Austin and had attracted the attention of the nation in 1950. The United States Supreme Court in the case of *Sweatt v. Painter* ordered the University of Texas to admit Herman Sweatt, a black from Houston, to its law school. In its majority opinion the Court made it quite clear that equality in state programs of higher education implied more than merely duplicating programs of study and physical plants for the sole use of blacks.

Fully a year before public school systems were ordered to desegregate as a result of *Brown v. Board of Education* Beto, in 1953, brought to Concordia its first black student, Henry Sorrel. Even though Concordia was a private Lutheran boy's school, the significance of Beto's bringing a black student to a school that had been all-white since 1926, and then totally integrating him into the student body and the life of the campus community should not be underestimated. These were, after all, dangerous times, and the question of racial integration rubbed a raw nerve across the South, and the presence of potential violence was understood by all. Beto thought the Southern custom of segregation loathsome, and his religious beliefs would not allow him to tolerate racial discrimination in any fashion.

Henry Sorrel was a quiet, polite, and well-mannered youth who was born in New Orleans but raised in Houston. His father was a missionary affiliated with the Missouri Synod, and a 1936 graduate from the Lutheran-sponsored Immanuel College in Greensboro, North Carolina.[69] His missionary work in Houston had brought him into contact with Beto. Pastor Sorrel mentioned to Beto that he was having trouble finding a quality high school that would admit his son so he could acquire a good education. Without any consultations, hesitation, or regard for the social conventions of the day Beto boldly told the father that Henry was welcome at Concordia.[70]

When Beto returned from Houston he assembled the faculty and students and told them Henry would be coming to Concordia and that he would brook no arguments or protests about his decision; Henry was going to be coming to Concordia and that was that. When Henry arrived at Concordia in August 1953, Beto called the faculty and students together once again and introduced

Henry to them. Afterwards, Beto invited Henry into his home where he told Henry that if he ever had any trouble to come straight to him. Beto was intent on doing anything to make sure that Henry felt comfortable at Concordia and was successful in his studies. Just to make sure everything went smoothly for Henry, Beto assigned the biggest and strongest upperclassman at Concordia to watch over him. At first the students and faculty were curious about Henry, but quickly accepted him into the campus community. Henry lived communally in the dormitory with the other boys, shared bathroom facilities with them, ate in the dining hall, attended class, and worshiped in the chapel. In 1953 this mixing of white and black in such a close and intimate way was truly out of the mainstream not only in Austin, but in Texas and the South as well.

While the question of racial tolerance on the Concordia campus was put to rest by Beto, things were not quite so settled in the Austin community. On Sundays the students at Concordia all attended St. Paul Lutheran Church. The first time Henry walked into the church with his classmates in late August 1953, the parishioners greeted him with icy stares. One parishioner got up and told Henry he was not to come again, but if he liked he could stay for that Sunday's service and sit in a pew at the very back of the church. Then Beto walked in, quickly understood what was happening, and informed the entire congregation that he would not tolerate their unchristian behavior toward a fellow Lutheran. Beto then escorted Henry to the pew at the front of the church closest to the altar. Nothing more was ever said, and that pew became Henry's permanent seat at Sunday worship for the next four years.[71]

By the late fall of 1953 word had spread around Austin about "the nigger boy at the church school."[72] Shortly before Thanksgiving a small confrontation occurred at the edge of campus when a group of Austin citizens gathered one afternoon to gawk and ostensibly to find out if indeed a black student was enrolled at Concordia and attending class with the rest of the white student body. Upon learning of the commotion Beto came out, undoubtedly wearing his Stetson, and without any thought of the possible consequences to himself informed the crowd that Henry had been there a couple of months already and it really was none of their concern. When the police arrived the crowd dispersed.[73]

Even though the campus was integrated and he was accepted by his fellow students, much of Austin remained segregated and fellowship with white students did not always insure service at all businesses such as certain soda fountains. After graduating from Concordia with his high school diploma, Henry joined the Baltimore Police Department, where he served for thirty-four years.[74]

Coeducation

At the same time Beto brought the first black student to Concordia, he began laying the foundation for transforming Concordia into a coeducational institution. His decision to admit young women was driven in part by his knowledge that there was a growing crisis in the educational system of the Lutheran Church; there simply were not enough women to teach in its elementary schools.[75] In addition to solving such minor problems as creating an education curriculum and hiring additional personnel, Beto needed to overcome the major impediment in making Concordia coeducational. That hurdle was the construction of a dormitory for women. Beto worked tirelessly for this cause. In a forty-five-day period in early 1954, he addressed more than thirty gatherings of Lutherans throughout the state. While his primary appeal to the two hundred Lutheran congregations in Texas was for funds to construct the new dormitory, he also publicized the program and recruited students.[76] Again he was successful in raising the money, and ground was broken on the new women's dormitory in September 1954, and women began matriculating at Concordia in September 1955.

Beto, however, was apprehensive about bringing women to the Concordia campus; he was initially not sure how life on campus with female students would work out. Prior to the arrival of the first female students, Beto spent considerable time talking with the boys and telling them in no uncertain terms they had to behave themselves and be mannerly and gentlemanly. He also cautioned them about girls and dating, saying that "if you go out with a girl and she allows you to kiss her on the first date, just think of those salt blocks lying out in the pasture and remember that every bull that comes along gives them a lick!"[77]

Once the women arrived, Beto watched both them and the boys like a hawk. If he thought a coed was wearing something inappropriate or behaving in a way he did not approve of, he pulled her aside and gently let his concerns be known. When Beto admonished a student he never made her feel guilty, but counseled her in the same manner that a loving father would his daughter. They always got the message, and as the 1955 fall semester progressed, an informal code of behavior based on what Beto thought right and proper permeated the campus.[78] One woman from that first class candidly remarked years later that "Dr. Beto had a presence about him; he was a big man, larger than life in all respects, and we were all in awe of him. To think I might do something to cause him to give me his piercing silent look of disapproval made my stomach hurt. No one ever wanted to tell their parents that he had to scold them for any reason. The girls admired, respected, and trusted him like a father."[79]

Beto's Service to Concordia

In May 1954 Beto had been given another opportunity to leave Concordia when he received another "call," this time to be head of the Department of Church History and Historical Theology at his alma mater, Concordia Seminary, in St. Louis.[80]

This call was not so easy to reject. Beto struggled with this call, as is evident from his response to Alfred O. Fuerbringer, President of the St. Louis Seminary:

> During the past three weeks there has been no time during my waking hours when the call to St. Louis has not been on my mind. After giving the call serious consideration and wavering from day to day between "to go or not to go," I am led to the decision that the call should be declined. A prime consideration which led me to this decision is the awareness of my own inadequacy in the area of Church History. In my opinion, a professor of Church History at the Church's leading theological seminary should be an expert and an authority in

this field. Quite frankly, I don't qualify. There is some regret in my heart; I believe that I would have enjoyed working with you.[81]

In the years following his returning the call to St. Louis, Beto continued to work tirelessly. Five buildings had been added to the campus during the ten years Beto served as president, and at the time of his ten-year anniversary in 1959, plans were already underway for a new men's dormitory.[82] But Beto was more than "the building president." He was, perhaps first and foremost, the spiritual guide and leader for many of the young men and women who went to Concordia.

In January 1959, colleagues and friends gathered to celebrate Beto's ten-year anniversary as president. His campus office and home were flooded with letters and telegrams of congratulations, including one from Gov. Price Daniel,[83] and a banquet was held in his honor. In attendance at the banquet, in addition to religious figures, were his friends O. B. Ellis, Director of the Texas Department of Corrections, and H. H. Coffield, Chairman of the Texas Board of Corrections.[84] Remarkably, Beto's unquestionable success at Concordia is only half the story of his years in Austin. Beto had a special relationship with Ellis and Coffield, and his close association with these two men during the six-year period from 1953 to 1959 is one of the truly great stories in American penology.

Chapter 3

THE TEXAS PRISON SYSTEM: THE FIRST
ONE HUNDRED YEARS (1849–1953)

In 1849, one hundred years before Beto's installation as Concordia's president, the first convict was confined in the partially completed penitentiary at Huntsville. During the hundred years that followed, the administrators of the state of Texas attempted to balance public safety, the humane treatment of prisoners, and fiscal responsibility. The perfect balance was elusive and the record of the prison system is a spotty one, alternating between neglect and reform. When Beto was appointed to the Texas Prison Board, the state agency created in 1927 to supervise the prison system, another attempt at reform had just begun, and Beto became an important participant in the movement. A backward glance into the prison system's hundred years not only establishes the context in which Beto would work, but also provides a yardstick for measuring the contributions made by Beto and his contemporaries to improve the prison system itself.

Economic Self-sufficiency

The goal of economic self-sufficiency was the most prominent and enduring theme in the history of the prison system, and that theme remained dominant in the Beto era. The key to prison self-sufficiency was prison labor, and with the construction of the first prison at Huntsville, appropriately named "The Walls" after its massive fifteen-foot-high walls, the legislature and prison officials searched for novel ways to achieve that goal. In the early years prisoners worked inside the prison as shoemakers, blacksmiths, carpenters, tailors, wagon makers, harness and saddle craftsmen and in the fabrication of basic agricultural implements. In the 1850s manufacturing was added to the prison workshop when the state introduced a cotton and textile mill. By 1859 forty looms were in operation and the profits flowed into the state treasury.

As the number of convicts increased, however, finding adequate tasks suited for prisoners within the prison became impossible, so the legislature, in 1866, adopted a practice that became a dismal chapter in Texas history: the convict lease system. Under one variation of this system a private entrepreneur leased the entire penitentiary, along with the prisoners, and used the prisoners in the production of goods. The contractor, in turn, assumed responsibility for the total operation of the prison including everything from the care of the prisoners to hiring the guards. A further refinement of this system enabled the contractor to sublease the prisoners to other citizens who could put the prisoners to work in cotton fields, stone quarries, tanneries, logging operations, and railroad construction. And under yet another variation, the state maintained control of the prisons, but contracted prisoners for work on projects outside the prison. The corporation that constructed the state capitol in the mid-1880s, for example, used 500 prisoners to quarry granite and limestone.

In spite of oversight mechanisms put into place by the legislature, abuse of convicts and mismanagement of state property were all too frequent. Texas newspapers were often the only watchdogs of prison conditions, and they graphically described physical abuse, inadequate housing, and malnutrition. Because of a meager diet and lack of medical care, sicknesses such as scurvy, chronic diarrhea, pneumonia, and malaria were common. For trivial offenses convicts were put into stocks, whipped unmercifully, or shot. Attempts to escape were almost daily occurrences, as was the practice of self-mutilation by heel string cutting. In this procedure the convict severed his Achilles' tendon running from the heel up the back of the leg. Without the tendon the foot was disabled and labor in the fields was not possible. And after a physician sutured the tendon together, complete healing could take place only with months of rest. Newspaper accounts of conditions aroused public opinion and public opinion spurred political action, so that finally, in 1910, the convict lease system was ended.[1]

Even though the system no longer existed when Beto joined the Prison Board, another method of utilizing prison labor outside of the prison itself did exist and it was an outgrowth of the convict lease system. The experience with leasing prisoners to cotton farmers had demonstrated the feasibility of using prisoners in the cotton fields, and prison administrators decided to enter into the agricultural enterprise itself. As a result, in 1883 the legislature appropriated funds for establishing the first prison farm, the 1,511-acre Wynne Plantation, located two miles north of Huntsville. Two years later the Harlem Farm (later Jester Units I and II), a 2,500-acre sugar plantation in Fort Bend County, was purchased. During the years that followed prison administrators added more agricultural units, so that by the time Beto came on the scene, agricultural products, especially cotton, provided the lifeblood of the prison system.

The expectation of creating a stable and continuous source of revenue from state-owned farms, however, was never realized. Poor farm management, internal corruption, and crop failures often failed to offset the investment the state made in property and equipment.[2]

The MacCormick Survey, 1944

The cycle of neglect and reform repeated itself in the late 1930s and following public complaints of inhumane treatment, the legislature, in 1943, passed a resolution to establish an independent committee to investigate. The public response was a cynical opinion that it was yet one more pro forma exercise to deflect public attention away from the legislature's failure to solve the problems.[3]

The press did not let the issue die, and finally in May 1944 the board took action and invited a recognized authority in penology, Austin H. MacCormick, to examine the Texas prison system and recommend reforms. MacCormick, known as "Spike" to his friends, spent sixty-five years in penology occupying various posts, including the commissioner of corrections for New York City. Later, at the request of the secretary of the Army, he restructured the military prison system, and for it received the Presidential Medal of Merit, at that time the nation's highest civilian award.[4] Eventually he joined the faculty of the University of California at Berkeley as professor of criminology and for several decades served as the executive director of the Osborne Association.[5]

When MacCormick arrived in Texas in the late summer of 1944 he found the prison system with a decaying physical plant, buildings in need of repair, and the grounds littered with broken and rusted machinery. The soil of the agricultural lands had been depleted by repeated cultivation of cotton, and it was tilled by the muscle labor of man and mule. The industrial operation inside the prison was limited to producing license plates. Living conditions provided for the convicts conveyed an image of misery and grinding poverty. Clothing was limited to a set of thin cotton clothes that would be boiled from time to time in iron cauldrons with soapless water. Convicts who were not in the "Walls" unit were housed in "tanks," one-room military-like structures thirty to forty feet in length and fifteen feet wide.[6] Sanitation did not exist and convicts suffered from malnutrition, scurvy, malaria, chronic diarrhea, and pneumonia. Personal abuse went uncontrolled. The personnel system was also inadequate. Wardens were hired, not because of their expertise, but because of "Good Ole Boy" Texas-style political patronage. Guards were often underpaid, untrained, indolent, corrupt, brutal, and sadistic. The turnover of personnel was high, and the number needed for proper management was lacking.[7]

MacCormick sent his report to the board on January 22, 1945, and set forth clearly all the problems he had encountered the previous summer. His report bluntly concluded that the system was among the worst in the United States, and the shame of the Lone Star State. He recommended that the board begin overhauling the system by reforming the agricultural program, constructing facilities for 700 inmates, creating a vocational industrial training program for the inmates, and upgrading the prison personnel. His report, while certainly more detailed, thorough, and more credible than the newspaper exposés, was, to no one's surprise, another scathing indictment of the Texas prison system. MacCormick remained on call as a consultant to the board for three years, but no one contacted him further and nothing of substance was undertaken to correct a single deficiency MacCormick had identified.[8]

In January 1947 the cycle was about to be repeated with the press reporting abuses and members of the legislature asking questions. The board decided to invite MacCormick to Texas to conduct yet another survey.[9] The otherwise placid and unflappable Mac-Cormick was livid. Why do another survey when nothing had been done in response to the first one? He then proceeded to work around the board and went first to the press. In the spring of 1947 he began a vigorous campaign of letter-writing to Texas newspapers describing the conditions. And then he broke his principle of keeping politics out of prison affairs and went directly to the governor. Beauford Jester, elected the previous November, had campaigned on a platform that included prison reform. In a telegram to the governor, Mac-Cormick denounced the Texas prison system as "deplorable, inhumane, and barbaric,"[10] and in the letter that followed he sent a synopsis of his 1944 report. MacCormick laid the blame for the conditions at the feet of the board and the general manager.

Governor Jester and Reform

Jester began making inquiries and soon concluded that Mac-Cormick was correct in his appraisal and informed the general manager to either resign or be fired. Finally in November the general manager resigned and the chairman of the board and the vice-chairman, in a display of solidarity with the general manager, did the same. Jester then had the unprecedented opportunity to restructure the composition of the board and provide it with a mandate that would have a lasting historical importance. Jester's vision for the board was to make membership on the Texas Prison Board "an honor conferred only on men who have been extremely successful in their careers," and appointment to it "regarded as a particularly high compliment."[11]

Jester's first appointment was for the chairman's position. He chose Wilbur Cunningham Windsor, a broad-minded and public spirited independent oil operator, rancher, businessman, banker, and civic leader from Tyler. Not only was he a successful business-man, but he was a confidant of Jester. The governor gave Windsor a copy of MacCormick's 1944 report and pointedly told him to establish board policy that would lead to meaningful reform and to look for a truly progressive and enlightened individual who could bring leadership and vision to the general manager's position. Windsor did both.[12]

During the summer of 1947 Windsor personally inspected every unit of the Texas prison system and realized conditions were worse than had been reported three years earlier. Windsor's pro-posal, in keeping with MacCormick's recommendation, identified five broad areas for reform: rehabilitation, living conditions for the inmates, increased salaries and improved living conditions for the guards, modernization and mechanization of farming, and legisla-tion that would enable prison industries to produce a profit.[13] The board adopted the proposal and the document remains as one of the significant documents in the archives of the Texas prison sys-tem. It also became Governor Jester's blueprint, and the stage was set for what is unquestionably the single greatest penal reform story in American history.

O. B. Ellis in Memphis

Windsor, in his search for the right person to translate the board's policy from paper to practice, toured various state prison systems and asked for advice from prison officials. The one name that was mentioned time after time was O. B. Ellis. Oscar Byron Ellis was born in Cleveland, Alabama, on August 27, 1902.[14] His father, a strict Methodist, was a farmer and school superinten-dent who had a widespread reputation for his honesty and integrity. Young Oscar worked on his father's land and by his early teenage years he had learned the basic economics of truck farming and had acquired an appreciation for the science of agri-cultural management.

After graduation from Birmingham Southern College in 1920 with a degree in chemistry, Ellis did some graduate work at the University of Tennessee and then went to Memphis where he took a position with the Florsheim Shoe Company. In 1927 he taught science at a Memphis secondary school, but after one year, became an accountant with the school system and eventually its business manager. He found his calling in 1937 when at the age of thirty-four, he won an election for one of the three seats on the Shelby County Commissioner's Court. The duty of the commissioners was to administer the county's roads, bridges, and its 5,000-acre penal farm. A few months after Ellis took office, the manager of the penal farm died so Ellis personally assumed management of the farm while he continued with his other responsibilities.

During the following eleven years, Ellis transformed the ramshackle county farm with its 600 inmates, into a model correctional facility. He reclaimed the farm's agricultural promise through soil conservation and scientific farming, and improved the quality of its livestock. His goal was not only to educate the inmates in modern farming methods, but also to provide a place for Southern farmers to see the latest scientific advances in farming equipment and methods and to acquire blooded livestock at reasonable prices. By 1947 the penal farm was recognized as one of the nation's premier experimental farms, and that year alone attracted almost 5,000 visitors from seventeen states and one foreign country.[15]

His treatment of prisoners was also enlightened, certainly by Southern standards. He opened a school for illiterates from both races and created a number of vocational programs to teach a variety of trades.[16] He established an isolation unit for that small percentage of inmates whose life was a litany of crime. "Toughies," as he called them, would remain "charges of society for the rest of their lives" but their absence from the remainder of the prison population simplified discipline and raised the morale of the other inmates. Those inmates who were able-bodied were expected to work a ten-hour day, but they were also given six hours of leisure time each day for recreation, education, and religious activity. Prisoners who broke the rules could be punished by loss of privileges, loss of good conduct time, and finally solitary confinement, but Ellis prohibited further punishment such as whipping or other forms of brutality, including verbal abuse and cursing.[17]

But a truly impressive practice, beyond the efficient management of the farm and the humane treatment of the prisoners, was his relation with the press. He kept the press and wire services fully informed on events at the farm, whether the news was good or bad. The press responded with laudatory articles, and Windsor soon learned about the Shelby County Penal Farm. Windsor and several board members inspected the farm and readily made the comparison between the Ellis' model farm and the deteriorated condition of the Texas prison lands. Windsor invited Ellis to Tyler for an interview with the entire board and then offered him a four-year appointment as general manager of the Texas Prison System. Before accepting, Ellis made a hurried inspection tour of the prison properties. Then, in full agreement with the Windsor policy, he accepted the appointment.[18]

Ellis in Texas, 1948–1961

Ellis arrived in Huntsville on January 1, 1948, and began working on a proposal for implementing reform. At the end of February he finished his blueprint and asked Windsor to schedule a board meeting for its presentation. He also asked Windsor to invite the press to the meeting, an unprecedented practice, but one that Windsor accepted. The presentation, delivered at Huntsville on the first day of March, brought unanimous endorsement from the board and ecstatic support from the press. By the end of the year more than one hundred articles and editorials appeared in Texas newspapers, all of which reported positively on the board, Ellis, and the program for overhauling the Texas prison system.[19]

But the program also had a price-tag of more than four million dollars, funds that only the legislature could provide. Following the March meeting Ellis and other members of the board stumped the state holding public forums and rallying citizen support for their appropriations bill.[20] Often they would speak in one town and then sleep in the back of the car as a driver carried them to the next town where they would present another talk.[21] When he was not on the road, Ellis used the resources at hand, such as soap, water, paint, plaster, and inmate labor, to make improvements. Ellis planted ivy next to the century-old red-brick walls of the Huntsville unit and was responsible for starting the colorful flower gardens at the entrance of the Walls Unit that still exist.

But the most pressing and immediate challenge Ellis faced was the prison's personnel. The problem was greater among the rank and file than with the administrators. There were incompetents in the ranks and others who could not change their ways.[22] During the first eighteen months Ellis summarily fired more than fifty guards and wardens for a variety of reasons, including brutality, incompetence, carelessness, and assisting convicts with procuring drugs and alcohol. But he also initiated a "Warden of the Year Award" to increase morale.

One year after taking the office, Ellis made a report to the board and claimed some successes. The inmate morale was high, and they believed that something was being done to improve their condition. To document his conclusion Ellis cited statistics of self mutilations and escapes, two indexes used by penologists to gauge inmate dissatisfaction and unrest. Both had declined dramatically. Self mutilations declined from eighty-seven to twenty and escapes dropped from 126 to ninety. But substantial change could only be achieved with a generous appropriation from the legislature.

The Fifty-first Legislature did not fail. The friendly press and the public meetings had helped create a favorable climate. On March 7, 1949, Governor Jester signed the bill appropriating four million dollars that had passed the legislature with a unanimous vote. There was even an additional emergency appropriation bill of half a million dollars to cover the increased size of the prison population.[23] Ellis' only disappointment was the failure to include a salary increase for the employees. In short order construction began on bath houses and laundries, and ground was broken for the segregation unit at the Walls. Ellis was also able to hire two qualified assistants, Richard Jones to oversee the building program and Byron W. Frierson to modernize the prison farms.[24]

A major project initiated by Ellis was the construction of the segregation unit. It was in keeping with his philosophy from Shelby County, which held that "toughies" constituted about ten percent of the population and their removal from the remaining inmates simplified management. The structure was built within the Walls Unit and designed in such a way as to require the minimum number of guards. Two long cellblocks stood four stories high. Each of the 566 cells, designed to hold one man, measured five feet in width, nine feet in length and eight feet in height and faced inward to a closed courtyard. Because no effort was made to engage them in work, these prisoners received two meals a day instead of the customary three. Three times a week they were permitted to enter the inner courtyard for two hours of exercise and fresh air. The first wing was completed in January 1951. The press dubbed it "Little Alcatraz," but the convicts cynically named it "The Shamrock" after a posh hotel built on South Main Street in Houston by Glenn McCarthy, a flamboyant and wealthy Texas oil man. Both were exclusive, but only one was luxurious.

While the building program was underway, so were improvements on the prison farms. One of the first purchases made was of tractors. Not only did they replace the mules used for plowing and cultivating, but they were utilized as the "Ellis Taxis." Instead of marching long distances to the fields, the inmates climbed on board trailers pulled by the tractors. Efficiency and increased productivity was an immediate result.[25] Then followed a program of improving the cattle herd and requests for assistance from Texas A&M University for such things as pasture improvement and insect control. By the fall of 1951 the prison system was supplying all of its meat requirement from a herd of 10,288 registered beef cattle, and the cost of keeping an inmate had dropped twenty-five cents per day from 1948, thereby saving the state treasury nearly $700,000 a year.[26]

Not everything about Ellis' first four years was a success story. The prison population constantly increased while the appropriations measures in the state legislature were considered only every other year. Forecasting the prison population to match the biennial budget cycle was next to impossible. Ellis also failed to persuade the legislature to appropriate a million dollars for an institution for the criminally insane. Along with the inmates in the segregation unit, this small minority was disruptive and difficult to control. They belonged in a separate facility and not in the penitentiary. And finally, there was the low compensation of the prison personnel. Without adequate compensation, hiring qualified people was difficult.

Compared to his accomplishments, however, these three shortcomings were insignificant, and on November 12, 1951, the board unanimously reappointed him for another four years and increased his salary to $12,500 per year. Governor Allan Shivers, who had assumed office following the death of Governor Jester, praised Ellis for his work and credited the Prison Board for hiring him for the position. Ellis went on to serve until his death in 1961.[27]

The influence of Ellis on Beto cannot be underestimated. He was the general manager of the prisons when Beto joined the Prison Board, and Ellis was the person Beto would replace when Beto became the general manager. For Beto, Ellis provided not only an example of an enlightened administrator, but he began the reforms on which Beto could build.

Above left: Louis Henry Beto, St. Louis, Missouri, 1914.

Above right: Margaret Beto, with a coal scuttle, Hysham, Montana, 1915.

Left: George J. Beto in a soldier's uniform, New Rockford, North Dakota, ca. 1918.

George J. Beto at Concordia College, Milwaukee, Wisconsin, ca. 1935.

Above: George J. Beto the "Deerslayer" following a hunt in West Texas, 1951.

Left: George J. Beto, President of Concordia College, Austin, Texas, 1950s.

Above: Beto family living in Austin, Texas, 1953. From left to right: George J. Beto, son Mark, daughter Lynn, wife Marilynn Beto, daughter Beth, and son Dan.

Cartoon from *The Concordia Record,* May 1958.

Above: O. B. Ellis, 1951.
Courtesy East Texas Chamber of Commerce

Left: H. H. Coffield, 1959.
Courtesy Texas Parade Magazine

(From l–r) Governor Price Daniel, George J. Beto, and former Governor Allan Shivers at a reception in Austin honoring Beto, 1959. *Photograph by Bill Malone*

George J. Beto in 1959, shortly before his departure for Springfield, Illinois. *Courtesy UPI, Inc.*

George J. Beto's installation as President of Concordia Theological Seminary, Springfield, Illinois, 1959. Beto's brother-in-law, Martin L. Koehneke, is to Beto's right.

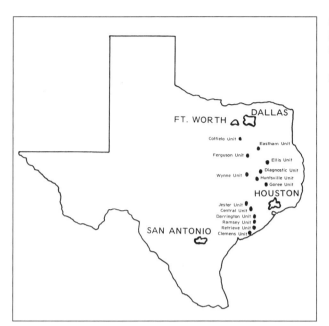

Left: Map of Texas Department of Corrections. *Courtesy 1971 TDC Annual Report*

(From l–r) George J. Beto, Governor John B. Connally, and H. H. Coffield, Chairman of the Texas Board of Corrections, at the director's residence in Huntsville, 1963. *Frank Dobbs, photographer*

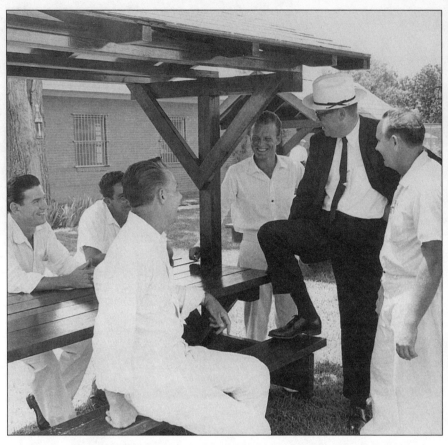

George J. Beto talking to inmates, 1963. *Frank Dobbs, photographer*

Opposite upper: Members of the Texas Board of Corrections. Standing from left to right: W. Irvin "Red" James (Houston), Walter Pfluger (San Angelo), Walter Mischer (Houston), Fred Shields (San Antonio), James Marvin Windham(Livingston); seated: George J. Beto and H. H. Coffield (Rockdale), mid-1960s. *Frank Dobbs, photographer*

Opposite lower: George J. Beto in a wheelchair, returning to duty after tractor accident on his farm, with a group of inmates on the "yard" at the Huntsville Unit, 1964. *Courtesy UPI, Inc.*

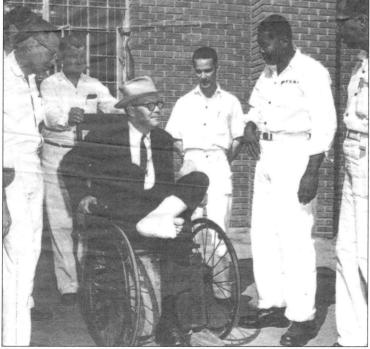

George J. Beto "walking the units," here speaking to an inmate, 1967.
Courtesy Concordia Historical Institute, Dept. of Archives and History, Lutheran Church-Missouri Synod, St. Louis

Above: (From l–r) Max Rogers, Jack Kyle, H. H. "Tubby" Sandel, and George J. Beto, 1968.

Left: George J. Beto and Arleigh B. Templeton, President of Sam Houston State University, 1968. *Frank Dobbs, photographer*

George J. Beto, with Marilynn Beto in center, receiving an award from Governor Preston Smith, 1972. *Frank Dobbs, photographer*

Opposite upper: George J. Beto in front of the Walls Unit at Huntsville, 1970. *Photo by Sam Pierson, Jr., copyright Houston Chronicle*

Opposite lower: (From l–r) Governor Preston Smith, Lieutenant Governor Ben Barnes, former Governor Allan Shivers, H. H. Coffield, and George J. Beto at a prison function, 1970. *Frank Dobbs, photographer*

George J. Beto in 1986 with trademark Stetson hat. *Photo copyright Houston Chronicle*

George J. Beto, Distinguished Professor in the College of Criminal Justice, Sam Houston State University, late 1980s.

The George J. Beto Criminal Justice Center at Sam Houston State University in Huntsville.

Chapter 4

THE TEXAS PRISON BOARD: BETO, COFFIELD, AND ELLIS (1953–1959)

Beto's appointment to the Prison Board was a political act, and politics played a role in the governor's decision. Even though Beto's mother was an ardent Republican, Beto, already during his years as a student in Milwaukee, believed that the Republican party lacked "a social conscience."[1] When Beto arrived in Texas in 1939 the Republican Party was a mere shadow, so Beto affiliated with the Democrats, the only party in town. Ever since the end of Reconstruction, the Democrats had easily defeated the Republicans, and the real struggles for political office took place not on the first Tuesday in November, but on the date of the party primary.

Although the Texas Democrats supported Franklin Roosevelt and his vice president, "Cactus Jack" Garner, a Texan, during the first two terms, an increasing number of voters became disenchanted with the New Deal. This was true especially after Roosevelt chose to run for a third term and Garner decided not to be Roosevelt's running mate. During the ensuing years this disenchantment grew into a division within the party between the conservatives, symbolized by W. Lee O'Daniel and Coke R. Stevenson, and the liberals, personified by Ralph Yarborough and Lyndon B. Johnson. Governor Buford Jester, a conservative, kept the party together in 1948 to support Harry Truman, and Beto joyfully reported Truman's upset victory over Thomas Dewey to his students. But Truman's stand on tidelands oil, whereby the offshore oil became the property of the nation instead of the various coastal states, widened the divide between the Democratic factions. In 1952, when Adlai Stevenson adopted the Truman position, and when Dwight D. Eisenhower came out in support of the oil belonging to the coastal states, the conservative Democrats, including Beto, joined with the Republicans to carry the state for Eisenhower.[2]

Following the death of Governor Jester, Lieutenant Governor Allan Shivers became governor and preserved power for the conservative Democrats. In the 1952 primary, Shivers handily defeated the liberal Ralph Yarborough and continued to serve as governor until 1957. Beto, although living in a precinct that favored the liberal faction, supported Shivers, and that support eventually turned into admiration. Referring to an event at a party convention, Beto wrote to Shivers: "Your handling of the extremely delicate situation of last Friday was masterful."[3] In 1957, Shivers was succeeded by another conservative, Price Daniel. Beto actively supported Daniel and received thanks from the party leadership for his role in helping Daniel achieve a "lopsided victory" in the election.[4]

Beto admitted to never having considered public service prior to the appointment, but when Governor Shivers phoned him in late January 1953, all that changed:

> Shivers, whom I didn't know, called me one day and advised me that he understood I was a friend of his, and that he liked to have his friends do things for him. He told me that he wanted to appoint me to the Prison Board. . . . He said it was Beauford Jester's policy and his policy to appoint prominent businessmen in the State to that board, but he believed I could make some contribution. He also told me that O. B. Ellis was doing a good job and that the prison had made remarkable progress, and he cautioned me against being a disruptive influence on the Board. He also asked me to survey all of the prison units and report back to him, which I did.[5]

Thus began Beto's involvement with penology. The person who had vacated the position that Beto would occupy was a college

professor, so Shivers was able to fill the post with another academi-
cian as well as a theologian. When the boys at Concordia, aware of
their own resistance to authority, heard of the new job for their
president, they heartily approved. After all, they had provided him
with all the experience he would need in his new position.

Not everyone was immediately comfortable with Shivers'
choice to fill the vacancy on the board with Beto. Shivers had not
consulted with either O. B. Ellis or H. H. Coffield, an influential
member of the Prison Board, and they did not know how a
"preacher" would fit in. So, shortly after the appointment, the two
men appeared at the Beto residence on the Concordia campus to
size him up. No record exists of how long the meeting lasted, what
subjects were discussed, or what was said. What is known for certain is that after this initial meeting both Ellis and Coffield left the
Concordia campus secure in the knowledge that Shivers had made
an excellent choice. Out of this meeting an enduring friendship was
formed among the three men. When Beto first met Ellis and
Coffield he could not have been aware that the impending association with these two men would irrevocably alter not only his life,
but the direction of the Texas prison system as well.

Following this first historic meeting, Beto returned the courtesy
by personally visiting and inspecting all thirteen units that comprised the Texas prison system, and used the occasion to prepare a
report for Governor Shivers. Beto later presented this same report
to the March meeting of the board. When the newspapers reported
Beto's appointment to the board, letters from inmates began arriving at his Concordia office. Beto read them all, investigated the
complaints, and made them part of his initial report.[6] Beto hit his
stride immediately, and maintained it for six years.

The Texas Prison Board

The Texas Prison Board was composed of nine members who
were appointed by the governor and confirmed by the Senate.
Each person was appointed for a six-year term. The members met
five times a year, generally in Huntsville, Houston, Dallas, or Austin.
Although the formal meeting convened at 9:30 AM and finished

before noon, most of the discussions and decisions were made informally the night before at a dinner meeting and in separate conversations.[7]

The board elected its own officers, but O. B. Ellis provided the board chairman with the items for the agenda. Ellis divided the operations of the system into certain subdivisions such as "Agriculture and Livestock," "New Construction," or "Legislation and Legal," and the chairman assigned each member to one of these categories. Every attempt was made to match the member's interest and skills with the appropriate category. Beto's predecessor had been responsible for "Inmates," and that task not only interested Beto, but it was also where he was most competent. Each member then became a committee of one who would report to the board on matters concerning his category. In the weeks between the meetings, when any issue arose, Ellis simply filed the material with one of the committees, and then prior to the next meeting wrote a separate memorandum to each of the board members. These memoranda then became the basis for the agenda.[8]

Being appointed to the board was an honor just by the stature of others selected for the board. Two men, a vice president of Texas Gulf Sulphur and an oil man and rancher, were appointed along with Beto. All three had attained a high level of achievement in their careers, and the appointment provided public recognition of their accomplishments. The honor of being appointed was also underscored by the responsibility assigned them. As board members they appointed the general manager of the prison system and supervised the entire system and its properties. Beto was not intimidated by his new colleagues or the challenge, but showed the same ease in dealing with these wealthy and powerful men in their board meetings as he did when he was with pastors and laymen on the Concordia campus.

Of all the members of the Prison Board, one of them, Hubert Hardison Coffield, became Beto's close friend and patron. "Pete" Coffield had been appointed to the board in 1949 and then was continuously reappointed until he resigned in 1974 because of ill health. At the November meeting in 1956 Coffield became chairman, and

Beto was elected secretary. Coffield continued as chairman for the next eighteen years. The amount of time a member of the board spent on the problems of the prison system, outside of the board meetings, was at the discretion of the member. The two who were most deeply involved, traveling to the prison units and inspecting conditions, were Coffield and Beto. Coffield's and Beto's leadership and presence at important legislative and state budget board hearings accounted in large measure for the continued success of the prison system.

Coffield's home was in Rockdale, about forty-five miles from Austin. He had been born in 1898 and was Beto's senior by eighteen years. Pete's father, who had been in the wholesale meat business, died when Pete was nine, leaving a widow and six children. The family lived in poverty and Pete helped out by selling newspapers. When he was thirteen he purchased a two-wheeled cart and a donkey and worked for a laundry service, picking up and delivering clothes. Following graduation from Rockdale High School he attended Baylor University, and earned money by operating his own laundry business.

After completing his second year, he left the university to help fight World War I by joining the Naval Air Corps. By the time his training was completed and he had earned his wings, the Armistice had been signed, and following his discharge in 1919, Coffield returned to Rockdale. He never lost his affection for airplanes, and later owned several and used them to travel between his various homes and properties as well as when he performed his service to the Prison Board.

He made his first fortune by selling military surplus materials. The government was eager to divest itself of these items, so he purchased pants, shirts, coats, underwear, sheets, and blankets by the train carload at low prices. Then, using three surplus military trucks, he crisscrossed the state selling the surplus items at auctions. His auctions were popular and often attracted 2,000 to 3,000 people. One of his most successful ventures was buying ten railroad box cars full of horse harnesses at Fort Sill, Oklahoma, and shipping them to Texas. Because they were a different type of harness than those preferred by Texas farmers, he hired leather craftsmen to adapt them. He continued this business for about five years during which time he averaged two to three hours of sleep a night.

He invested his army surplus profits in oil leases when the Rockdale-Minerva oil field was discovered. Unable to finance the actual exploration, drilling, and extraction, he sold part interest in his leases to someone who could bankroll the entire operation. The leases proved profitable, and during the 1930s, when the country was enduring the Great Depression, Coffield was prospering. In the late 1930s he diversified and invested in cattle ranching, industrial enterprises, and Houston real estate. At the time he was appointed to the Prison Board in 1949, his estate was valued at $50 million. As an active member and treasurer of the Texas Democratic Party, he was a delegate to the tumultuous 1968 convention in Chicago, and for a time was considered second only to Lyndon Johnson when it came to political power in Texas.[9]

In spite of his wealth and success, he continued to live a simple life and retained his modest two-story house in Rockdale. He also retained his humble, gracious demeanor and his quick, keen wit. At the same time, however, he knew how to live the good life and derived great pleasure from entertaining his friends in an opulent style. One of the holdings he acquired in the 1940s was the Diamond H Ranch, 13,500 acres near Catarina, on the upper Rio Grande Valley in Dimmit County. Here was a complex comprising a hunting lodge of ten rooms and ten baths, a swimming pool, and an airfield with hangars, where he could entertain his friends and engage in hunting deer, quail, and javelina. For something closer to home, he owned a mansion on Lake Travis, which earlier had been the Austin Yacht Club. Coffield's frequent guests included members of the Texas Senate, the justices of the Texas Supreme Court, influential politicians, and Dallas bankers.[10]

Later in life he suffered from Parkinson's disease and died in 1979. He had married Marjorie Prewitt of Rockdale, and the couple had had a son, but both preceded him in death. With no immediate family, he left his fortune to the Boy Scouts of America, the Salvation Army, and the Episcopal Diocese of Texas. His contribution to the Texas prison system was enormous and his influence on Beto and his career was considerable.[11]

Conditions in the Prison System

Beto took his seat on the committee at the March 1953 meeting. Ellis had already been at work reforming the system for six years, and by the time Beto joined the board, public attention was being drawn to the major improvements that had been achieved. The Ferguson Honor Farm, for example, opened on August 1, 1952, and established a working environment without guards, guns, or bloodhounds. Sixty convicts, all carefully chosen for their exemplary records while in prison, worked on the farm and lived in a clean residence with handsome furniture. A prisoner, sentenced to life, worked in a modern kitchen and served palatable food. The only authority figures on the farm were the supervisors, all agricultural specialists who provided direction to the men. The journalists were impressed with the low cost of maintaining a prisoner. Because of the productivity of the prison farms and factories, the cost in Texas was only fifty-nine cents per day while the cost in other states was $2.33.[12]

Two indexes for gauging prison morale across the entire prison system were also positive. Instances of self-mutilation, in which prisoners severed their Achilles' tendons or cut off a finger or hand, were down from eighty-seven in 1947 to a single incident in 1953. And the number of escapes declined from 126 in 1947 to only twenty-nine. Those numbers were especially impressive considering the increase of the prison population from 5,099 in 1947 to 7,063 in 1953.[13]

The next year, 1954, Beto had yet one more visit at his faculty home from a person who also later became his close friend and ally, W. S. "Bill" Heatly. So close a bond was formed that Beto was later asked to give the sermon at Heatly's funeral and then a speech at the dedication of the Brown-Heatly State Office Building. Heatly, a Baylor Law School graduate, readily confessed to being an alcoholic, but happily added that he had consumed his last drink at 1:30 PM on April 19, 1949. He became an active member in Alcoholics Anonymous (AA) and in 1953 Governor Shivers appointed him to the state's Commission on Alcoholism. Heatly and his associates recognized the role alcohol played in the lives of many incarcerated people and attempted to establish AA chapters in the state's prisons and to conduct meetings with the prisoners. The reception by the corrections officers was generally lukewarm, and often the AA representatives were kept waiting in the sun before they were admitted to the prison, or had the meetings terminated prematurely.

Heatly called on Beto for help and the new member of the Prison Board opened the doors for Heatly's cause. Heatly, although first elected to the State Legislature in 1954, was appointed to the House Appropriations Committee that same year. From that time on, until his retirement in 1982, Heatly served on that committee and occupied the position of chairman for twelve of those years. Heatly used the power the position provided to the fullest, and at times used it to reward friends and punish opponents. Agencies that received sufficient funding were those agencies who looked after the poor, or as Heatly said, "Those who did not have an alumni association," such as the mental health department, the Texas Youth Commission, and of course, the state's prison system. Later when Beto was the director of the Texas Department of Corrections, he wrote, "Mr. Heatly has been of inestimable help to me; without his aid in the Legislature, my road would have been a rocky one."[14]

At the meeting of the board at the Rice Hotel in Houston on September 22, 1954, Beto was once again elected as the Texas delegate to the American Prison Association's annual meeting, scheduled to be held during the last week in October in Philadelphia. One week before the Philadelphia meeting, Austin MacCormick (the penologist who had written the scathing report on Texas prisons in 1944) returned to Huntsville at the request of Ellis for a second look. The results of MacCormick's visit put Texas in the national spotlight. After the two-day inspection MacCormick flew to the meeting in Philadelphia, where he praised the Texas prison system's remarkable progress under Ellis and the board during the past seven years, and stated that he considered the changes achieved nothing short of miraculous. He told the assembled prison administrators that he ranked the Texas system on par with California, and placed them both as the best in the nation. Mac-Cormick was not one to lavish praise indiscriminately, and when he talked, people listened. As a result of what he had to say about the Texas prison system, the states of Oklahoma, Louisiana, Alabama, and Mississippi arranged to send delegates to tour the prison system and meet with Ellis and the board.[15]

At the Philadelphia meeting Beto became acquainted with some of the great luminaries of American penology, and later reported back to the board that such meetings were of inestimable value in providing him with insights into prison problems. Given what MacCormick was telling people, and after listening to the concerns expressed by prison administrators from around the country, Beto came away from the Philadelphia meeting convinced that the Texas prison system was on the verge of comparing favorably with the innovative and reform-minded systems in other states and the federal government. He also informed the board that "it was regrettable that state laws prevented more people from attending these meetings.[16]

After the Philadelphia meeting, MacCormick sent the formal assessment of his inspection tour, and the report was the highlight of the board meeting held on November 8. In his report he singled out some specific aspects. Improvements in inmate living conditions, Beto's responsibility, received the lion's share of the praise. The reforms that MacCormick expressly mentioned included those dealing with good food and clean clothing, efforts at rehabilitation through vocational training, general education, religious services, and the construction and reconditioning of buildings. He approved of the modernization of agricultural methods and improved working conditions. No longer were the men marched to the fields, but were now transported in trailer wagons, and no longer were the men walking behind mule-drawn implements, but sitting astride tractors. The focus of the farms had become productivity.

"You have," wrote MacCormick, "now reached a level of quality and a degree of dignity where [the titles "Prison System" and "General Manager"] are no longer appropriate: Texas has now more than a prison system. I recommend that steps be taken to establish a [Texas] Department of Corrections, that you change [the name of] the Prison Board to Texas Correctional Commission, and change the title of General Manager to Commissioner of Corrections."[17]

Beto agreed with MacCormick's suggestion, and told the Board that "the changes in terminology suggested by Mr. MacCormick are a trend," and pointed out that "after eighty years the American Prison Association has recently changed its title to American Correctional Association."[18] Beto also said the name changes would definitely be good for Texas, but thought it would take a legislative act to accomplish this. He was right. In 1957 the legislature changed the name of the Texas Prison System to the Texas Department of Corrections, and the Texas Prison Board was changed to the Texas Board of Corrections, and the position of General Manager was changed to Director.

Both MacCormick and Beto, however, did not believe the system was as good as it could be, and that there were still problems that needed to be resolved.[19] A major problem MacCormick alluded to and one that every board member recognized was the increasing size of the prison population. As Texas increased in population and as the urban areas expanded, it was safe to assume that the trend would continue. The most obvious instance of overcrowding was at the Eastham Unit. There, half of the inmate population of 1,000 was sleeping on the floor every night. Such conditions were conducive to riot and with that the destruction of lives and property. Ellis asked the legislature for $3,500,000 for the construction of a 1,000-cell prison, and promised that with the use of convict labor and utilizing bricks made at the prison factory, he could construct a facility worth twice as much.

The Eastham Unit was not completed until 1957, and then it too became overcrowded when 1,700 men were assigned to it. The problem of housing persisted throughout Beto's term of service on the board, and the prison population was growing at the rate of 700 a year. Returning from a meeting of the American Congress of Corrections, Beto reported that the housing conditions in Texas facilities were sub-standard and that those conditions were the cause of numerous incidents. Seventy-five percent of the population lived in open rooms, which were called "tanks," instead of in cells. Penologists said it should be twenty-five percent. Good rehabilitation programs, Beto believed, depended on "good celling practices."[20] In a typical month, 403 new prisoners were arriving, while 328 were discharged because they had completed their sentences or received some form of clemency. Construction always lagged behind the demand for space, and annual requests for appropriations became almost a ritual. In 1959, the year Beto moved to Illinois, the board asked the Legislature for $7.5 million for capital improvements.[21]

Alternatives to Incarceration

Even with the legislature's funding for construction, other solutions were needed to restrain the growth. One program was adult probation. Although probation was a concept adopted by most states in the 1930s, it was not an idea Texans readily embraced. The legislature did not authorize the practice until 1947, the year of MacCormick's final report and the year Ellis was hired as general manager.

Typically, probation was granted to a first offender of a misdemeanor or felony, so that instead of being incarcerated, he was granted freedom. However, that privilege carried requirements such as restrictions on his movements and scheduled meetings with a probation officer. Any transgression of these obligations could result in imprisonment for his earlier offense. The Texas precedent for probation was the practice of granting a suspended sentence. Under this procedure the judge, upon conviction on a misdemeanor or felony charge, pronounced the sentence, but then released the person into the community. As long as his behavior was law-abiding he remained a free man. The major problem with this procedure was that there were no guidelines so the judge could easily be accused of corruption or favoritism. A second problem was that there was no supervision of the convicted person to help him avoid a second offense.

In 1947 The Texas Legislature addressed both of these shortcomings with the Adult Probation Law. It established guidelines for implementing probation and authorized the appointment of probation officers by the district court judges. The authority of supervising of the officers was assigned to the Texas Board of Pardons and Paroles. The major problem, however, was that the legislature repeatedly failed to provide funding for the program. Without funding, the probation system would not work, and this method of reducing the crowding of prisons was not an option. In 1957, however, ten years after the probation system was established, the legislature modified the law by removing the oversight function from the Board of Pardons and Paroles and assigning it to the county governments. The county then became responsible for both funding and the employment of probation officers.[22]

A second device for restricting the growth of the prison population was parole. While probation was intended to avoid incarceration, parole was designed to extract a prisoner before his sentence had been completed. Most states had adopted programs of parole by the 1920s, but Texas once more lagged behind and would not pass a comprehensive parole law until 1957. Instead Texas utilized the practice of executive clemency. Under executive clemency, as practiced for decades, when the governor issued a pardon, the prisoner was freed from serving the remainder of his sentence and regained all rights and privileges of citizenship. In the nineteenth century the requests for pardon became a burden for the governors, and this onus increased until 1893 when the legislature provided relief with a Board of Pardons Advisors. This two-member board screened and reviewed all requests and forwarded them to the governor with the board's recommendation. But that procedure fell prey to the charge of influence peddling, so in 1929 the legislature replaced the advisors with a Board of Pardons and Parole appointed by the governor but ratified by the Senate.

That 1929 law also provided for a second variation of the pardoning power, which was called executive parole or conditional release. Under this procedure the prisoner was released to the community, on the condition that he commit no further offenses, but he did not enjoy the return of his civil rights. Neither was he placed under any form of supervision unless some volunteers in the county provided it. Not until 1957, upon the urging of Ellis, did the Texas Legislature create an enforcement arm of the Board of Pardons and

Paroles called the Division of Parole Supervision, and accompanied its creation with funding to make it work.[23]

A third solution for reducing the prison population was to confront the problem of mental illness. Too many of the inmates were psychotic and should have been in mental hospitals instead of the penitentiary. The problem was not easily resolved because the mental hospitals themselves were overcrowded. When Beto attended the Philadelphia meeting of the American Correctional Association in 1954, he learned more about the mentally ill in prisons. He had no statistics for Texas but he was certain that many of the inmates were mentally ill. In 1956 Beto and others called for the creation of a hospital for the criminally insane. In May 1959, when he was struggling over the call from Springfield, a million-dollar treatment center for mental patients, just outside of Huntsville, was opened.[24]

The Great Impostor

In 1955, while General Manager Ellis and the board were fine-tuning the system, they became unwitting participants in a deception that was one episode in a long collection of escapades. In 1959 Robert Crichton used these events as the basis for a book titled *The Great Impostor,* and that, in turn, became the framework for a movie of the same title starring Tony Curtis. Because no injury or human suffering resulted from the Huntsville incident, it can be told in a light-hearted and entertaining way, especially when professionals in the matter of security, the best in the craft, are duped. Crichton, attempting to bring interest to his story, misrepresented the actual conditions within the prison system by describing conditions that existed prior to Ellis' reforms. But even those inaccuracies left no permanent scars because by the time the book appeared, the reputation of the institution was secure. Beto, in Illinois at that time, called the book's description of the Texas Department of Corrections a caricature, and was "somewhat disturbed" by its "looseness with the truth."[25]

The impostor, Ferdinand Waldo Demara, Jr., in this case known as Benjamin W. Jones, was a short, rotund, and baby-faced man with a crew-cut who gained the confidence of people with his courteous and charming manners. Before he applied for a position with the Texas Department of Corrections in 1955, he had successfully impersonated a ship's surgeon in the Canadian Navy, a college professor, a Trappist monk, and a state trooper. Demara, or Jones, was residing in the Houston YMCA and was working as an auditor (also under false pretenses) for a hotel, when he saw a notice in the classified section announcing openings in the prison system. Beto later reported receiving a letter from Jones in the spring of 1955 and referred him to the general manager, Ellis. Using false letters of recommendation and credentials (including a Ph.D. from the University of Texas), Jones made a formal application. After an interview with Ellis, he was offered a position.

Given the rank of lieutenant, he was assigned to guard duty on the fields of Wynne Farm, near Huntsville. In June, after serving only one month, he was advanced to captain and given the task of recreational officer in the prison of the Wynne Farm. He worked well with the inmates and on one occasion even ended a fight between two prisoners by persuasion rather than force. Soon thereafter he was advanced to the post of assistant warden of the segregation unit within the penitentiary itself. Inmates in this unit included discipline cases, sexual deviants, psychotics, and prisoners in protective custody. During Jones' employment Beto reviewed Jones' folder, talked with him, and concluded from what he observed and heard that Jones was working out well in the position. Beto's only doubt arose when he talked to Jones about professors at the University of Texas. Jones did not remember the names Beto mentioned, but Beto dismissed the doubts because Beto had taken his courses during the summer sessions when many of the regular faculty were not in the classroom.

Ellis was also highly impressed with Jones and on several occasions remarked to Beto that "Jones is too good to be true." Jones found his employment fulfilling and even envisioned becoming a professional penologist. However, it all ended when one of the convicts read a back issue of *Life* magazine containing an article about Demara's escapades, and recognized that Demara in the picture was Jones, the guard. The photograph quickly made it to Ellis, and when Jones was confronted with it, he denied being Demara.

Afraid of making a false accusation, Ellis excused Demara while Ellis began verifying the Jones credentials. Demara used the opportunity to leave Huntsville and departed from the state of Texas. Ellis admitted his error in judgment to the press, but insisted that he would hire Demara again if he were to appear with legitimate credentials.[26]

Service on the Board

Several incidents took place during the years of Coffield's and Beto's presence on the board that illustrate the unpredictability of events as well as the procedures the board members followed when these incidents arose. The first of these was called the Shamrock Disturbance and took place in 1955. The "Little Shamrock" was the name the prisoners ironically used to refer to the high security segregation unit. It was the segregation unit where the Great Imposter was exposed, and which housed 432 of the hard-core inmates who were not permitted to work on the farms or the factories.

Fifty-two men from one section of the building, having completed their morning meal at 9:00 AM, were released into the yard three times a week for their two-hour exercise period. The yard was a small area forty feet by one hundred feet and surrounded by concrete walls and patrolled by armed guards. There was no chance for escape. When it was time to return to their cells, they refused and instead insisted that they receive three instead of two meals a day.

The prison policy for the two meals was based on the fact that these men did not work and therefore did not need the caloric intake of those who did work. Another reason was time. Because these were dangerous men, serving the meals in the dining hall was done carefully and in shifts, thereby making it time-consuming. If three meals were served, the personnel would spend much of the day serving meals.

Ellis was at one of the farms when these events began to unfold and returned to Huntsville at about 4:00 PM. He was not greatly concerned because conditions were secure and it would not be long before the men would get thirsty, hungry, and tired. He did, however, talk to them and informed them that while he would not consider any demands, he would listen to requests, and that they could stay in the yard as long as there was no violence. They complained about the food and asked for three meals a day. They also threatened to sever their Achilles' tendons if the guards fired or used tear gas. Otherwise, everything was stable.

Simultaneously the other units were notified to stand ready for any possibility of the resistance spreading. The governor and the board members were notified by phone. Several of the board members, including Beto and Coffield, flew in to give their support to Ellis and authorized him to take any measures needed to control the situation.

True to Ellis' prediction, the strike ended in about thirty hours and, after the men were stripped and searched for weapons, they returned to their cells. As punishment, they lost privileges such as exercise periods, books, and the weekly movie for one month. Correspondence with their families, however, was permitted. The two meals per day practice was continued, but for one month the recalcitrants would be served those meals in their cells instead of in the small dining room.[27]

The second incident that illustrates Beto's involvement came very close to seriously altering the course of events upon which Ellis and the board were embarked. While returning to Huntsville from a peace officer's banquet on the evening of January 30, 1957. Ellis and his son John, age twenty-one, were severely injured in a head-on automobile collision in heavy fog on U.S. Highway 73, about three miles north of Conroe, Texas. Ellis was hospitalized in critical condition with a broken leg, shattered patella, and fractured jaw. His son underwent surgery for a ruptured spleen. In the ensuing years, Beto and others noted that after the accident Ellis was never quite as hale and hearty as before, was in occasional pain, and both the frequency and duration of his health problems increased. During Ellis' period of recuperation, the prison system was managed on an *ad hoc* basis by Coffield and Beto.[28]

The third incident was the 1957 "buck." A buck was a general term for resistance, or strike. This buck took place at the Harlem

Prison Farm # 1, in Sugar Land, southeast of Houston. It was on Saturday, the day was hot and humid, and it was the first day of the cotton-picking season. The Hispanic inmates, numbering almost 300, refused to work and insisted on a five-day work week. Four years earlier Ellis had reduced the work week to five days except for one month in the spring planting season and two months during the fall harvest.

Ellis first notified Coffield, who was in Dallas, and then spoke to the inmates reminding them of the work policy. He also reminded them that all farmers picked on Saturdays when the cotton was ready, and that they would be kept in the fields until they had picked their 160-pound quota. They refused. Coffield, in the meantime, boarded his plane and flew to Austin where he picked up Beto. They arrived at about 3:00 PM and found more guards and police, but the workers were still sitting. At 5:00 PM the inmates decided to return to work, and were given water and a sandwich. They, however, were kept in the fields overnight and then worked the next day to finish their quota.[29] The willingness of Coffield and Beto to drop everything in order to assist Ellis was typical of the earnestness with which they assumed their responsibility. But there was also a close personal friendship between Ellis and the men he called his "bosses." Later Beto considered himself one of Ellis' "disciples."[30]

Beto not only responded to the dramatic incidents, but he paid attention to routine details as well. He spent more and more time at the prison facilities and at one point admitted that the prison board took more time away from his full time duties as president of Concordia than he wished.[31] During his weekly visits to one or another of the facilities he spoke with the wardens and guards and read the disciplinary reports. He interviewed prisoners and listened to their grievances. He went everywhere to inspect the fields and working conditions, to the kitchens where he ate the food, and to the sleeping quarters to examine living conditions. Little escaped him and he acquired intimate knowledge of all aspects of the prisoner's life. Beto usually spent several days a month in personal interviews with prison inmates and many hours writing to or interviewing their kinfolk.[32]

This thorough knowledge was reflected in his reports. Even his first report was impressive. But as he learned more, his reports grew even more detailed and insightful. They generally included statistical data (on escapes, mutilations, disciplinary infractions, inmates killed by inmates, inmates killed by guards, other infractions, and the average daily population of the prison system), and progress reports on the rehabilitation programs (including education, library, recreation, religion, music, and medical treatment), and medical aids (such as glasses, hearing aids, and artificial eyes). His reports became increasingly more analytical and included data on inmate population trends, descriptions of prison population by age, and an accounting of prison system activities in education, recreation, and counseling. The board members were impressed, and Beto generally presented the motions in the meetings that were then adopted. The board also realized his ability to write clear, sharp reports, so they invariably appointed him to attend the national conferences and then report to them on the proceedings.

Many of the ideas that Beto learned at these national conferences, or solutions he thought of himself, led to reforms that were later implemented. These included the expansion of Alcoholics Anonymous in all prison units, the adoption of the guidelines used by the Federal Bureau of Prisons for feeding men in solitary confinement, hiring a prison psychiatrist, the installation of television sets for use by the inmates, and the employment of a musician and choir director.

An unusual project he encouraged was the construction of a chapel within the prisons. As the theologian on the board he was active in its planning and construction. Using revenues from the prison rodeo and with bricks they made in their kiln, the inmates built the chapel at no cost to the state. A name frequently used for a prison chapel was The Chapel of St. Dismas, the repentant thief on the cross. Beto proposed calling it The Chapel of Hope. When he noticed that only a piano was available for services, he and Coffield purchased an organ. It was only fitting that the board asked him to be the speaker at the chapel's dedication.[33]

But the most widely heralded contribution made by Beto, and for which he received the Texas Heritage Foundation medal, was bringing secondary education to the prison. It was called the

Texas Training Institute, and it conducted night school at all the prison units to help inmates prepare for the General Education Development (GED) program. Even though participation in the program was voluntary, it had potential because eighty percent of the 10,000 inmates lacked a high school diploma. The certificate, although not a diploma, made the inmate eligible for admission into college when his prison term had been served. This educational program was the only one of its kind in the nation.[34]

Beto launched the program in 1956 with the cooperation of Dr. H. E. Robinson of the Texas Education Agency and employed students from Sam Houston State College to administer the American Council of Education exams. One hundred and twenty inmates, including a former school superintendent, served as instructors. Four hundred students enrolled in just the first year. The first graduating class, in 1956, numbered twenty-nine, and by July of the next year, 135 had received their certificates. Twenty-five of the graduates were female and a dozen were African Americans. With the completion of each term, graduation exercises were held in the chapel, with all the fanfare of a high school graduation, and before a capacity crowd of prisoners and guests.[35]

At one of these ceremonies as the group filed out of the chapel, an inmate, age thirty-eight and serving a life sentence, stopped in front of Beto and Robinson and said, "You have meant more to me today than anyone has in the 21 years I have been here."[36] By 1963 more than 3,000 inmates had received certificates.

The hectic pace seemed to energize Beto. He was able to manage both his vocation at Concordia and his avocation at Huntsville. Complaints from fellow Lutherans directed to Beto were not based on an inadequate job at Concordia, but on the amount of time he spent on the Prison Board.[37] If anything suffered it would have been his family or his personal recreation. Unlike his father, he did not play golf, and he held sports, especially those associated with educational institutions, in low esteem. His only recreation was occasionally riding a horse, or deer-hunting with his friends, if "hunting" can be loosely interpreted. But like his father, Beto volunteered his time to help enrich the life of young people. He served as chairman of the Regulations Committee of the Capital Area

Council of the Boy Scouts of America, and in 1958 was presented with the Silver Beaver Award, the highest Boy Scout honor for volunteer adult leaders. He also maintained a subtle presence in the political arena, and delivered the invocation at the opening rally of Governor Price Daniel's campaign for a second term as governor.[38]

The Call to Springfield

Two events took place in 1959 that broke the hectic, though satisfying, pace of Beto's life. The first, in April, was a call to become the president of Concordia Theological Seminary in Springfield, Illinois. After its president, Walter A. Baepler, died suddenly of a heart attack in October 1958, the Missouri Synod convened a seven-member committee to select a new president. Beto was selected to fill the position from a list of sixty-one candidates nominated by congregations of the Lutheran Church throughout the United States and Canada.[39] Life in Austin was fulfilling, and Beto was content with both his work at Concordia and his work with the Prison Board. In the past he had turned down calls to fill vacancies in the Lutheran church, but the call from Springfield Theological Seminary was different. The seminary not only produced pastors who immediately filled vacant pulpits in the church, but it needed strong leadership to expand and develop. Why, he wondered, should he tear up the roots of a life he found so gratifying and forsake the circle of intimate friends he had cultivated?

When Beto received the call from the seminary, he was initially torn between his desire to serve the church by accepting the challenge of building up the seminary into a quality institution, and his desire to remain in Austin where he could serve the church, continue his work on the Texas Prison Board, and reside in a place he and his family treasured. However, his work at Austin had been successful, and the major challenges he undertook for both Concordia College and the Prison Board had been met. Concordia in Austin had reached a level where little direction was needed, and the fact that he could spend as much time as he did with the prison system proved that Concordia had momentum, as well as a faculty and staff that could manage it. Also his work on the Prison Board had borne fruit, and the system was in good hands. Now the church was asking him to relinquish the familiar setting of Austin and accept the challenge of upgrading Springfield and overseeing the education of future Lutheran pastors.

The decision of whether to stay in Austin or go to Springfield was an agonizing one for Beto, and his wrestling with what to do was not made any easier by those who wanted him to remain in Texas. The Board of Control at Concordia Austin pleaded with him not to leave. Despite the high dignity of the call to take the reins of the Springfield seminary, neither Ellis nor Coffield were thrilled by the prospect of Beto's leaving Texas, and they immediately beseeched him to stay where he was. Governor Price Daniel also weighed in and tried to dissuade Beto from leaving by offering to reappoint him to another term on the board. "Because of his outstanding service to the State of Texas," the governor said, "I expressed to him my hope that he would stay in Texas rather than accept the new position. I fear that we will lose him."[40]

Marilynn observed that the pressure he was under to make a decision finally took its toll:

None of us wanted to leave Austin. [George] was miserable and couldn't sleep. That is the only time I can remember ever seeing him break down and sob so hard. It was heart-breaking. Finally, one morning while we were still in bed he quietly said to me "Let's go." I knew what he meant. We were going to Springfield. Later I asked him what made him decide to leave Austin. He answered "My conscience."[41]

After six weeks of consideration, Beto reluctantly accepted the call to Springfield on May 26, four days prior to Concordia's commencement. In announcing his decision to accept the call to become the seminary's tenth president, Beto released a public statement in which he acknowledged his ties with the Board of Corrections but remained strangely silent about Concordia, his twenty-year project. It is also interesting to note that in his statement Beto relied on the sage advice given to him in 1931 by his uncle, George Witsma, Jr., when Beto was a student at Concordia

College in Milwaukee, and he was concerned about his ability to rise to a challenge:

> The recognition of the indisputable challenge which the theological seminary in Springfield offers forces me to accept the presidency of that institution. If I fail to respond to that challenge I would have extreme difficulty living with my conscience. . . . It is with considerable sadness that I leave Texas. I shall miss particularly my associations with the Texas Board of Corrections. It has been a distinct privilege for me to know and to work with the distinguished Texans who make up that Board, especially Mr. H. H. Coffield. His unselfish and unflagging devotion to the great cause of prison reform in Texas will always be an inspiration to me. [42]

The second disruptive event was the death of Morris Dunbar. Dunbar, an elderly African American from Algiers, Louisiana, had done time in the Texas prison system for the murder of his wife. But Dunbar was a man of great dignity and inner calm and Beto believed that Dunbar was the ideal individual for rehabilitation. In 1953 Beto helped secure Dunbar's release on parole and hired him as the groundskeeper for the Concordia campus at a salary of $1,800 per year.[43] The arrangement worked out well, and Dunbar became an intimate friend of the entire Beto family. He soon brought an almost parklike look to campus, but he also brought his skills in barbecuing. Dunbar was well liked by the students, whom he always greeted with a smile and a cheerful word, and he patiently tolerated an occasional prank perpetrated on his tractor.[44] But then in 1959, two weeks before the end of the school year, Dunbar did not report to work. Concerned that he might be ill, Beto drove to Dunbar's home, and when he received no response, alerted the police. The police entered the home and discovered Dunbar's body and later found the body of his common law wife. Dunbar had taken her life and then hanged himself. The deaths devastated Beto. It was not so much a matter of his error in judgment because he knew that no one could predict the effectiveness of rehabilitation, but they had become friends. Also, suicide, an act contrary to Beto's religion, was an act of despair, while Beto focused on hope. At Concordia's graduation on May 30, 1959, when Beto announced his farewell to his fellow Lutherans, he included a prayer for Dunbar and commended his soul to "Him who judgeth all things righteously."[45]

Beto's last Prison Board meeting was on March 9, 1959. During his entire six-year term on the board, Beto had never missed a single scheduled meeting. Now, at age forty-three, he was leaving. Perhaps the greatest tribute to Beto was made by the editor of *The Echo*, the official inmate newspaper of the Texas prison system. When word of Beto's departure for Illinois reached them, the front page banner headline set in bold type eloquently summed up the situation for the 10,000 convicts in the Texas Prison System: "Buddy, You Have Lost a Friend."[46]

Chapter 5

CONCORDIA THEOLOGICAL SEMINARY, SPRINGFIELD, ILLINOIS (1959–1962)

As any schoolboy knows, both Austin and Springfield are capitals of their respective states. But as any Texan will tell you, Austin is the more beautiful and exciting of the two. While Austin is situated on the lovely wooded hills of the Balcones Escarpment along the impressive Colorado River, Springfield is built on a flat, glaciated plain surrounded by some of the most productive farmland imaginable. In addition to being the political center of the state, Austin is also the home of the University of Texas, the state's flagship institution of higher education, whereas the premier University of Illinois is ninety miles from Springfield, at Champaign. Although on occasion some university educators in Texas may have lusted after a location far away from political meddling, the interaction between the political and educational mentalities has often contributed to not only the intellectual vibrancy of the institution, but entertainment in the guise of comic relief as well. Concordia, the college that Beto left behind, was a small part of the larger Austin scene. The seminary that Beto chose to lead, although not much larger than its sister school in Austin, was by virtue of Springfield's smaller size, proportionately more important to the city.

The seminary campus was located within walking distance of downtown in a northeasterly direction, and it occupied the building and campus of a small university that had been forced to close. One of the students who had attended the ill-fated university in 1856 was Robert Lincoln, whose father was a country lawyer with political ambitions.[1] The university was conveniently located about ten blocks north of Abraham Lincoln's home. At the time Beto arrived in Springfield the size of the campus was approximately fifteen acres, but it was not contiguous, and a street separated one portion from the other. Because the part of town surrounding the campus was declining, a seminary with ideas of expansion promised to be an increasingly beneficial civic asset.[2]

Throughout its history the Missouri Synod had supported two seminaries, both named Concordia.[3] The seminary at St. Louis, attended by both George and his father, was the older of the two. It had been founded in 1839, and later served as the seminary for those students who had completed programs at one of the junior colleges of the synod. In 1926 the seminary was moved from its location in St. Louis to seventy-one acres of wooded hills west of the city, in the community of Clayton. It was the premier institution, with an excellent library, handsome stone buildings, a highly qualified faculty, and it enjoyed the generous financial support of the Missouri Synod.

The seminary in Springfield actually had been founded in Fort Wayne, Indiana, in 1846, the year before the Missouri Synod was organized. Like the St. Louis seminary, it too was based on a German model, but with a very practical and utilitarian purpose. The focus of the curriculum was not ancient languages or philosophical issues of theology, but the practical essentials of faith and everyday tasks of a parish pastor. A number of German missionary societies already utilized this practical variant of a seminary for preparing overseas missionaries, and the concept was adopted by the seminary in Fort Wayne to provide pastors for the German immigrants flooding the United States. With that goal in mind, the founders directed their energies toward recruiting young German-Americans who had not completed a *Gymnasium* program, as well as lay German immigrants, encouraging them to enroll and become "emergency helpers" (*Nothelfer*).[4]

After a brief sojourn in St. Louis from 1861 to 1874, the practical seminary was moved again, this time one hundred miles away to Springfield, Illinois. During the next decades, as the demand for Lutheran pastors declined, the school was considered expendable and earmarked for extinction on several occasions. It survived each threatened closure, but never received adequate financial support from the synod. Finally, in 1944, after yet another attempt to close it failed, the synod endorsed the seminary, although restricting it "to students from special groups, such as foreign, Finnish, Slovak, etc., [who were of an] advanced age [twenty years], and such as have a limited aptitude for ancient languages."[5]

But no one anticipated the post-World War II years, and instead of withering away, the seminary, bolstered by returning war veterans who seldom fit the St. Louis mold, soon doubled its enrollment. Another change after World War II was the expansion of the synod's mission fields from a narrow focus on China and India to the entire globe. The demand for pastoral candidates increased. The seminary already possessed a small college department that offered preparatory and remedial courses for new students who were deficient in their studies, and could thereby customize their program for seminary study. Although there were no language requirements for entrance, some exposure to Greek, Hebrew, and Latin was part of the curriculum of the seminary.

The difference between the two seminaries at St. Louis and Springfield, both as to their purpose and facilities, was common knowledge in synodical circles. Springfield's campus and buildings were much inferior to those in St. Louis, the faculty was not as highly credentialed, and the financial support of the synod was barely adequate. Often, because of its less rigorous course of study, the Springfield graduates received less respect than their fellows from St. Louis, and most of the highly prized and sought after administrative and elective posts in the Missouri Synod were occupied by St. Louis graduates. Springfield was, in essence, the poor sister of higher education within the synod. In spite of it all, enrollment at the Springfield seminary held at approximately 300 in the 1950s, with the exception of 1950, when it increased to 387.[6]

In 1957, however, the synod implemented a slight modification in its educational system for those in the theoretical course of study. The educational leaders purchased 187 acres of land on the outskirts of Fort Wayne, Indiana, and at a cost of seven million dollars, established a residential senior college. Under the new program, following graduation from one of the Lutheran junior colleges scattered across the United States, including Concordia Austin, a student matriculated at Fort Wayne prior to entering the St. Louis seminary. All the graduates of Fort Wayne Senior College earned a bachelor's degree, something Beto had done under the previous system by attending Valparaiso University during his vicarage year. But the practical result was that it added one more year of study to an already lengthy program of eleven years.[7]

One of the unintended consequences was that an increasing number of prospective students believed that the additional year, along with such a thorough training in the ancient languages, was not what they wanted. Some preferred a broader education at a secular institution by way of preparation for the Lutheran ministry, and others went directly from the junior college to Springfield. And there were some students who were married, or were contemplating marriage, who found the cloistered life at the senior college unacceptable. At the same time, Springfield had improved its image by slowly strengthening the curriculum and upgrading its faculty in the years following World War II. In 1956 the enrollment at Springfield began to increase, so that by 1958, the year before Beto's arrival, the student body numbered 411.[8]

Walter A. Baepler, Beto's predecessor, responded to the growth by hiring six additional professors in 1958 and initiating a construction program. Even before Beto was installed as president, a new residence hall costing $375,000 was under construction.[9] Additional recommendations to the Missouri Synod, made prior to Beto's installation, included the entrance requirement of a bachelor's degree, and therefore the elimination of the college department, as well as the introduction of a summer school program and authorization of six more professorships. Upon the death of President Baepler, the synodical leaders recognized the need for a person who could continue the aggressive program of improvements and lead the school to a new level of excellence. George Beto, with his Austin record, was the logical choice.[10]

Seminary Presidency

After attending the June convention of the Missouri Synod in San Francisco with his family, Beto returned to Austin, and in the early summer of 1959 moved his family north and settled into the president's house on the Springfield campus. On September 20, at Trinity Lutheran Church, just across the street from the state capitol, the new president was installed. Martin L. Koeneke, his brother-in-law and president of Concordia Teachers College, River Forest, Illinois, preached the sermon. Although Pastor Louis Beto did not live to see this installation, his wife, George's mother, was present. Realizing the need to create the public support he had enjoyed in Texas, President Beto held a large reception after his installation. A handpicked group of guests included not only church officials, but professionals, businessmen, and civic leaders, such as the president of the Rotary Club. At the reception the guests met the new president and learned about the plans for a two-million-dollar seminary expansion project.[11]

Beto adapted his administrative style at Springfield just as he had done from time to time during his twenty years in Austin. In Springfield he relied extensively on other administrative officers, although he maintained his focus on public relations. In the months that followed his installation as president, Beto expanded his contacts with the community, joined the Rotary Club, and was often seen at a "nearby watering hole," The Old Mill, sitting at a table, "front and center" with businessmen, "doing deals."[12]

One of the most important challenges that Beto faced in upgrading the seminary was developing the faculty. In a situation reminiscent of the concerns that employees of the Texas prison system had when Ellis began to implement his program for improving the quality of his staff, it was only natural for some of the existing faculty at Springfield to be somewhat apprehensive. The tenor of the school was changing, and it seemed as if it would change even more with Beto. A few professors even feared that Beto was too liberal. Most of the professoriate had calls, and with that, tenure, and Beto made no attempt to remove anyone. Instead, he provided study leaves and sabbaticals so professors could complete doctoral programs, and turned his attention to recruiting new faculty. He searched out young promising scholars, preferably with doctorates in hand, and hired seven the first year and five the second year. He encouraged scholarship and helped the faculty publish and gain visibility within the Missouri Synod.

Hiring faculty in Springfield required a slight adjustment from the way it was done in Austin. In Austin he had needed a faculty with a broad, general training in many academic disciplines, while at the seminary the faculty would be largely in religious studies. At Austin the lower salaries and greater teaching demands made it difficult to attract highly credentialed people, while at Springfield the inducements were greater for prospective faculty. In addition to improving salaries, Beto secured both a housing allowance for the faculty as well as a group insurance plan for them and their families.[13] The older professors, who may have had their doubts as to what Beto was trying to accomplish, could clearly see that the new president was certainly interested in their welfare.

The academic program that Beto inherited was acceptable and required little adjustment. The seminary was not accredited, however, and he took the first step toward gaining accreditation with the American Association of Theological Schools.[14] For all practical purposes, Beto implemented the administrative plan set in motion by the previous administration, and closed the pre-seminary, or college program. All that he retained was the program that provided remedial work in religion and foreign languages. In its place he introduced a summer session in order to utilize the facilities more efficiently and to make it possible for students to accelerate their academic progress and expedite their degree plans. The summer program was well received because the students were often married and eager to complete their studies.[15]

Without doubt, the most demanding aspect of Beto's position as president of the seminary was planning, funding, and completing the construction of buildings. His experience in Texas with construction projects could be directly transferred to Springfield. In

Texas, however, he was successful in raising funds because of his direct solicitation and his name recognition; in Illinois, his name was not as widely known, and establishing a donor base takes time. To compensate for these handicaps, Beto relied heavily on the Missouri Synod's Board for Higher Education. Fortunately for Beto, the board had already adopted a new, positive attitude toward the Springfield seminary, which called for greater appropriations. Requests for funding remained in the hands of the synodical conventions, but favorable endorsement from the board ensured approval. Even though he was dependent on the good graces of the board, he did not always wait for their approval on every aspect of the seminary's physical plant. In the case of the library, a crew was already clearing the space for the new structure by tearing down a house while Beto was on the telephone with the BHE executive asking for permission! It was easier to get forgiveness, Beto maintained, than it was to get permission.[16]

The size of the campus may have been suitable in the early days of the seminary, but as more buildings were added, space became inadequate. Although the seminary was landlocked, the neighborhood was aging and the existing housing remained relatively inexpensive. Under Beto's direction the seminary purchased more than thirty parcels of property and then removed whatever structures were on them. Three blocks of Moffatt Street, which had divided the campus, were closed from public use so the campus could be unified. Abandoning the older method of hodgepodge expansion, Beto pursued the idea of a master plan in which the placement of buildings and playing fields was well thought out and purposeful.[17]

During his first year as president he completed Selke Hall, a dormitory for seventy-two men, at a cost of $340,000. The second year the Schulz Library was erected for $600,000 and that same year saw the renovation and expansion of the heating plant for $250,000. In his report to the Synodical Convention of 1962, Beto requested funds of more than $2,500,000 for such projects as married student housing, a chapel, and an administrative building.[18]

As the seminary president, Beto was instrumental in making Concordia the first synodical institution to grant an honorary doctorate to either an African American or to a female. He did both in 1961 when Rosa Jinsey Young, of Selma, Alabama, was named Doctor of Letters. After Young had affiliated with the Lutheran church, she organized the first thirteen black Lutheran congregations in her state. In addition to being a missionary, she taught school and wrote articles and a book titled *Light in the Dark Belt*. Unlike Concordia Austin, Concordia Springfield had been integrated already at the turn of the century through a synodical resolution, so the recognition was not only to honor Dr. Young, but to call attention to the role of African Americans in the church.[19]

Just as Beto had modified his interaction with students in Austin when he added the junior college and coeducation, so he again adjusted to yet another setting. In Springfield the student population was older than in Austin, and in many cases the students were heads of households. He treated them appropriately and with respect. No longer did he walk the hall of the dormitories, and in his relationships with the student body he was more distant. The "King George" of his Austin days had become "Lonesome George" in Springfield.[20] He did admonish them as a group on occasion, however, as he did in an editorial for the *Sem Quill*, the seminary's student newspaper. "We have observed that our students are particularly adept in witnessing orally to their faith. We need to remind ourselves periodically, however, that our lives are also an effective form of witness. . . . The Lord of Life and Death once remarked that we (what we are and believe) are known by our fruits." And on another occasion he directed their thoughts to their careers. He reminded them of the Lutheran teaching of the priesthood of all believers, which held that every person could speak directly with God and need not go through the clergy. When they occupied a parish, Beto wrote, pastors were not part of a "priestly caste," but were "priests among priests."[21]

Theological Views

While he adapted his administrative style to his new position and its unique demands, his religious views did not change. His interest continued to be in Scripture and its application to daily life, and his religious stance was orthodox and very much in the mainstream of the Missouri Synod's practice. He was critical of the trend among certain clergymen to adopt vestments, such as the surplice and stole, which he did not find in the Lutheran tradition. He himself continued to wear his black doctoral gown. Neither was he fond of borrowing liturgical practices from either the Roman Catholic Church or the Episcopalians, especially when the innovations were chosen for theatrical effect rather than for teaching a doctrine. He preferred a service that was traditional. On one occasion Beto said that if he were not Lutheran, he probably would be Baptist, because of the simplicity of the service.[22] High church practices did not fit into his mentality.

In 1959, when Beto took over as president at Springfield, a current of theological upheaval was beginning to flow in the Missouri Synod. This controversy grew and eventually led to the student walk-out at the St. Louis seminary in 1974. Beto himself was not a theologian in the strict academic sense of the word, and "had little interest in the questions that were being raised."[23] Or if he did, he did not show it. Some of the older members of the faculty were disappointed that he did not sit down and chat about theological matters. For them it was doctrine; for Beto it was practice. He was never fond of pastoral conferences with their theological topics, and he avoided them at every opportunity. After he retired he attended a pastoral conference in Texas and observed that he had not attended a conference in the area for forty years, but "they are talking about the same things they talked about forty years ago."[24]

When Beto added new faculty to the seminary he was more concerned with their credentials and their academic ability than he was with their theological inclinations. Yet a number of the men he secured for the faculty were theologically liberal, and later became part of the conflict against those who were theologically conservative. Many people in the Missouri Synod preferred the middle position similar to Beto's and hoped to avoid the debate, but as the conflict intensified they were drawn or pushed to one side or the other. Beto's return to Texas extracted him from that unpleasant situation and he was never forced to choose sides.[25]

Although he was not drawn into the fray, the "controversy" escalated during his brief tenure at Springfield. Beto preferred the word "unrest." He acknowledged the unrest and mentioned some of the issues, but in his public statements he steered a middle course and expressed himself judiciously. He did have definite opinions on some of the issues, but they were on opposite sides of the debate. On the one hand, he adhered to a conservative view of the doctrine of the Word. To Beto, Scripture was more than a collection of writings that *contained* the word of God; it *was* the Word of God, divinely inspired.[26] His approach to the Bible, and the ways of interpreting it, was traditional. Already in his days at Austin, when students advanced Darwinian evolutionary theory as an alternative to the Genesis account, Beto generally gave the response in a mocking German accent, "Voss you der, Charlie?" And he agreed with Dr. Hermann Sasse, a conservative Lutheran in Australia, about the liberal faculty at St. Louis. In joint faculty meetings between the two seminaries, Beto, like Sasse, was disturbed by what seemed to be the St. Louis faculty running after "the train of liberal Lutheranism" just in time "to catch it for the great catastrophe." Instead of mature behavior, Beto noted that the St. Louis faculty frequently displayed "an almost sophomoric 'smart alec' attitude."[27]

At the same time, his views on relations with other churches placed him in the liberal camp. His political activity in both Texas and Illinois required him to work with people of other faiths, and like his mother, he attended their religious services and events. His ecumenical stand was a liberal one and he was interested in the religious affiliation of his friends. In his letters appear lighthearted phrases such as "apparently you Campbellites were not breaking bread with the Baptists." Or, to a Southern Baptist friend of his, he wrote, "Incidentally, I ran into a Southern Baptist who is residing in Springfield. Apparently that subversive group is surreptitiously infiltrating the North for the purpose of taking it over."[28] No one to whom Beto ever spoke or wrote in this manner ever mistook his good-natured banter for malice or ill-will. It was this very question of the relationship of members of the Missouri Synod with other Christian bodies that gave rise to the theological controversy in the synod in the first place, and Beto approved of the greater "evangelical" spirit.

Beto put his ecumenism to the test in this continuing debate and maintained friends on both sides. Most likely, because he did not see things in deep theological terms, he concluded that the source of the problem was not doctrinal, but rather the result of the Missouri Synod passing from "a cultural and social isolation into the American mainstream."[29] Once the church had completed that transition, Beto assumed the problem would be resolved.

Eleven years after his departure from Springfield he attended the synodical convention in New Orleans, which proved to be one of the most contentious meetings of the period. Several months after the convention he still held the middle ground, and wrote "I am somewhat disenchanted with both extreme elements in the Missouri Synod. When I listen to that agate-headed Bavarian from Michigan on the one hand, and on the other hand observe those clowns from the St. Louis faculty picketing Preus' installation, I begin to wonder whether or not I still have a church home."[30]

But he remained in the Missouri Synod "in part because of my loyalty to a human institution in which I was born and reared, and in part because of my recognition of the frailty of all human institutions, regardless of whether they be visible church bodies or some other types of bureaucracy."[31] In contrast to the local pastoral conferences, which he avoided, Beto rarely missed the national synodical convention. The conventions, with all the accompanying socialization, were his ties to the past. He also continued to serve on those synodical boards and committees that, by their nature, were not theologically controversial. Most of them met quarterly, and Beto was often absent because of his responsibilities in Huntsville. His first appointment, already made during the presidency at Springfield, was to the editorial board of *The Lutheran Witness*. He served from 1959 to 1965. From 1962 to 1968 he served on the Lutheran Church-Missouri Synod Foundation, whose principal function was to invest the funds that were contributed to the church. From 1966 to 1976 he was on the Board of Public Relations, a body assigned the task of disseminating favorable publicity for the Lutheran church and its celebrities. And finally, he served on the Board of Managers-Pension Funds from 1980 to 1983, whose responsibility it was to manage the health care and retirement programs of the employees of the Missouri Synod and it member congregations.

Illinois Criminal Justice

Even though Beto threw himself into the task of building up the seminary, just as he had done with the school in Austin, there never was even a hint that the seminary and its administration would be his exclusive concern. Beto's interests were not parochial, and because his interest in the field of corrections was more than just a passing fancy, he never severed the connections with the friends in Texas who shared his interest. If he was not involved directly on a board or a committee, as he had been in Texas, at least he could learn more about the topic and gain a wider appreciation of its challenges. Illinois was the home of a famous prison and warden, both of whom were praised in the United States and Europe, and both attracted the interest of penologists and scholars. The prison was Stateville, in Joliet, and the warden was Joseph E. Ragen. Beto first met Ragen in the summer of 1953, just a few months after he was appointed to the Texas Prison Board. Beto's father had died in 1950, and so he often traveled to Lena to visit his mother. After one such visit in 1953 Beto traveled the short distance across northern Illinois to visit Ragen and tour the famous prison.[32] Beto and Ragen became fast friends, and Beto always referred to Ragen as his mentor. Ragen kept two residences, one in Springfield where he resided during the first three or four days of the week so he could monitor the pulse of the legislature, and the other in Joliet, where he stayed for the remainder of the week. When Ragen was in Springfield he and Beto lunched together about once a week. Undoubtedly, prison management and Illinois politics were topics of conversation between the two men. In Beto's opinion, Ragen needed to broaden his social horizon beyond the political orbit, so in March 1961 Beto invited twenty-five bankers and non-politicians to a stag party to feast on venison and meet Ragen. Beto estimated that they consumed enough whiskey "to float a battleship."[33] The lessons Beto learned from this mentor, both in conversation and in visits to the Stateville Penitentiary, remained with him the remainder of his life. The similarities between the two men and their philosophies are numerous, and warrant a deeper study of Ragen and his approach to penitentiary management.

Ragen had followed in his father's footsteps by being elected sheriff of a rural Illinois community. In 1933, however, he became the warden of Southern Illinois Penitentiary, in Menard. Even though his education was limited to the ninth grade, his performance at Menard was creditable, and he was appointed warden of Stateville in 1935. The prison there was in dire need of reform, so Ragen applied what he had learned at Menard, and in the ensuing years continued to develop his philosophy about convict management. He was successful in turning Stateville from one of the toughest prisons in the country, dominated by Chicago gangsters, into a clean, orderly, and well-run institution.[34]

Because his system of convict management was not unique and was practiced by other wardens, scholars have labeled it as "charismatic authority," or "monolithic," and point to Ragen as its quintessential practioner. Opponents of Ragen's approach to convict management called it authoritarian, while proponents have called it effective. It is basically a tradeoff in which the convicts give up personal freedom and in return gain security, order, and decent living conditions. Ragen summed up his philosophy for Beto in one sentence: "Either you run it [the prison], or they [the convicts] run it."[35] Aside from Ragen's prison management model, Beto learned anew the subtle but important interplay between corrections and politics. Ragen's residential arrangement symbolized what Beto knew from Texas. A warden lives not only at the penitentiary, but also at the state capitol.

Not all elements espoused by Ragen became part of Beto's penal philosophy, but many did. By the time Beto arrived in Illinois, Ragen had completed more than twenty-five years of service, and in his later life had given up some of the more oppressive aspects and in keeping with the fashionable trend in the 1950s, had begun to focus on rehabilitation. At the core of his philosophy, however, Ragen believed that inmates were entitled to nothing more beyond the basic human essentials. Anything beyond these essentials had to be earned by cooperative behavior, a positive attitude, and physical labor. Prison industries, Ragen held, not only eliminated the idleness that was the cause of many prison problems, but also reduced the cost of maintaining the prison. Work also taught skills that could be applied in the outside world, and Ragen supported vocational training, which broadened an inmate's options for future employment. He firmly believed that rewards, including extra privileges and reduced sentences, should be granted for good behavior.[36]

From himself, Ragen expected total involvement. He attended to every little detail in the day-to-day running of the prison. When he was in Joliet he toured the prison daily and talked to the guards and inmates, most of whom he knew by name. Using a system of informants, he was able to anticipate trouble and resolve problems before they escalated. The best way of eliminating riots, he maintained, was to prevent them through "good prison administration."[37] Beto and Ragen both have been identified as "charismatic," and possibly the type of penal management espoused and practiced by both could be effective only when it was administered by a person with that type of personality and one who was constantly in touch with the prison.

When Ragen took charge of Stateville he was confronted with a prison that had lost direction, and through the use of his philosophy, he brought order. But could Ragen have made his system work in the 1960s, when reform-minded penological scholars proposed new philosophies for prisons with a focus on civil rights, and the prison population changed so that racial minorities predominated?[38] Ragen relinquished his post at Stateville in 1961, before these changes set in. Yet Beto, building on the old Ragen philosophy, and serving in the context of the 1960s, was able to make the philosophy work once again in Texas.

Beto's loyalty to Ragen remained steadfast until Ragen's death on September 22, 1971. In August 1961, for example, Ragen was hospitalized for gall bladder surgery, but complications set in and he hovered near death. After a few weeks, when his condition was stabilized, he returned to his home in Joliet. Visitation was restricted, but Beto flew from Springfield to be with him.[39] After his recovery, Ragen resumed his position as Director of the Illinois Department of Public Safety, a post to which he had been appointed by Gov. Otto Kerner in 1961. But then, four years later, on May 27, 1965, Ragen resigned under pressure from Kerner for "irregularities" during his days as warden at Stateville. The charges included secretly recording conversations in his office, making excessive payments to two trucking firms, and maintaining two residences at public expense.[40] In response to Ragen's forced resignation, Beto wrote a letter from Huntsville commending Ragen for his years of service and expressing the desire that "our friendship and association continue undiminished."[41] And then in August, Beto attended a testimonial banquet for Ragen in Chicago where Kerner was the principal speaker.[42]

Ragen was equally impressed with Beto. When a vacancy occurred on the Illinois Board of Pardons and Paroles in 1961, Ragen urged Governor Kerner to appoint Beto to the board. Service on the board was part-time, but the salary was $9,000, only $6,000 less than Ragen himself earned.[43] Beto, in contrast to his actions in 1959 when he was asked to fill the vacancy at the Springfield seminary, actively sought support for the position from others. He telephoned Illinois Congressman Paul Simon, another Lutheran pastor's son, for help, and he received the support of J. A. O. Preus, the former governor of Minnesota and father of Concordia's classics professor. Pete Coffield, Beto's Texas friend, also helped by soliciting Eugene McElvaney, Senior Vice President of the First National Bank in Dallas, to prevail on the presidents of the three largest banks in Chicago to support the Beto appointment.[44]

Kerner's letter of appointment was dated May 3, 1961, and Beto responded on May 5 with the pledge to "discharge the duties of the position faithfully, always keeping in mind my responsibility to the people of Illinois, my loyalty to you, and my personal integrity." Beto credited the appointment to the influence of Ragen and to the "heat" three Chicago bankers were able to generate.[45]

As a member of the Illinois Board of Pardons and Paroles, Beto's responsibilities were to attend monthly meetings and then make decisions based on the parole applications from inmates from all the correctional institutions in Illinois. They decided on three types of matters; first, setting the conditions under which parole would be granted; second, granting parole; and third, determining parole violations. The board also advised the governor on cases of executive clemency, but the final decision in these cases rested with the governor.[46]

The same day Kerner named Beto to the Board of Pardons and Paroles, he had also, just a few hours earlier, appointed Beto to chair a committee to evaluate the activities and services of the Illinois Youth Commission (IYC). The IYC was the state agency responsible for the care, control, and custody of juveniles adjudicated delinquent by the juvenile courts in Illinois and placed in its system of juvenile reformatories. The commission had recently lost its director, so Kerner seized the opportunity to evaluate the entire agency. In the early 1960s the juvenile reformatories in Illinois were in a state of decay and neglect similar to the conditions found in the Texas prison system before the arrival of Ellis in 1948. As chairman of the commission, Beto was charged with the responsibility of organizing and managing a survey of the entire juvenile corrections system in the state. Under his direction a committee of nine people surveyed the physical facilities with a view to making recommendations to the legislature for program development and funding. Beto's experience, expertise on inmate welfare, and his accomplishments while on the Texas Prison Board made him uniquely qualified to chair Kerner's commission.

Despite his busy schedule, Beto found time to personally visit the juvenile institutions, and duplicating the practice that made him famous in Texas during his years on the prison board, walked the facilities, talked with the juvenile inmates and staff, ate the food in the dining halls, and met with administrators. He was not impressed with what he saw and heard.

Although the report was a collective effort by a group of nine individuals, Beto wrote the report and his point of view and ideas are presented.[47] In keeping with his Texas focus on the inmates, he recommended better sanitation in the kitchens and greater cleanliness in the living quarters. Inmates, after being screened in a diagnostic center, should be separated into groups according to age and criminal history. Beto also recommended that more emphasis be given to humane treatment by supplying health care from medical personnel and eliminating degrading punishments, such as shaving the heads of inmates. His confidence in the role of education in the rehabilitation process was also visible when he recommended the establishment of an academic program, reminiscent of his Texas Training Institute, and an extensive vocational training program.

In addition, the report recommended the standard topics for the improvement of most prison systems, including new construction to alleviate overcrowding, expansion of institutional research, upgrading of personnel through increased compensation and in-service training, and an expanded utilization of probation. The last page of the report, however, was vintage Beto when it first identified the causes of criminality to include the rural-urban shift, the breakdown of the American home, the deterioration of American character, and the failure of the church to assist the lower socio-economic segment of society, and then concluded with a quotation from Edward Gibbons' *Decline and Fall of the Roman Empire.*

The study was completed in February 1962, but by the time of the final scheduled meeting in March, Beto had already moved to Texas. He obtained permission from the Texas Board of Corrections to attend the meeting in Chicago, and then filed the final report with Governor Kerner.[48]

Beto admired Kerner, and they continued to maintain a friendly and cordial relationship that spanned fourteen years. It is easy to understand why Beto held Kerner in high regard, for he was a self-made man of many accomplishments. Kerner had served in the army during World War II, and retired with the rank of brigadier general. After the war he was appointed U.S. Attorney for the Northern District of Illinois. From 1954 to 1961 he occupied the bench in Cook County, Illinois, as a County Judge. Beginning in 1961, two years after Beto arrived in Springfield, Kerner was twice elected governor of Illinois. In 1967, one year before the expiration of his second term, President Lyndon Baines Johnson appointed him chairman of the President's National Advisory Commission on Civil Disorders (better known as the Kerner Commission).

After Kerner completed his second term as Illinois governor, he was nominated by President Johnson, and confirmed by the United States Senate, to fill a vacancy on the United States Seventh Circuit Court of Appeals.[49] It was at this point that his fortunes began to wane. In the early 1970s he was indicted and later convicted of bribery in connection with the purchase of race track stock. Following his conviction in 1974 Kerner resigned from the federal appellate bench, and earned the infamy of being the highest level sitting federal judge in the history of the United States to be sentenced to prison. Beto's admiration for Kerner prevented him from accepting the decision even after a federal appellate court affirmed Kerner's conviction. Writing to the United States Board of Parole, Beto stated, "I am unwilling to believe that he is wittingly guilty of the crimes with which he is charged."[50]

Despite Beto's unsuccessful attempt at obtaining an immediate parole for his friend, he corresponded regularly with Kerner while he was incarcerated in the Federal Correctional Institution in Lexington, Kentucky. Kerner was released from prison before completing his sentence when it was discovered he was ill with terminal lung cancer, and he was paroled to a hospital in Chicago. Beto promised to visit Kerner there on his next trip to see his mother in Lena.[51] But the planned visit never happened. Kerner died in Chicago on May 9, 1976, and because of his distinguished military career, was buried in Arlington National Cemetery.[52]

European Tour

During his stay in Illinois, Beto could not forget about Texas. Although busy on new construction projects and recruiting new faculty, he found time to return periodically to the state. In April 1960, less than a year after he left Texas, Beto spoke in Dallas and to a Lutheran group in Houston. His friends, such as Coffield, also kept in touch. In May 1960, for example, Coffield shipped a mare and a colt to Springfield, and Beto, with the assistance of Frank

Mason, a Springfield realtor who helped with the expansion of the seminary campus, secured a stable and pasture for the animals.

In July and part of August of that year Beto and his eldest son Dan made an extensive tour of Europe, and Beto scheduled his departure from Houston instead of Chicago. That itinerary permitted him to deliver a speech to the Criminal Law Section of the State Bar Association. After the speech he spent another week in Texas visiting with his friends. On July 6, early in the morning, he and Dan flew to Houston aboard Coffield's Beachcraft Bonanza airplane and then continued to Europe. Marilynn and the three younger children meanwhile remained in Austin, living in the Knippa family's home.[53]

Beto's ostensible reason for the European tour was to attend the Second International Congress for Lutheran Research at Westfälische Wilhelms-Universität in Münster, West Germany, scheduled for early August. The father and his teenage son, however, arrived in Europe a full month earlier for a tour of nine countries. Beto planned the itinerary, and the sites they visited symbolize Beto's broad focus in his life at that time. His first sphere of interest was religious. In addition to the conference he visited Lutheran pastors in the German cities of Hamburg, Heidelberg, and Frankfort, and in London he attended a meeting of Lutheran pastors from England, Australia, Germany, and India. He also spent some time with his brother-in-law, Jay Behnken, who was an Air Force chaplain stationed in Germany.

His second focus was on European prisons. Already in May, two months prior to his departure, Beto corresponded with the embassies of various countries and requested assistance in examining firsthand the "inmate welfare programs" in each of their respective prison systems. In support of his request, Beto included a formal letter of introduction from Gov. Price Daniel, complete with a gold-colored sticker embossed with the seal of the state of Texas. He identified himself as a former member of the Texas Board of Corrections and a current member of the American Congress of Corrections. Ragen also assisted by requesting the General Secretary of the American Correctional Association to provide Beto with a letter of introduction.[54]

Beto gained access to prisons in England, France, Switzerland, West Germany, Denmark, and the Netherlands, and the institutions he visited included maximum security facilities, juvenile reformatories, and minimum security, or open prisons. In London, Beto met with Sir Lionel Fox, the legendary Director General of the English prison system, and toured the well-known Wormwood Scrubs prison. Following a visit to another English prison, the governor of the prison, overcompensating for the dreary, rainy day, provided transportation to the train station in a prison wagon. It was an unmistakable vehicle and the locals stared as the "Black Mariah" speeded by. At Arnhem, Netherlands, he visited a prison built on the panopticon concept and designed by Jeremy Bentham. The design, also utilized by the prison at Joliet, allowed the prison guards to observe prison cells from a central post.

His third focus was that of a tourist, although his interests reflected his years of classical education and his study of western civilization. The sites included the religious ones associated with the Reformation, the Cologne Cathedral and St. Peter's in the Vatican as well as locations made famous during the Nazi Era such as Dachau and Berchtesgaden. Cultural activities ranged from viewing the art and architecture of Florence to attending a George Bernard Shaw play in London to the nightlife at Soho, and to observing the speakers at Hyde Park. He thoroughly enjoyed the European social life in the pubs, the sidewalk cafes, and the beer gardens.

Beto had little to say about the Münster conference, and there is no evidence that he produced any study of Luther, but he did use his tour of European prisons to prepare for an address to the American Congress of Corrections in Denver in late August. The report of his observations was later printed in a series of articles in the *Austin American Statesman*. In it he admitted that his observations were "admittedly superficial," but that some general comparisons with American institutions, and some specifically with Texas prisons, could be profitable.[55] He ended the report with high praise for the Texas Department of Corrections:

> Nowhere did we see that which an American penologist would call a well-guarded prison. In Switzerland, for instance, at the Berne Canton

prison, there were no walls, no guns, no fences. In not one of the maximum-security prisons of northern Europe were guards mounted on the walls.

Exclusive of Switzerland, where approximately 50 escapes per year occur at Witzwil prison, we had difficulty understanding why more men "don't go over the wall." The comparatively short sentences may furnish a partial answer. Rarely do European sentences run beyond six years. Too, the internal security of the countries of Europe may serve as a deterrent. When registration at a hotel requires a passport or some form of identification, you receive the impression that the entire population is under surveillance. In that type of atmosphere an escapee would undoubtedly have some difficulty remaining free very long.

We always inspected the kitchens and checked the menus. The entire prison-feeding program in Europe left us cold. The kitchens lack modern equipment; the prisoners are fed in their cells; the menus are unimaginative; and the food when served appeared wholly unappetizing. At Melun in France, an inmate who had spent seven years as a student in England told us in an aside that the only places serving poorer food than the French prisons were English boarding schools.

Nowhere did we see men in "tanks" or dormitories. Individual cells were the rule. As a rule, sex perversion and "the strong ruling the weak" are not the problems they are in American prisons.

Usually items made by prisoners were either used in the institutions themselves or were sold to other state agencies. We saw furniture manufactured for state use, boots and shoes being made for the armed forces, uniforms tailored for those state employees requiring distinctive garb, periodicals and books bound for state libraries, and printing done for state agencies. Prisoners were paid for their work. Usually one-half of their remuneration was reserved for them for disbursement at the time of their release.

There was some "leasing" of convict labor. In some countries "free world" industrialists would bring machinery, materials, and supervisors to the penitentiary for the manufacture of items not requiring a high skill. The state in turn was reimbursed for the labor of the convicts.

The employment of convicts is a difficult problem. We cannot escape the conclusion, however, that the costs of prison operation in America could be considerably reduced if prison labor were used on a wider scale to serve other state agencies. We recognize that the prejudices of certain vested interests make this desirable goal almost unattainable.

At Melun there was an employee for every 4.5 prisoners. At Copenhagen the ratio was 1.5. In Holland generally the ratio ran 1 to 2. When we expressed amazement at the large number of employees, we were told to go to the Netherlands juvenile institution at Zutphen where 70 employees work with 70 boys. These European ratios are a far cry from Texas' 1 to 9 ratio.

While we made a serious effort to secure accurate data on costs of operation of European prisons, we experienced considerable difficulty in this area. The information we did receive, however, left us with the definitive impression that the high employee-inmate ratio and the comparative lack of efficiency in operation resulted in costs roughly equivalent to those in the United States. Nowhere did we see a prison or a prison system operated as efficiently as the Texas Department of Corrections.[56]

The Death of O. B. Ellis and the Beginning of the Beto Era at the TDC

Following Beto's return from Europe he settled back into the routine of seminary president, all the while maintaining his ties to Texas. That changed in November 1961. In the early part of that month, Beto's friend and head of the Texas prison system, O. B. Ellis, suffered a fatal heart attack.[57] Ellis had not been feeling well and, despite a minor, unspecified illness, he continued to go to his office every day. Although he spent Saturday, November 11, in bed with a fever, he got up the next day and drove to Houston to dine with the members of the Texas Board of Corrections prior to their scheduled meeting on Monday. On Sunday evening, November 12, 1961, Ellis, along with eight other prison officials, was eating and talking with members of the Texas Board of Corrections when, to the horror of everyone present, he suddenly collapsed in his chair at 9:30 PM. An ambulance was quickly summoned and he was rushed to Houston's Methodist Hospital, where he was pronounced dead on arrival. He was fifty-nine years old.[58]

Word about Ellis' death spread rapidly across the state, and the press, which had for years chronicled the rising fortunes of the Texas Department of Corrections, was eager to learn who would be chosen to succeed him. Coffield told the press that he and the board were not going to make any hasty decisions about filling the vacant prison director's position. "It's a big job and we're in no rush to name a director," Coffield said.[59]

On the morning of November 20, a little more than a week after Ellis' death, Coffield sent a Western Union telegram to Beto, informing him that "The Texas Board of Corrections today unanimously elected you director. Our action has the support of the governor [Price Daniel] and the entire official family plus the prison administrators."[60] Coffield and the board expected Beto to reply immediately to the offer, but getting none by early afternoon, Coffield turned to the telephone. Beto was in Joliet attending hearings of the Illinois Pardon and Parole Board at Stateville Penitentiary when he was called from the room to take an urgent telephone call from "a representative of the Texas board." It was then that Beto first learned of the board's decision to hire him as director. The sudden and unexpected offer came as a shock to Beto. Stunned, he returned to the hearing room and continued with his business.

Early in the afternoon, newspapers in Illinois learned of the appointment from the Associated Press wire service, and reporters immediately began to search out Beto for a comment. They also found him in Joliet. After the board concluded its business a number of reporters rushed Beto as he was leaving the hearing room and asked him about the offer. "It's my first knowledge of it," he answered, "and I haven't had time to think about it."[61]

In the days that followed Beto was deluged with congratulatory letters and telegrams urging him to accept the position. Among those who contacted Beto and encouraged him to accept the offer were Gov. Price Daniel, Robert W. Calvert, Chief Justice of the

Supreme Court of Texas, Homer Garrison, Director of the Texas Department of Public Safety, University of Texas President J. R. Smiley, and Baylor University Chancellor Dr. W. R. White, and various other state legislators, bankers, and Texas industrialists. Austin MacCormick, the Executive Director of the Osborne Association, wrote Beto, telling him that:

> O. B. [Ellis] talked to me some time ago about his feeling that you would be a good man to succeed him when he finally decided to step out, and I gave my blessing to the idea. He put the Department of Corrections on such a firm footing that I do not see how it could ever slip back into the state in which I found it in 1944. It could, however, retrogress unless it has firm leadership. I believe you can give it that leadership, [and] you can count on me personally to help you in any way.[62]

Marvin Vance, a Methodist minister in Austin and member of the Texas Board of Corrections, wrote Beto, saying: "I accompanied Pete [Coffield] yesterday morning as we conferred with Price [Governor Daniel] and made known our desire to have you head up the Prison System. He respects our judgment, and I am sure that Pete told you via phone that he concurs in our choice. You are assured of our support in every way."[63]

But not everyone was pleased. In a tersely worded statement, the Board of Trustees of Concordia Theological Seminary quickly made clear its position that Beto should remain at the seminary. The board cited as reasons for its displeasure with the offer from Texas "his comparatively short tenure at the institution, the unfinished plans for expansion of the seminary which he has initiated, and his responsibility to the future ministers enrolled, as well as to the large number of new faculty members which he had recruited." The board resolved that "we would be reluctant to grant Dr. Beto a peaceful dismissal to accept an office outside the church. It is hardly possible for us to pass favorably on permitting Dr. Beto to leave the full time service of the church as a minister of the Gospel."[64]

In the weeks that followed the offer, Beto was obviously torn between remaining at the seminary or returning to Texas to head the prison system. He confided the depth of his anguish when he wrote to Austin MacCormick saying, "As you may well realize, the choice is not easy,"[65] and he also wrote to another friend remarking that "These have been difficult days for me."[66]

Following a meeting with the seminary's Board of Control on December 11, Beto announced that he was declining the offer to become director of the Texas Department of Corrections. In a telegram to Coffield the following day, Beto said that while he recognized the humanitarian character of the directorship of the Texas Department of Corrections, he felt compelled to respect the judgment of his board and remain at the seminary.[67] Coffield, obviously surprised and disappointed with his decision, wrote back simply, "Regret you have declined the prison position."[68]

But Coffield and the board were not to be deterred. These were, after all, powerful and influential men who were not used to taking "no" for an answer. Three days later, on December 15, Coffield called Beto with a new offer, one that would allow Beto to be involved in the ministry and keep him on the clergy roster of the Lutheran Church: "Recalling Beto's deep interest in the religious welfare of the inmates and the many hours he spent in counseling individual prisoners spiritually, we are [now] asking him to serve concurrently as Chief of Chaplains. We believe that the combination of Beto's ministerial and administrative background should be used fully in the Texas Department of Corrections and will aid substantially in the achievement of the objectives set for this Department."[69]

Beto did not immediately refuse this second offer, but neither did he immediately accept it. The board was secure, however, in its belief that Beto was the only man who could fill Ellis' shoes, and they were willing to wait for Beto's response. After six long weeks of agonizing and soul searching, Beto finally accepted the second offer on February 9, saying, "Inasmuch as the provisions of the original appointment offered by the Texas Board of Corrections have been altered and expanded to include a spiritual ministry, I am moved to accept the appointment."[70] Beto had crossed his Rubicon. As he had often said in his history classes, "*Alia jacta est*." The die is cast.

In accepting the offer Beto observed to a friend that "Some people are of the opinion that I am off my rocker for leaving the security [of the] citadel for the Department of Corrections job. Perhaps I am. Perhaps also these are the days in which we must live dangerously."[71]

Beto was receiving $25,000 a year as president of the Concordia Theological Seminary in Springfield. His salary as TDC director would be $18,500, plus emoluments, including a car, house, utilities, and prison food products valued at $4,500 per annum.[72] Despite a not inconsequential reduction in salary to take on the enormous responsibilities of care, control, and custody of 12,500 convicts scattered across thirteen separate prison units, the issue of money did not enter into his decision: "I was never concerned about the salary. I had to make peace in my mind about my life—whether I could better serve mankind in the ministry or in prison work."[73]

Putting aside their bitter disappointment, the Concordia Board of Control was gracious in bidding adieu to Beto when they wrote:

> In granting Dr. Beto a peaceful release from his office as president of Concordia Theological Seminary so that he may assume the dual office of Director of Corrections and Chief of Chaplains for the Texas Department of Corrections, the board does so reluctantly, realizing that our seminary is not only losing an effective administrator, but that the church is losing one of its outstanding leaders in the field of education.[74]

The *Sem Quill* student newspaper reported the event with the headline "Beto Goes to Prison." To many of the seminarians it was all in good fun, but Beto failed to see the humor in it. Many factors, including the wishes of his family, had gone into the decision.[75] It had been especially agonizing because he had had to choose between his two callings. Before his acceptance of the Texas offer, Beto was primarily in the ministry, and only secondarily in corrections. Under the new arrangement he would be largely in corrections with his hand in the ministry. Changing the focus of his life was wrenching, and he was irritated with the flippancy of the student journalist who was unaware of and unsympathetic toward his soul-searching.[76]

Beto left the seminary before all his goals had been met, but it is useless to speculate what would have happened if he had stayed in Springfield. In fact, in 1976, the Missouri-Synod once more revised its educational program by closing the Senior College in Fort Wayne and moving the Springfield seminary to the Senior College campus. There is a bit of irony in this because the campus was sold to the state of Illinois and the buildings Beto erected for training Lutheran pastors became a training facility for Illinois State Troopers and offices for correctional personnel. Even so, Beto's administration was impressive and during his tenure the enrollment of the seminary reached 494, larger in number than any other Lutheran seminary (excluding graduate students) in the country.[77]

Beto assumed his duties as Director of the Texas Department of Corrections on March 1, 1962. He was forty-six years old and halfway through his working life when he gave up his successful career in church work. But it was the second half of his working life that brought him to a pre-eminent place in the history of American prisons. The directorship of the Texas Department of Corrections would change not only his life, it would define it.

Chapter 6

TEXAS DEPARTMENT OF CORRECTIONS (1962–1972)

Huntsville, Texas, home of the famed Walls Unit and the administrative center of the Texas Department of Corrections (now the Institutional Division of the Texas Department of Criminal Justice), is the county seat of Walker County, approximately seventy-five miles north of Houston. Founded in 1835 as an Indian trading post, the town is situated in the lush "Big Piney Woods" area of deep East Texas. The green, gently rolling hills dotted by stands of tall pine trees sustained an economy driven principally by farming, ranching, timber harvesting, and the Texas Department of Corrections. The population of Huntsville in 1962, not counting prisoners, was approximately 12,500.[1]

The school year no longer dictated Beto's schedule, and on March 1, 1962, within three weeks of accepting the appointment, he occupied his new post. The moving van left Springfield in the snow and arrived at Huntsville in the rain. Dan, a senior in high school, remained behind to complete the school year with his friends. The rest of the family moved into the director's mansion across the street from the Walls. Built for Ellis in 1951, the mansion was a spacious building and provided 5,000 square feet of living space. Constructed of red brick and in keeping with its Georgian design, the building was fronted by a portico, supported by six large white columns with Ionic capitals. In sharp contrast to the high walls of the penitentiary that were built right up to the sidewalk, the mansion was set back from the street and graced with a circular drive and a spacious lawn. The main floor, which included a den and guest rooms, was semipublic, open to frequent visitors. The upstairs provided the private area for the family. Trusties, or prisoners whose behavior qualified them for greater responsibilities, staffed the building and looked after the household duties. But only when asked did the inmates go upstairs. Initially the staircase was open, but Mrs. Beto, seeking more privacy and security, had a door installed at the top of the stairs. The new living conditions were comfortable, but there were also rules such as the one that prohibited Lynn and Beth from staying home alone when the trusties were present.[2]

For Mrs. Beto, life at the director's mansion proved to be very different from that to which she had grown accustomed as the wife of a college and seminary president, and her contribution to Beto's success as a prison administrator should not be underestimated. Mrs. Beto not only ran the household, but often met with the family or friends of inmates who were seeking solace:

> There were so many guests eating meals with us, attending meetings in the den (which George used as an office at home), or staying in the guest quarters of the house that I often felt as if I were running a hotel or restaurant. We had prison officials, legislators, and judges from throughout the United States and from other countries as house guests.
>
> Often on Sundays when the children and I returned home from church, the doorbell would ring, and there would stand the family of an inmate. Since George was usually in his office on Sunday mornings, or out of town, I took the family members into the den of the house and visited with them. They needed someone to help with a problem involving their son, daughter, or loved-one in prison. Sometimes they were in tears when they arrived, but they left smiling because someone had taken the time to listen to their problems. I missed many a meal with the children, but trying to help them by just being a compassionate listener was so important to them.[3]

The Betos were back among old friends and on April 12 a wel-
come-home dinner was held at the Houston Club. Coffield and
W. S. Bellows, Jr., both board members, planned it and invited one
hundred dignitaries including Gov. Price Daniel. Mayor Lewis
Cutrer of Houston gave Beto the keys to the city. Beto enjoyed an
advantage which other directors such as Ellis did not have. He
knew and understood Texas politics. He not only knew names, but
he counted the people who were the key players as his friends.[4]

Two days after he took office, approximately twenty or thirty
Latin American prisoners on the Number One Hoe Squad at the
Harlem Unit, convinced about 300 other men to stage a "buck."
Instead of working in the fields with hoes, they just sat down,
refusing to talk to anyone except Dr. Beto. Beto and Coffield traveled to the unit, west of Houston, and Beto walked into the fields
and asked the men for their "beefs," only to be rebuffed. Years
later Beto recalled the circumstances of the incident:

> After I walked out there and attempted unsuccessfully to communi-
> cate with them, I went to the warden's office. In the office there were,
> I think, five or six wardens from the various units in the Fort Bend
> and Brazoria Counties, and we discussed what we were going to do.
> In a sense, it was a test of me [with the wardens], because some of the
> wardens didn't know me [and] they didn't know what I would do.
> One of the wardens, though, did know me from my years on the
> Prison Board, and as we were discussing strategy to deal with the
> buck, he said, "You've seen a lot of these in your days, haven't you?"
> I replied that I had, and he said, "You know, we've never won one.
> They either end in a draw or we lose 'em." I agreed with that, and I
> recognized that this was a critical moment, so I put four or five of
> those wardens on horseback armed with wet rope . . . and instructed
> them to go out and put number one hoe squad to work. I told them to
> use whatever force was necessary. There was a flurry of excitement
> and then the number one hoe squad went to work in a hurry and the
> rest of the inmates followed.[5]

The convict grapevine carried an account of the incident
through the prison system, and the inmates knew that the new

director was not a pushover and there were no more challenges. The only other buck during Beto's ten years was the Ferguson Buck later in the same year. Ferguson housed first offenders, who in all likelihood were unaware of the strong response to the Harlem buck.[6]

The story of Beto's putting down the Harlem work buck evolved into a fable, a mingling of facts, hearsay, myth, and romantic fantasy. In subsequent years the storytellers embellished the incident with extra elements of drama that had Beto confronting the strikers personally with a Bible in one hand and a baseball bat (or a club or a trace chain) in the other and declaring "Gentlemen, I can go either way, with the bat or with the Bible. Which would you prefer?" Within minutes a spokesman for the mob gave Beto the word: "We'll go the Bible route, all the way."[7]

Even though the confrontation had been successfully resolved, the first six months continued to be stressful. For the first time in his professional life Beto was not working for the church and he feared that he would not live up to the expectations people had for him. Marilynn noticed that during this period he lost weight, did not sleep well, and lived on coffee and cigarettes.[8] After a while he gained confidence, but he continued a strenuous schedule that kept him on the job from fourteen to sixteen hours a day for the work week, as well as shorter hours on Saturdays and Sundays. His usual daily schedule began between 6 and 6:30 AM. As he got in his car, he used his radio to call either the Huntsville or Eastham units for some information. Other employees could hear the conversation and realized that Beto was on the job. Soon there were more messages from people who knew that Beto could hear them and was able to recognize the voices of those already at work. He traveled by car, by airplane if necessary, or on horseback if he chose to go the fields to observe and talk with inmates. During the inspections he walked among the prisoners and any prisoner could give him a letter or a request. Beto was what the Germans call a *Menschenkenner*, a person who has the ability to analyze people. That ability along with his gift for remembering names and faces enabled him to assist prisoners who did not know how to solve problems or were caught in the web of bureaucracy.[9]

Within months he was known as "Walking George" for his frequent visits or "The Man" for his forceful response to the strikers. Beto made it a practice to visit every prison unit at least once a month. Sometimes he was accompanied by a member of the legislature or a visiting dignitary from another state or county. He walked very fast during these visits, regardless of who might be with him. It was not uncommon for people who accompanied him on his tours of the prison units to later remark that they had difficulty in keeping up with him. He also visited units alone, often at night. On one occasion he drove to the Jester Unit shortly after midnight and rattled the back gate to gain entrance. Beto gave his name to the guard and expected to be admitted. The guard, not being personally acquainted with Beto, insisted on some identification. Beto complied, and instead of reprimanding him, spoke to the guard for a few minutes and complimented him for properly following procedure.[10]

On Sunday morning he generally walked through the Walls Unit and the courtyard. He also used the day to make himself available to meet with relatives of the inmates who wished to speak with him. Most of the relatives usually came to meet Beto just to satisfy themselves that their son or husband was in good hands. A few, however, came to complain to Beto that their loved ones deserved special consideration or that they were being ill-treated by the guards. Marilynn remembered two incidents in particular that demonstrate how Beto the *Menschenkenner,* handled these types of encounters:

> On one occasion a mother of a young inmate tried to convince George how good her son was, and that he should be treated differently from the other prisoners. George finally said to her, "Well, it's a sure bet that he didn't get into prison for singing too loudly in church!"
>
> On another occasion a mother of a young prisoner attempted to tell George that her son was being mistreated by the guards, that he was not receiving sufficient food, and that he was not getting proper medical attention. When George asked how she was aware of this, the woman replied, "My son told me, and I know it is the truth because my son has never lied to me." George responded by saying to the

woman, "Madam, you are indeed fortunate, because I have four children, and all four of them would lie to me!"[11]

As an ardent subscriber to Joe Ragen's maxim that one could not run a prison from behind a desk, Beto adhered to a schedule that made him an omnipresent fixture at the prison system. Beto's son Mark noted:

> I was given many opportunities to observe the man in action first-hand, as he often took me with him on his visits to various prison units. Any inmate who wanted to discuss a problem with him could approach him and do so. The visits demonstrated the versatility of his leadership style, such as unannounced, early-morning arrivals on a prison farm: talking with anyone, anytime, anywhere; attention to detail; employing a disarming sense of humor and friendliness; and gracefully shifting between listening, commenting, counseling, advising, admonishing, complimenting, rewarding, and disciplining. He had a knack for telling people what they did not want to hear and then being agreed with and thanked for it.[12]

Beto received an average of thirty letters a day from the inmates and about fifteen letters from parents of the men in prison. He answered each letter the day it arrived, beginning the response with "Dear Sir." Inmates wrote or spoke to "Dr. Beto" with personal problems, for parole recommendations, requests for trusty jobs, for help in locating their family members and some for just conversation.[13]

Shortly after moving to Huntsville, Beto purchased a forty-acre farm about six miles north of Huntsville. He named it Wit's End Ranch, and it was a place he could go to for a change of pace. It was a peaceful and isolated place off a rough dirt road and home to many species of Texas wildlife. The "ranch" initially served as a retreat, and then in 1972 it become a home. The telephone and doorbell seldom beckoned, and Beto found the physical work associated with maintaining the place invigorating, or, as he said, "sweating the slugs out of my system." Eventually he ran about twenty-five Angus cattle and for the first time in his life he was not "all hat and no cattle." After it became a home the number and kinds of domesticated animals increased and the responsibility for caring for the animals during Beto's absence fell on Marilynn.[14] Years later, she wrote the following about the bucolic life at Wit's End Ranch:

> It was so peaceful out there—like living in a different world compared to the very public life we lived in all the previous years. The only disadvantages there were the rough country road, the well water, constant flats on our [vehicles], and having dirty cars and trucks most of the time.
>
> We had as very large front yard out there, and we did a lot of yard work. George always felt so good after a good work-out. . . . He rode a horse out there on the ranch to check on the cattle and fences, and sometimes when he hauled hay to feed them. We had a zoo out there with all the cattle, horses, Nubian goats, Mouflon sheep, dog, ring-necked turtle doves, and geese. We could have done without all the snakes, skunks, rats, and armadillos.[15]

On a Tuesday afternoon toward the end of September 1964 Beto went to the ranch to cut weeds with a bush hog (rotary cutter) attached to a tractor he had borrowed from a friend. The tractor hit a stump and Beto was thrown off and suffered a broken ankle, several broken ribs, and a punctured lung. Fortunately, when he was thrown off, the tractor slipped out of gear and stopped, thereby preventing certain death. His car stood about a hundred yards away and he crawled all the way. He drove to a neighbor's house and they telephoned for the ambulance.[16] After the required stitching and setting of bones, he spent several days in the Huntsville Hospital. When Coffield came to visit him, Coffield decided that the care was not adequate and had Beto transported to Methodist Hospital in Houston where he was placed in intensive care. He remained in intensive care for a week and survived two bouts with pneumonia. Beto believed that he would have died had it not been for his old friend's concern. Marilynn recalls that the near brush with death gave Beto a different outlook on life. "After his recovery he said he appreciated life, the blue sky, and the sunshine so much more than before."[17] Altogether, Beto lost thirteen weeks of work.

Time away from his office was not only spent on health matters; absence was frequently necessary for developing relationships with political leaders and journalists outside of town. Huntsville, being a small town, did not provide many opportunities for that purpose, but it is situated in relative proximity to two centers of influence. Houston lay within seventy miles and Austin was 175 miles away, short distances by Texas standards. Houston's significance was based on newspapers, finance, and courts, while Austin served as the political center and home to newspapers that featured a sharp political focus.

The legislature generated funds for the prison system, so Beto's presence in Austin was to be expected. It was reminiscent of Joseph Ragen's presence in Springfield, Illinois, and Beto followed Ragen's example. Beto was well prepared for the task because he had honed his craft of winning appropriations on thrifty Lutherans and had also gained insights into the intricacies of the political system as a Prison Board member. A first step in obtaining appropriations required the identification of those politicians who held power and those who could be counted on to lend support. That task was not a problem because he already knew most of the power brokers before he had moved to Illinois, and not much had changed during his brief absence from Texas. On one occasion, Beto, then a professor, conducted a workshop on the Texas Legislature and stated that five to ten legislators exercised predominate control over the prison appropriations. Another advantage was his natural affection for people and his memory for names and faces. Wherever he went, be it the halls of the capitol or the back roads of Texas, he stopped for quick, yet unhurried, casual visits in offices, homes, or business. He paid a call to make a comment, tell a humorous story, or ask about the person's welfare. No one seemed to mind the interruption and instead considered it a compliment. Besides, the interruption was brief. He was comfortable with people on all levels of society and spoke to each person's frame of reference. People liked him in return, liked his sincerity, and trusted him. In addition to dropping in the offices as he proceeded down the halls of the capitol, he phoned politicians, and if a secretary, whom he also most likely knew, asked for his identity in an attempt to filter out the unimportant calls, he would say that the call was from "an irate taxpayer." His message was a happy blend of wit and wisdom.

Beto also sought out social centers of community where state leaders gathered, and joined them. During his early years in Austin he joined the Kiwanis Club and soon became its president. As a result of his association with Coffield on the Prison Board he learned of locker clubs. These clubs, which catered to the elite, scrutinized potential members and charged a membership fee. In an elegant atmosphere the service was of the highest quality. The management assigned a locker for each member's liquor to be used solely by the member and his guests. Mundane matters such as charges were tastefully camouflaged, although the management sent out a monthly bill. Beto continued his strategy in Springfield, and then when he moved to Huntsville, he joined the Old Capitol Club in Houston's Rice Hotel. This club, which had been founded in the 1950s and closed in 1977, was at its zenith during Beto's years with the Department of Corrections. It was known as Houston's power center and the watering hole of lawyers, judges, oilmen, newspaper men, and politicians eager to make deals.[18]

At large affairs, such as dinners or banquets, Beto was the master of working a crowd. Guests at political events generally had been carefully selected for the occasion, so opportunities for influencing people were abundant. Social events for him were not events to be dreaded; they were opportunities to meet new people and renew friendships. While shaking hands or giving compliments, he was comfortable and relaxed. As often happens when a celebrity is mingling, the recipient of the attention, while enjoying the brief limelight, has the feeling that the celebrity is looking over his shoulder for the next person to meet. No one got that feeling with Beto, and you were the center of attention until he moved on.

With politicians the contacts were often in offices, in hearing rooms, and at receptions, but with journalists the medium was the telephone. Again, in harmony with the example of a mentor, in this instance his predecessor O. B. Ellis, Beto won over the press. He knew the journalists, read their newspapers, and phoned them. The calls could be to compliment a journalist or to provide new information. But he also made himself available to journalists if they needed information. When they phoned him, day or night, weekdays or weekends, he took time, often at the expense of his family, to speak to them. If they needed a statement, he gave them one. He treated them with respect and he responded honestly. He was available and he was quotable.[19]

Whether speaking to politicians, journalists, or even theologians, Beto avoided being confrontational. He preferred to "cultivate" people and did not wish to take the risk of alienating them or getting bogged down in petty controversies. If he did not agree with someone and wished to move on, he said "You may be right." If on the other hand, he chose to make a further point, he often cocked his head to one side, raised his eyebrows, squinted slightly and said, "Now, friend, you may want to consider . . ." As a result he maintained friends on both sides of an argument and people went away feeling that they had been heard. Later he could look to them for support. If someone attempted to pin him down to one side of a controversial issue, and he decided not to express his view, he deflected the question with humor.[20]

His method of handling politicians and journalists yielded positive results. Politicians responded generously—not only because Beto was likable—but because he could demonstrate accountability and reassure public servants of the stewardship of state funds. Journalists throughout the state gave him good press, and long after he relinquished his position with the Department of Corrections, the press remembered him.

Beto's focus on the prison system was so intense during his early years that he developed only a few close friendships in the Huntsville community. The three persons who did become his friends and confidants included a lawyer, Joe Davis, a rancher, Herbert Sandel, and a judge, Max Rogers. Rogers served as a district judge and was also the presiding judge in the Second Administrative District. When both Rogers and Beto were in town, hardly a day went by without a telephone call or a face-to-face conversation.[21]

As a public figure and the new director, Beto was frequently asked questions about controversial topics such as capital punishment. Capital punishment was not only a widely debated issue at that time, but Beto himself became directly involved with the executions. Within three months after assuming leadership, he presided over four executions. Realizing the potential for public outcry over rash statements, Beto was cautious during his first years about giving his opinion. When queried about his views on the death penalty Beto's response during his years as director of the TDC was always measured and ambiguous: "As an agent of the State, I am not permitted the luxury of an opinion in the area of capital punishment. I am simply carrying out the mandates of the Court. No contribution to my activities as an agent of the State would be made by a public expression of my opinion on this matter." And neither was Beto about to be drawn into a debate on the efficacy of capital punishment. Typically, Beto, when asked for his opinion on the objective of the death penalty replied with "no comment."[22]

But there was no question about Beto's views regarding abetting the public's oftentimes morbid curiosity about death row and the electric chair. When an attorney wrote Beto seeking permission for his son to tour death row as part of a class project, Beto wrote that "as a matter of policy we do not allow visitors generally, and young people particularly to view the electric chair. The chair happens to be situated in the same areas in which the condemned cells are located. The bringing of visitors to that section of the prison represents a rather disturbing influence. Accordingly, I must regretfully deny your request." Likewise, when an Amarillo television station sought access to death row for the purpose of making a documentary on capital punishment in Texas, the request was denied.[23]

After his retirement from the TDC directorship in 1972, Beto mused that "the memory of the [executions I presided over] haunt my mind. It wasn't one of the most pleasant aspects of the job."[24] This aspect of Beto's job was undoubtedly made more difficult for him given his position as a Lutheran minister and his understanding of the Lutheran church's interpretation of Scripture, because he did "not believe . . . that the Scriptures prescribe capital punishment."[25]

In actual fact Beto agreed in principle with the right of the state to execute, because certain conditions could warrant it. However, in practice he opposed the death penalty because it was not equally administered. The prison held 130 murderers, but only forty-three were on death row, and one young man whose death Beto witnessed, was executed not for murder, but for armed robbery.[26]

The Ellis Legacy

The Texas prison system came to fruition during Beto's tenure as director. Like his contemporaries, Beto served during an era that gave full rein to his special genius. When he took over as director of the TDC, his health was good, the challenge was stimulating, and his determination to succeed in continuing with the program of reform begun by Ellis was total. Beto inherited a prison system that was ranked among the top three systems in the nation. Beto was intimately familiar with the prison system because, as a member of the Board of Corrections, he had helped bring it to that level.

But Beto saw where improvements could be made, and he had ideas about the direction he wanted to take the prison system. He expressed his vision for the department this way:

> Mr. Ellis enjoyed an enviable reputation throughout the state. When I came here there was some opposition to my appointment. I was a clergyman for one thing, and an educator. There were some misgivings . . . [about my ability to do the job]. So when the papers asked me what my program was, I stated that I simply wanted to continue the progress that O. B. Ellis had begun. And in a sense I meant that. He had established a work program that I think was somewhat enviable throughout the United States. He had clean prisons, the inmates were well fed, and the morale was high.
>
> In my own mind, however, I had a couple of programs which I wanted to implement that I did not announce. Had I announced them at that time they probably would have failed, [so] I quietly endeavored to implement them. One was an industrial program. The industrial program in the [TDC] was limited, through no one's fault, but we had reached a point in mechanization of agriculture and

inmate numbers where it was necessary, or desirable, to institute an industrial program.

Another item that I wanted to improve was in the area of education. Progress under Ellis was remarkable. We needed to do more [though], because the world was changing. Another area that filled me with some concern was inmate housing. We had too many inmates in double decked beds in tanks, and the population was growing.[27]

He preserved the TDC administrative organization structure that Ellis had established in 1948 and made it his own until his retirement in 1972. The top three administrative levels were Director, Assistant Director, and Warden. The four assistant directors were each responsible for one of the following: Agriculture, Construction, Custody, and Treatment.

There were thirteen separate prison units,[28] each under the control of a warden, with 12,190 prisoners, 1,500 employees, 83,000 acres of land, 12,000 cattle, 14,000 hogs, 69,000 chickens and turkeys, 700 horses, and 500 man-tracking dogs. The industrial operation, other than the license plate operation, produced items only for the prison system, and was small compared to agriculture. Even so it included a textile mill, a garment factory, a shoe factory, a mattress factory, a packing house, and a canning factory.

Beto also inherited the Prison Rodeo, a widely publicized event that had been initiated in 1931. It was held every Sunday in October at a 30,000-seat stadium adjacent to the prison and produced as much as $175,000 a year. The funds were used for many services that were not provided by tax dollars, such as hearing aids, dentures, television sets, and art supplies. The inmates played the parts of cowboys, clowns, singers, and musicians but made no pretense that they were not prisoners. A typical gag heard on the loud speaker announcing a participant was: "This prisoner has twelve years more at this mailing address. He first came here for stealing—learned to read and write in prison—and came back the second time for forgery."[29]

Coffield was an enthusiastic promoter and supporter and each year helped obtain a different celebrity such as Red Foley, Minnie Pearl, Roy Acuff, or Dizzy Dean. Mrs. Beto remembered them fondly, and often the entertainers came to the director's house to change into their costumes or eat lunch. She quite often helped with things such as sewing on a button or repairing costumes. Even so, she found the month of October a trying time and invariably checked the calendar to see if the month had four or five Sundays. Beto generally was at the prison with officials and guests while she was in the mansion preparing for guests who dropped by before and after the rodeo.[30]

Beto hoped to build on the Ellis program with some modifications. His only significant change was closing the segregation unit (Shamrock). Beto disapproved of the policy that permitted several hundred men to escape physical labor by sitting isolated in their cells. Also, instead of being grouped and labeled as "incorrigibles" he believed that even they could change for the better, but that when malcontents, troublemakers, and agitators were put together the opposite resulted. So one of the first changes he made was distributing the "toughies" throughout the units. His other goals, although long-range, were to increase the salaries of guards and correction offices, improve inmate housing, expand industries, and improve educational programs, both the vocational and academic. He also hoped to delegate more authority to the four administrative assistants and unit wardens, and to use the talents of the men on the Board of Corrections.[31]

One significant change made by Beto that he was "pardonably proud of" was reminiscent of his days as president of Concordia Austin: he hired the first black correctional officers. Some prison staff and inmates were uneasy about this policy, and there was some initial resistance, but the transition went more smoothly than many people expected. Years later, one black correctional officer reminisced with Beto's son Dan, telling him that "Before your daddy came to the prison system, if a black man applied for a job, he would have been cursed and physically abused. That all came to a stop when Dr. George took over." Many of the blacks Beto hired went on to distinguished careers and made significant contributions to the operation of the prison system.[32]

Beto's leadership of the Texas Board of Corrections was more pronounced than that of Ellis. In the meetings he provided extensive commentary and initiated policy and procedural motions. When the chairman called for a vote on a motion, it passed, generally with a unanimous vote. He showed the same impatience with meetings that he demonstrated as college president. One observer noted that "Beto would just as soon hold a horse in the rain as sit in a meeting." And Beto himself wrote that "busy men with vision waste little time in formal meetings."[33]

Agricultural Program

The agricultural program had been an Ellis success. The assistant director in charge of agriculture, Byron Frierson, had been hired by Ellis and remained at the post during Beto's entire tenure. Frierson, after serving in World War II, had returned to Texas A&M University to complete his studies. Then in 1948, after three years as a county agent, he had joined with Ellis. During his term with Ellis, he had been instrumental in modernizing the equipment, upgrading the facilities, rehabilitating the farm land, improving the bloodlines of the livestock, and providing food for the prisoners. By the time Beto assumed the leadership, the agricultural program was efficient and stable, and Frierson earned the title of "The State's No.1 Farmer." A board member who aided Frierson, especially in improving the livestock herd, was Walter Pfluger, board member for twelve years and cattleman from West Texas.[34]

The primary purpose of the agricultural operation was to provide as much food for prison consumption as possible and to supply raw materials for prison industry and construction. Some products, such as cotton, were produced for the prison textile mills as well as for sale on the market. All profit from agriculture was returned to the state treasury. Agricultural activity not only reduced the cost of operating the prison but also taught skills and work habits to the inmates.

Approximately 10,000 acres were planted in cotton each year and the average yield was an impressive one bale per acre. Thirty-one thousand additional acres were used for field crops such as corn, sorghum, and hay. Edible crops on 6,500 acres produced about six million pounds of vegetables including everything from cushaws to okra. There were ten dairies with milking machines and pasteurization facilities that produced one quart of milk per man per day. The program even included a mill for making syrup from cane.

During the Beto administration the primary focus shifted from agriculture to industry. More and more workers were diverted to construction and the trades, leaving fewer men for agricultural tasks. Even the educational program decreased the time men could spend in the fields. The change from agriculture to industry was in harmony with the change of the population of Texas from rural to urban settings. Fewer men entered prison with an agricultural background and few could benefit from agricultural training. The demand for food, however, increased as the prison population grew, so in keeping up with the times, the agricultural operation during Beto's tenure became increasingly mechanized and modernized.[35]

By 1970, shortly before Beto's retirement, the TDC held 101,721 acres with 40,000 acres in production of food and 50,000 acres of grazing lands. There were 15,800 beef and dairy cattle, 17,000 hogs, 112,000 chickens, 3,000 turkeys, 345 horses, 290 mares, 10,000 cultivated catfish, and 387 dogs. Annually, the farms yielded 819,490 dozen eggs, 83,500 pounds of cheese, four million pounds of potatoes, 3,500 bales of cotton, and 500,000 bushels of corn.[36]

Even though Beto's energies were drawn away from prison agriculture toward prison industry, Frierson, of all the TDC personnel, was the one person who remained closest to Beto. In Frierson, Beto found someone to whom he could talk, not only about prisons, but also about a wide range of interests, including issues of the state and nation, spiritual matters, and farming, an interest dating back to the Lena days. Frierson was the only staff member to spend the night in the guest room of the mansion, and host and guest often continued their conversations into the early morning hours. These visits occurred weekly, when Frierson, who lived in Sugar Land, traveled to the Huntsville area to inspect the "upper farms." Beto also respected Frierson's experience and sound judgment on prison matters, and he liked Frierson's decisive, hardbitten personality.[37]

Industrial Program

While the agricultural sector enjoyed increased productivity, Beto brought a significant change to the industrial program. When he took office the TDC produced items only for its own use. Beto created a market for prison goods by initiating a modification in the purchasing regulations of the state institutions. Largely through his efforts, the Fifty-eighth Legislature approved Senate Bill No.338 (The Prison Made Goods Act) in 1963. It authorized the TDC to manufacture articles and compelled state agencies to purchase these materials, provided the quality and price were satisfactory. The purpose was to expand opportunities for inmate rehabilitation and generate additional savings for the state. The state provided no funds but set up provisions for a revolving fund that permitted profits to be used for the program's expansion. As the demand for agricultural work declined, the expansion of industrial activity was needed to provide work for the increasing number of prisoners. Prior to the new law the facilities produced license plates and goods only for prison consumption such as shoes, clothing, textiles, mattresses, brooms and mops, and canned goods. In addition to the traditional problems of custody and training, the TDC became businesslike and attended to quality control, production quotas, marketing, accounting, and supply.[38]

Under the direction of S. D. "Sammie" Bradley the industrial program increased production of the materials it was already making by adding a second eight-hour shift at the garment factory at Goree and a third shift at the textile mill at the Huntsville Unit. Bradley brought in new machinery for the textile mill, which by 1972 used 2,500 bales of cotton, and added new and modern equipment for license plate production. The canning factory at the Central Unit and the garment factory at Wynne were enlarged to meet increased state demands for food and clothing. And new standards were established to improve the quality as well as the quantity of shoes at the Ellis Unit and mattresses at the Wynne Unit.

New industries such as a broom and mop factory at the Ferguson Unit utilized the broom corn grown on the farms and fabrics from the textile mill. Then came a dental laboratory making false teeth, a coffee roasting plant, a tire recapping plant, a cardboard carton factory, and a detergent and wax factory.[39] By 1972 the seven small and poorly equipped factories had grown to twenty-two modern shops and factories providing training for 1,500 inmates and producing goods valued well in excess of six million dollars.

The productivity of prison industries was great enough so that in 1969 *Texas Business & Industry* magazine addressed the issue in an article. Some manufacturers of products such as janitorial supplies objected to the state's production of those materials. At Beto's invitation the reporters visited the prison and interviewed both Bradley and Beto. The journalists were not convinced of the need for prison industries, and called attention to some prison assignments that were almost devoid of vocational training. They also found Bradley and Beto unsympathetic toward the needs of private businessmen and expressed their fears that the industrial activity would be enlarged and further take business away from the private sector.[40]

Construction

Construction of new facilities and repair of old properties was an ongoing activity. Ellis had formatted an extensive physical expansion program and most projects were implemented and completed under the administration of Beto. Prison projects were generally long-range, demanding time-consuming approval by the state legislature and a slower pace of construction caused by the unique security requirements associated with using prison labor. The use of bricks made at the Jester Unit and prison labor, however, was cost effective, and projects invariably cost one-third less than projects completed by a contractor. Just as with agriculture and industries, the construction projects were training sites for the prisoners.

In some instances parcels of agricultural land that had been developed were sold and the proceeds used to purchase other blocks of land for the establishment of new units. In 1964, for example, tracts of land at the Central, Harlem, Blue Ridge, and Goree units were sold for five million dollars. Using three million dollars, the Board purchased 22,453 acres of land in Anderson

County. The next year it was named the Coffield Unit, and would be the largest of the units.[41]

During 1966 there were thirty-nine projects in progress valued at more than eight million dollars. The projects included not only prisoner facilities, but the administration building at Huntsville, which was completed at a cost of $735,000 and a soap and detergent factory at Central for $168,000.[42]

The most pressing need was the construction of facilities with single cells to replace the "tanks," euphemistically called dormitories. When Beto took office, seventy-five percent of the prisoners lived in tanks; by 1964 it was sixty percent. Depending on the size of the tank, there were between fifty to 150 men packed in large rooms, sleeping on double-decker beds, separated only by a narrow aisle. Beto knew the problems and reported: "With the best of supervision, it is impossible to curb sex perversion and to prevent the strong from preying upon the weak in this environment. This inadequate housing situation is not a result of a lack of funds. The Legislature of Texas has been particularly generous to the prison system in granting funds for the building. The problem lies in the inability to build as rapidly as the prison population grows. Our present count is 12,400." In 1964 Beto reported that three studies, each made independently of the others, concluded that the population at the end of 1966 would be approximately 14,500.[43]

But the convict population did not increase during the next five years, and remained below 13,000. In 1969 Beto reported that the prison population had remained static for several years with about 5,000 convicts released and about 5,000 felons entering the system. Beto asked the legislature for money to continue building separate cells for inmates so that by 1969 the number of prisoners in tanks had been reduced to less than fifty percent. However, at the same time the TDC population was steady, crime statistics showed a significant increase and should have served as a warning to prepare for another surge in prisoners. Beto discounted the information and explained the statistics as due to better reporting of crimes.[44]

Throughout the period from 1962, when Beto took office, to 1969, when the prison population was stable, the steady pace of construction continued. In 1965 the TDC opened a new building at the Goree Unit providing facilities for 204 women. At Retrieve, two new cellblocks with modernized utility services were completed at a cost of $1,230,000 and occupied in 1971. Also in 1971 work was completed on remodeling the main unit at Clemens, including the addition of two new cellblocks and four dayrooms. Work continued on additions including two cellblocks and remodeling of the main unit at Ramsey II. Construction on the Coffield Unit near Tennessee Colony was initiated in 1965 with a capacity for 4,000 prisoners. But six years later, in 1971, it was still under construction and by then the prison population had increased by 2,000. At that rate, a building that took seven years to construct would be filled to capacity in two years. Forecasting prison populations was difficult, but by discounting the press reports of the increase in crime, Beto failed to take advantage of the lull in prison population to construct even more facilities with individual cells than he did.

Even though the State Legislature was his primary source of funds, Beto did, on occasion, solicit support from private funds. Henry Rockwell, a Houston philanthropist, became interested in the pre-release center at the Harlem (after 1967 Jester) Unit, and provided funds for the Rockwell Building, which was completed in 1969. During one of his visits to the facility, Rockwell noticed the absence of a chapel and an auditorium at Harlem. He asked Beto the cost of a building that could serve both functions. Beto subsequently visited with Rockwell and informed him that the cost would be about $150,000. Rockwell had been thinking about $50,000 but Beto persuaded him to make it $100,000. The remaining funds were taken from the TDC's budget. Beto also lobbied the legislature for funds for chapel construction at the Darrington Unit, Clemens Unit, and Retrieve Unit. Each chapel cost about $90,000.[45]

Beto's Philosophy of Prisons and Its Implementation

When Beto took office in 1962, he believed the prison system existed for three purposes. First, it served as a deterrent to crime. The fact that at least some people were apprehended and imprisoned deterred them and others from committing similar crimes. Second, it segregated certain people from free society. They, by their acts, forfeited their "right to breathe the air of free men." And imprisonment removed "a menace to the physical welfare of their fellow men." Finally, the prison must try to rehabilitate the inmate.[46] Two years later, in 1965, reflecting a more contemporary attitude, Beto revised his philosophy by dropping the "prison as a deterrent to crime" and replacing it with the "prison as a place to provide a program of humane treatment."

Rehabilitation, however, was a constant theme for Beto. He liked to remind people that ninety-five percent of the prisoners, whether they were paroled or whether they served their sentences, would at one time walk the streets again. Even though elements of an earlier era such as revenge and restraint remained, the predominant goal of contemporary penology was reintegration of the prisoner into society. In his first annual report he wrote: "We cannot be judged by the profitability of our agricultural endeavors, by the efficiency of our industrial program, nor by the economy of our construction projects; ultimately the citizens of Texas must and will judge us by our success or our failure in rehabilitation, by our efforts in keeping them from coming back."[47]

Rehabilitation began with self-discipline. Beto believed that many people who entered prison had never learned discipline. It may have been the fault of a dysfunctional family, the schools, or the church, but prisons must provide an environment of discipline. Approximately forty per cent of the prisoners had no sustained employment record. The prison must teach the dignity and necessity of labor. And finally, the educational level of inmates was low and many were illiterate. The prison needed to educate and train. The records showed that relatively few of the prisoners who earned a high school education while in prison were among the recidivists.

At the recognition dinner shortly after his return to Texas, Beto heralded the completion of the new Ferguson Unit. The focus of the entire unit was on the education and rehabilitation of seventeen- to twenty-one-year-old offenders. Acknowledging Texas' new resident, Governor Daniel said, "Dr. Beto is probably one of the best men in the country in the knowledge of how to rehabilitate men so they can be returned to society."[48]

In the rehabilitation triangle of discipline, labor, and education, Beto's major innovations were in education. The General Education Development (GED) program, which he had initiated in 1956 as a member of the Board of Corrections, was still in place when he became the director. But he wanted to expand educational opportunities, so in 1965 he replaced it with the Adult Basic Education Program. This program took over the instruction of inmates preparing to take the GED tests and in addition offered educational opportunities in a classroom from first through the ninth grades. The new program also attacked the problem of illiteracy. State law required that those inmates with a score lower than 3.0 on a standardized educational achievement test must attend school one-half day a week. At the very least the program's objective was to assist the illiterate inmate to meet the mathematics and literary skills set by the state and achieve a second grade education. During 1965, for example, 966 felons entered the prison who could not read or write. In cooperation with the Huntsville Independent School District, which acted as the funding agent, the department in that year employed twenty-two additional full-time certified teachers to teach academic classes from the first to the eighth grade level. More than 4,000 inmates were enrolled in the system. Taken by itself, the GED program continued to grant certification for completion of a twelve-year education, and from 1956 through 1972 more than 3,000 inmates received GED certificates.[49]

A more formal structure, however, was needed for classroom education, awarding diplomas instead of certificates, and providing relief to the Huntsville school district. Beto decided to create an independent school district within the Texas Education Agency with a student body made up solely of prison inmates. The foundation for the school district was laid at the November 8, 1965, meeting of the board when the board approved the concept and named the proposed district after James Windham, long-standing member of the Prison Board.

Three years later in 1968, the legislature passed Senate Bill No. 35 to take effect in September 1, 1968, making the Windham

School District a reality. The Prison Board served as the board of trustees and Beto was the administrative agent for the board of trustees. Each unit of the TDC was a school and provided classrooms. The schools were accredited and offered a program of studies that was similar to that of the public high school. Financial costs were met by the state and the district qualified for participation in the surplus property program. The legislature provided an initial budget of two million dollars so that a staff could be employed that included a superintendent, six principals, 174 classroom teachers, forty-four special education teachers, thirty-four vocational teachers, four counselors, and eight special services personnel such as librarians and school nurses.[50]

The Windham School District modified its program to reflect the nature of its student body. It absorbed the academic program operated for the previous three years under Adult Basic Education and continued to offer its courses. Under the new district, attendance was compulsory for inmates with less than a 5.0 score on an achievement test, and students were required to attend class for at least six hours a week. Many of the inmates with low literacy scores were placed in Special Educational classes with a small teacher-student ratio and specially designed materials and methods. At the end of 1970 more than 350 inmates were in these Special Ed classes and 1,500 were expected in 1971.

Although the district used state adopted textbooks, the teachers made curricular changes to appeal to older students. Inmates attended only one day a week to accommodate the need for their labor in agriculture and manufacturing activities. Because the teacher taught a different group of students each day, the teacher saw as many as 450 students a week. Another difference was the constant change in the student population. Each year, 7,000 convicted felons entered the prison and the majority of them would be enrolled in Windham classes.[51] After four years of operation the program had 125 professionally trained and certified educators with more than 7,000 inmates attending weekly classes.

Once Windham was established, the next step was to make college courses available. By 1965 the TDC had initiated a pilot program in cooperation with Alvin Junior College to offer college-level courses at the Ramsey Unit. All inmates, except the women from Goree, could attend. In 1966 college extension courses at Goree, Ferguson, Ellis, Eastham, and Darrington were taught by professors from Lee College of Baytown. During 1966, 565 inmates earned college credits.[52] In 1969 the first Associate of Arts Degree was awarded through Alvin. Later Brazos Junior College and Henderson County Junior Colleges joined in both academic and vocational courses. In the fall of 1970 there were 1,230 inmates enrolled in college programs.[53]

Education played so great a role in Beto's philosophy of correction that he thought it should be part of every parole plan. When asked in November 1978 what he thought about educational release, he replied: "I think it should be part of parole conditions. I'd parole [an inmate] for educational reasons. If his educational experience in prison shows that he can profit by further education on the outside, then this would encourage people."[54]

In addition to academic studies, the schools and junior colleges also provided vocational training and counseling. These courses included welding, truck and car repairing, machine work, body work, leather craft, saddle and boot making, carpentry, bricklaying, electrical engineering, barbering, butchering, food servicing, sign making, sheet and iron working, agriculture, air conditioning, appliance repair, furniture upholstering, cooking, and typing. For a time eighteen convicts were trained at Texas A&M as heavy equipment operators in a program financed by a $22,800 grant from the Texas Criminal Justice Council.[55]

Another major contribution Beto made to rehabilitation was the creation of the Pre-Release Program, which began on September 1, 1963. It was a program that assisted the inmate in making the transition from prison to the free world. Many of the people who had served long sentences of ten to twenty years did not know how to use a dial telephone or how to cope with a freeway. Beto observed that "It is sheer folly to keep a man in prison . . . and then release him with a few dollars, a cheap suit, and the perfunctory ministrations of the dismissing officer." In the months between taking office and the implementation of the new program, Beto interviewed at least five prisoners each day who were being discharged and counseled them. Simple mathematics indicated that something more was needed.[56]

The pre-release centers, established at the Jester, Ferguson, and Goree units, received the inmates six months prior to parole or completion of their sentences. At these centers there were no guards, no firearms, and no bloodhounds. The program consisted of half of the day at on-the-job training, and the other half with counseling and job placement. The counseling came from business-men and civic leaders who spoke about buying clothes, insurance, social security, finances, manners and courtesy, how to buy a car on the installment plan, and family relations. There were even driver education classes and help in obtaining a driver's license. For those with alcohol problems there were strategies to deal with alco-holism. The last five weeks were totally devoted to classroom study and during the last six weeks the inmates were taken to sports events and church services outside the prison. Families of the inmate could travel to the center and visit in a relaxed atmosphere around picnic tables. At the time of Beto's retirement in 1972, more than 24,000 inmates had completed the program. The recidivism rate had been reduced from thirty-three percent to twenty percent, one of the lowest in the nation.[57]

Work Release, another rehabilitation program, made it possi-ble for prisoners to go back and forth between prison and jobs in the free world on a daily basis. (Work Furlough enabled them to return to prison only on weekends or for specified check-in peri-ods.) The Work Release Program was approved by the Texas Leg-islature in 1969. Initially, in the experimental stage, the program was limited to sixty men from the Jester Unit. These men were taken by bus to industries along Houston's Southwest Freeway. The same bus then returned the inmates to prison that evening. Only men who had less than a year left on their term were consid-ered, and men associated with alcoholism, narcotics, sex devia-tion, or crimes of violence were excluded. The men were paid the same amount as their free counterparts, but a portion of their compensation was withheld for prison sustenance and trans-portation. The men either deposited their paychecks or sent their funds home.[58]

Despite the look and feel of this program as a therapeutic modality, to Beto it was the legislature's window dressing, something to tout to the public as evidence of continuing reform and modernization of the prison system. When he was asked in the early 1980s about his thoughts on the work release program that had been started during his tenure as director, Beto said, "Work release isn't used much even though there is a law allowing it. I think work release can be a Mickey Mouse operation. For example, at a unit near Houston inmates are bused each day to the industries in Houston and bused back at night. They are under no supervision all day long. If they are that trustworthy they ought to be paroled. Why let them work with free citizens all day and bring them back at night into the prison environment? This is an unnatural situation."[59]

As head of the chaplains, Beto also saw the chaplaincy program as part of the rehabilitation process. Even as a seminary president, while he viewed religion as a means for providing the salvation of souls, he also saw it as a power in changing lives here on earth. Although records or newspaper accounts are few in describing his role as head chaplain, that position was important to him and had been the incentive in accepting the position as director. But Beto believed that chaplains contributed more through counseling in day-to-day conversations with prisoners, than they did through sermons.[60] The counseling provided by chaplains was both of a religious and a non-religious nature. Chaplains also were frequently the only link between the confined person and his family so they often wrote letters to family members and notified them in the event of an inmate's death.

Although the primary exchange between chaplains and prisoners was voluntary, prison policy encouraged chapel attendance in the Point Incentive Program, a practice which Beto admitted, "may or may not be ethical." Before a prisoner could be considered by the Parole Board, he needed a score of eighty points, and chapel attendance added points. He frequently stated that the church had failed the prisoner and in most instances the church had not been part of the felon's life. In an attempt to create a supportive agency, part of the chaplain's function was to establish a connection between a prisoner, soon to be freed, with a home church or congregation.[61]

With the intention of providing the service of chaplains more effectively, in May 1963 Beto led the chaplains in revising the religious program and submitted the new Chaplains' Standards to the board for adoption. The standards stipulated that chaplains must be credentialed with college and seminary degrees, must have experienced a successful pastoral ministry, and must continue to maintain the endorsement of their communions. If chaplains had no clinical training they were required to enroll in such a course during their first year with the department. In order to implement clinical courses, a Clinical Pastoral Education Program was initiated in 1964 and received accreditation in 1965.[62]

Beto also worked to increase the number of chaplains, either through additional state subsidy or through support from denominations. Shortly after Beto became the director he spoke to the Texas Council of Churches and asked them to supplement the state's appropriation for the chaplaincy program with chaplains whom they financed. Instead of a commitment for more chaplains, he got "a lot of hot air with a halo." However, the Baptists, who were present not as members but as observers, took his request to heart and earned his "eternal gratitude" by sending him two highly qualified chaplains.[63] The TDC staffed only one clinically trained chaplain in 1961; when Beto retired from the TDC there were thirteen full-time chaplains, six intern chaplains, and several part-time chaplains.[64]

Like the chaplaincy program, the medical services also served a major function, by indirectly contributing to rehabilitation. Although all units were equipped with modern medical facilities and staffed by trained medical assistants, the central medical facilities were located at the Huntsville Unit. The hospital maintained 209 beds, and the TDC doctors received assistance from specialists from the University of Texas and Baylor University medical schools. Physicians and dentists made routine calls at each unit and patients who needed specialists were taken to the John Sealy Hospital in Galveston and to the M. D. Anderson Hospital in Houston.

The rehabilitation aspect was present for inmates with psychological problems who were institutionalized with the TDC. They were first assigned to the Wynne Treatment Center, and then personnel from Baylor University's College of Medicine cooperated with the TDC to develop a treatment program for each inmate. It was also a testing center for new medications, and two widely used tranquilizers, Mellaril and Librium were developed while Ellis was the Director. The clinical field trials had been conducted at the Wynne Unit, whose prisoners voluntarily agreed to participate in the research.[65]

Plastic surgeons from Baylor's Medical School repaired a multitude of disfiguring scars or unsightly features such as claw hands, jug ears, lopped-off noses and ears, and obscene or gang-related tattoos that might handicap the integration into society. But before a prisoner could undergo such plastic surgery, it was necessary for him to accumulate a certain number of points from the Point Incentive Program as an indication that he was truly interested in rehabilitation.[66]

After ten years of setting up programs that focused on rehabilitation, Beto was forced to admit that "no one can be rehabilitated, whether he's a drug user or a hot check writer or any kind of chronic transgressor, unless there's a desire on his part to be rehabilitated."[67] The recidivism rate in 1971, nevertheless, was at a respectable eighteen percent.

Personnel

Just as the identity of the "prison" had been changed to "corrections," so the concept of "guard" was changed to "corrections officer." These officers were no longer viewed as persons who maintained security but were considered vital participants in the correctional process. They spent the most time with the inmates. Upgrading the quality of the personnel was therefore a goal, and recruitment and training were two methods to achieve the goal.

The low salaries paid to the TDC custodial personnel were a serious source of disquiet and anxiety to Beto. Immediately on assuming office, Beto, hoping not only to recruit but to retain good officers, championed the cause of increased compensation. He said that it was "immoral and wrong for the state" to pay such low wages, especially for a sixty-hour work week. He asked the legislature to increase the minimum wage from $256 to $330 a month.[68] Not waiting for the legislature, in 1962 Beto permitted custodial officers to buy surplus vegetables from prison farms at nominal prices. He also permitted employees to bring their own trailers to the various units thereby reducing transportation costs, and he proposed the development of trailer parks near the prisons with a modest charge of five dollars a month for utilities.

Beto did not reach his target of $330 a month immediately, but in 1964, when 150 guard positions were vacant, he was able to increase guard salaries to $305 per month. He also introduced merit pay increases starting on March 1, 1964. The raises were approximately ten dollars per month, and were given on the basis of recommendations of the unit wardens and department heads.[69]

The personnel department placed advertisements in newspapers and sent out news releases but because the turnover rate was generally about twenty-five to thirty percent, the staff was still 111 officers short near the end of 1964. Beto hit upon the idea of using university interns to relieve the personnel shortage at the TDC. Internships had long been a part of the curriculum in many degree programs. In such a program a student could earn credit toward completion of his degree program by working in a state agency or private business enterprise under the direction of a supervisor. Internships were intended to translate the theoretical knowledge acquired in the lecture hall from paper into practice.

In May 1964, Beto established contacts with a number of colleges and universities in Texas and told them that he was prepared to offer paid internships for juniors. Designated by the TDC as "trainees," they would be paid $268 per month and given free room and board. Beto proposed to use the interns in all areas of the TDC, and he encouraged students from a broad range of majors to apply, including architecture, engineering, business, agriculture, psychology, and sociology. Beto hoped that a number of them would come to work for the prison system full-time after they graduated from college.[70] The program was "eminently successful," and

Beto thought it should be continued (which it is to this day).[71] In
the years that followed there was great competition for the forty
internship slots at the TDC.

With the help of interns, the TDC made it through the summers, when guards were in greatest demand.[72] But with continual
efforts the minimum salaries for custodial officers in 1971 had
risen to $424 along with fringe benefits such as insurance programs
and recreational facilities. In 1971, TDC was competitive with private industry for manpower even though the guard turnover rate
continued to be high.[73]

Along with being more selective in hiring personnel, and requiring at least a high school education for custodial officers, more
attention was given to training. Beto implemented an in-service
training program in which all custodial officers spent two weeks at
the Ferguson Unit. Half of the time was spent in studying the *Manual for Training Officers* published by the American Correctional
Association and the other half working at assignments at the Ferguson Unit.[74]

Beto also modernized the correctional officer staff by racially
integrating it. In 1962, after he made the decision to place the first
African American at Ferguson, the rumors circulated among the
employees that some would resign because of it. The warden at
Ferguson, Jack Kyle, told his subordinates that if any employee
made a statement about resignation for that particular reason, the
resignation would be accepted on the spot. Euriah Mayes was the
first black employed.[75] By February 2, 1971, fifty-two blacks and
thirty-two Hispanics were employed at TDC. White personnel
numbered 2,162.[76]

Beto's Control Model of Prison Management

Beto never forgot the Ragen maxim on controlling the prisons.
Control was to be in the hands of the keepers and not the kept.
Discipline need not be harsh, but it was to be swift, sure, and
consistent.[77]

An important element in prisoner control was the modernization of living conditions. The best living facility in the TDC for the

inmates and the simplest to control was represented by the Ferguson Unit. It was built with individual cells and each cell had a radio. Each cellblock, which was a number of cells grouped together, had a dayroom with a television and domino tables. The entire unit included a library, chapel, gymnasium, classrooms, a shop, two dining halls, and a fourteen-chair barbershop. For additional diversion a movie was scheduled for each Friday night. In contrast, the most difficult setting for prison control were the tanks. Privacy was unknown and opportunities for violence and abuse were all too frequent.

One way to avoid problems such as homosexual rape, was through the separation of inmates. Certain wings or cellblocks were set aside at each of the prisons, except Goree, to separate persons who were aggressive sexual deviates. Those cellblocks were more closely supervised and Beto felt that "we do a pretty good job by segregation." Youthful prisoners were protected by being placed in individual cells in an area that was monitored with closed circuit television surveillance.[78]

Work, in addition to teaching skills and helping to pay for the corrections program, also helped with control. It not only took the men out of the crowded tanks and cells and gave them a different setting, it prevented idleness. After a day in the field or factory the men returned to their bunks tired and less inclined to confrontation. Even though many states paid prisoners for their labor, Beto opposed paying convicts in principle, and believed that no prisoner could be paid enough to make it worthwhile.

But more than anything, prison life was a life of rules. There was even a rule for the dining halls which said, "Take all you want, but eat all you take." The punishment for not eating everything taken was doing menial chores, such as polishing brass, for three hours, five nights a week. One of Beto's first administrative actions after he took office was to appoint a committee to study the uniformity of punishment and rewards throughout the system. As a result of this study, in May 1962 the TDC implemented a revised set of rules governing punishment and rewards. Many forms of petty punishment were abolished, and a limit was placed on the length of solitary confinement.[79]

A positive motivation was the good time law. Instead of paying prisoners for their labor, Beto preferred to reward prisoners with reduced sentences. When a convicted felon entered the penitentiary, he was made a first-class prisoner, which meant that he was eligible to earn twenty extra days a month provided that he behaved himself. In other words, for every thirty days he served, he reduced his sentence by fifty days. If he was classified as a second-class prisoner, he earned ten extra days a month. In addition to that, the law allowed certain men to be made state approved trusties. If a trusty was willing to conduct himself properly while doing a specific type of work, he would receive an extra thirty days a month or a reduction of sixty days for every thirty days he served. If, however, a prisoner was recalcitrant, he served the sentence day-for-day. Trusties could build up this time, but the officers could take it away as a punishment for violating the rules of the prison.

Beto considered this good time policy important and effective. It not only encouraged good behavior in general, but it simplified supervision of the men doing labor in agriculture and industry. In agriculture there were as many as two hundred inmates riding pasture every day looking after the cattle or checking the fences, without supervision. And there were another ten crews out almost every day building fence under moderate supervision. Men who worked at the dairies or at the textile mill, like the trusties, received two days good time for every day they served.[80]

Not everyone agreed with the good time law. Grady Hazelwood, member of the Texas Senate from 1941 to 1971, pointed out that if a murderer sentenced for 2,000 years took advantage of all the options such as trusty time and blood donations, he could walk out in nine years, seven and a half months.[81]

For those who did not respond to rewards, there was also punishment. Beto did not "believe in any form of brutality or corporal punishment," but he knew that on occasion use of physical force was necessary.[82] Guards were never permitted to strike prisoners and if they did, they were dismissed on the spot. Weapons were not carried in the prisons, but lethal force was an option for the "high rider," a prison guard on horseback supervising the field hands. He was armed with a rifle and a pistol with orders to shoot anyone who tried to escape.

The ultimate punishment was solitary confinement. It was used not only for recalcitrant prisoners but also for those who were not willing to work. The prisoner was confined in a darkened concrete and steel cell with two blankets, but without a bed or mattress. He received two slices of bread a day and all the water he desired. After a seventy-two-hour period, the prisoner received a full meal. If there was no change of heart, he received bread and water for another seventy-two hours. The sequence was followed for fifteen days. If the prisoner refused to comply, he was examined by a physician, provided with regular meals for three days and then returned to the cycle.

The extent of violence within the prison was an issue of debate. It was not only a question of guards abusing prisoners, but prisoners abusing each other with either the approval of guards or with the inability of guards to prevent it. Prisoners exaggerated its existence and officers diminished it. In keeping abreast of the growing number of lawsuits filed by prisoners alleging brutality at the hands of guards, Beto began to grow anxious about the court's tendency to believe the inmates and not the guards. Beto responded to criticism by inviting the critic to tour the system. His frequent unannounced visits were intentionally made to discover irregularities. Board members such as Windham also visited units with the express purpose of finding evidence of brutality. Bruce Jackson, a Harvard Fellow, did research in Texas because the TDC permitted him complete and free access to inmates. That indicated to him that the TDC had nothing to hide.[83]

But there was an aspect of prison life that lent itself to abuse in spite of frequent inspections, and that was the Building Tender (BT) system. Building Tenders were not unique to Texas, but were widely used in American prisons during the late nineteenth century and early twentieth century. The BT was an inmate who helped control the prisons and in return gained some benefits. The most important service performed by the BT was not in cellblocks with individual cells, but in the tanks where as many as a hundred inmates lived in one large room. One of the services the BT provided was that of informant or "snitch." He told the guards of escape plans or any unacceptable behavior. He also assisted in duties such as taking head counts, locking and unlocking doors, and protecting the unarmed guards from the prisoners whenever the guards entered the tank or block. The BT also supervised an area by resolving conflicts between inmates and looking after the general maintenance of the facility. In return the BT was given more desirable work assignments or increased good time. But there were liabilities with the system. Physical force was inherent in the system and violence could be used to resolve problems or enforce the rules.

When Beto took office the BT system was still utilized, even though most prisons outside of the South had discontinued it. Ending the BT system could have been accomplished by erecting more buildings with individual cells and closing the tanks, or by hiring more guards to control the tanks. But retaining the tenders helped keep the costs in line. Beto also believed that careful selection of tenders and close supervision of them would reduce the liabilities. On one occasion as he was walking through a part of the prison he learned that a particular inmate had been made a BT. Beto, however, knew the person and his background and immediately removed him from the position. Beto observed that the inmate, if given the opportunity, "would rape a snake through a brick wall."[84] In spite of Beto's close supervision it is difficult to reconcile his tolerance of the BT system and his statement given during the Cruz trial that he opposed any situations that provided "an unconscionable control [of one inmate] over other inmates. . . ."[85] It was the BT system that Ellis and Beto perpetuated that was most out of step with Beto's general philosophy and with the evolving standards of contemporary prisoner treatment and which later provided examples of abuses in court hearings.

Beto defended his actions in testimony before Judge Carl O. Bue. He rejected allegations that building tenders exercised guard functions and denied that they were ever armed. Even the guards inside the prison were not armed for reasons of safety and Beto maintained that the quality of the guards had been improved. He also denied that brutality was permitted and said that while building tenders sometimes broke up inmate fights, they used only their hands. Beto believed he knew the conditions of the prisons because in his walks through the facilities, he personally listened to any inmate who wished to tell him something.[86]

Control, a condition Beto considered necessary in managing a penitentiary, was viewed as oppression by convicts. Mike Middleton, a former inmate, described it as follows:

> In dehumanizing men, Texas has got to rank with the worst. . . . Every man that works goes through a strip shakedown twice a day in all weather, when he comes in for lunch and when he comes back in the evening. On construction jobs you can get strip shakedowns four times a day to keep you from taking anything in and bringing anything out. Inmates were brutalized by building tenders or by others while officers turned their backs. The building tender system can lead to real violence and even death for somebody. The bad agitator is sent to solitary and stands a good chance of getting beat up.[87]

Critics have called the Beto system an "autonomous and authoritarian system" and stated that the inmates were under the "absolute authority of prison administrators."[88] It is safe to say that Beto never envisioned a prison system that was democratic but neither did his system, *ipso facto*, incorporate the abuse of prisoners. Labeling a system as autonomous and authoritarian implies that all events that transpired in the facilities were under the control of the administrators, and that abuses which inevitably take place must therefore be an intentional part of the system. Excessive violence, Beto repeatedly pointed out, took place at prisons such as Attica, New York, that were convict-run. While the discipline in TDC was admittedly strict, Beto had no intention of relinquishing control to inmates.[89]

To properly appraise Beto's contribution to penology, it is only reasonable to assume that his desire was to eliminate all abuses. If anything, it was the inability of Beto's system to protect the inmates from each other and the dependence on the building tenders to help maintain some order that defines the weakness of the Beto system.

His extensive improvements and reforms justifiably attracted attention and drew high praise. If he erred, it would have been in his failure to anticipate the rapid growth of the convict population and the failure to extract more tax dollars to construct individual cells and to eliminate the role of prison tenders.

Often in his speeches, Beto, always with the disclaimer that he was not a prophet nor the seventh son of a prophet, predicted trends or issues. Toward the end of his administration he missed two predictions. The first was his belief that prisons "are largely obsolete as treatment centers for criminals." Prisons in the future, he maintained, were the answers for only a small hard core, approximately twenty-five percent, of offenders. The large majority would be looked after in community-level programs of courts, social agencies, probation and parole authorities, and concerned citizens. Beto also believed that the TDC's Coffield Unit, under construction in Anderson County, could well be the last prison built in the United States.[90]

He also did not anticipate the extent or the intensity of court intervention in prison affairs. In his Presidential Address to the American Corrections Association in 1970, in which he talked about the future of corrections, he was silent about the role of the courts. Given the number of court cases in which the courts had ruled on cases involving prisons, his silence must have been intentional. He continued to see corrections officials and the state legislature as the agencies responsible for initiating reforms.[91] As a result, he was blind-sided when the courts vigorously intervened on behalf of the prisoners who appealed to them for their newly defined civil rights.

"The Most Sued Man in Texas"

While Beto was maintaining his control system and fine-tuning it, the civil rights movement was spreading far beyond racial inequality and into the realm of the rights of institutionalized citizens. In 1964 the Supreme Court in *Cooper v. Pate* ruled that inmates could bring legal action against prison officials under the Civil Rights Act of 1871. Encouraged by this ruling, inmates, as well as their advocates, began filing an increasing number of writs claiming that the conditions in which they were incarcerated constituted an abridgment of their civil liberties. Penal practices and policies that in earlier times were considered acceptable were soon falling under the definition of unconstitutional acts. While prison administrators in many states were implementing changes in keeping with the "evolving standards of decency," Texas leaders, proud of their self-initiated reforms that had brought praise from journalists, penologists, and politicians, saw little need to accelerate the reforms or depend on the courts for incentive.

From hindsight, one can be critical of Beto's failure to accept the new trends in civil rights. But from his perspective, penologists and not jurists administered prisons. For decades, one of the hallmarks of a good system was the low cost in tax dollars for prisoner maintenance. Under the new emerging standards economic costs were not part of the equation. He should have used the court rulings as leverage to extract funds from the taxpayers for new facilities and more personnel. Neither did he know what the ultimate goal of the movement was or even if it would prevail. If he had known the extent and its durability, he might have made accommodations. Instead he responded with resistance that was ineffectual in the long run. His response to threats at his "system that works" was similar in spirit to the resistance of Richard Daley, the mayor of "The City that Works," at the Chicago Democratic Convention in 1968. Beto supported Daley and wrote, "I am persuaded that your approach, which involved meeting insolent disrespect for law and order with force, is the only solution to the problem of lawlessness in this country."[92]

The first indication that court cases were becoming a significant part of the Texas Department of Corrections was a discussion in a board meeting of *Gideon v. Wainwright.* In that case the Supreme Court granted the plaintiff a retrial because he had not been properly represented by legal counsel at all stages of the proceedings. Many Texas inmates became active in filing appeals on similar grounds.[93] Then, following the ruling of *Cooper v. Pate* the Texas prisoners based their claims on the argument that some aspects of prison life were cruel and unusual punishment and therefore in conflict with the Eighth Amendment. They named Beto as the defendant and soon Beto was called "The most sued man in Texas." At first the federal courts generally refused to hear the cases but of those that were heard three can be used as instructive of the issues and of Beto's resistance to accommodate the changing concept of civil rights and to the larger picture of prisoner's rights.

Two individuals played significant roles as Beto's adversaries in these cases. The first was a prisoner, Fred Arispe Cruz, who was serving a fifteen-year term for aggravated robbery. He was one of the most prolific of the "writ-writers," a term used to designate those prisoners who wrote and submitted appeals to the courts. The TDC had set aside a room equipped with resource documents and writing materials in which prisoners could prepare their writs. But there were also restrictions. The research and writing, for example, could only be done in that room and not in their cells. And neither could prisoners become "jail-house lawyers" in which skilled inmates could provide assistance to other inmates. On one occasion in an attempt to increase his productivity, Cruz smuggled some legal documents to his cell. The documents were found and he was disciplined. He appealed his punishment to the November 7, 1966, meeting of the board. Windham reported Cruz's letter, but the board upheld the action of the Ellis Disciplinary Unit.[94]

The other individual was Mrs. Frances T. Freeman Jalet. She was a fifty-seven-year-old lawyer from New York and an activist who tried to help the inmates in pursuit of their rights. She had received specialized training in poverty legislation at the University of Pennsylvania and in 1967 came to Texas to work for the Legal Aid and Defender Society of Travis County. Cruz learned of Jalet through a newspaper article and sent her a letter asking for help. His earlier requests to the American Civil Liberties Union for assistance had gone unanswered and he hoped that Mrs. Jalet could help him so he would win a hearing. The more Jalet met with Cruz and other writ-writers, and as she learned more about the prison, the more she became persuaded that the practices and procedures were excessively restrictive and brutal.[95]

The first of three cases that involved Cruz and Jalet was *Novak v. Beto*. Ronald Novak was joined by Cruz as a co-complainant and together they challenged the constitutionality of various aspects of the Texas prison system, especially the prison rules that prohibited "jailhouse lawyers" from giving legal assistance to fellow inmates. Cruz, testifying in the federal court at Houston, stated that he had deliberately violated the rule prohibiting giving advice because the restrictions were unconstitutional based on the decision of *Johnson v. Avery*. He maintained that the decision gave him the right to assist other inmates in legal matters.

The suit stimulated discussion in both the Board of Corrections and the State Legislature. The chairman of the appropriations committee proposed the employment of an attorney solely for the purpose of helping inmates write habeas corpus writs. This was done so the prison officials could testify to the court that a "writ room" had previously been available and that the state had also employed a lawyer to assist those inmates who needed help. Beto testified that a lawyer and not a fellow inmate should provide the assistance in order to prevent "an unconscionable control over other inmates by setting himself up as a lawyer."[96]

Cruz and Novak also complained that their punishment for having given legal aid to their fellow prisoners had been solitary confinement and that the system of solitary confinement violated the Eighth Amendment's prohibition of cruel and unusual punishments as it was administered, and that the punishment was disproportionate to any possible offenses. Cruz further complained that prison guards continued the practice of punishing prisoners by making them face the wall and then touch the wall with both their nose and toes for at least two hours or as long as an entire night. The court, on October 15, 1970, ruled in favor of the defendants on all counts. The right of prisoners, as articulated in *Johnson v. Avery*, was to receive assistance and not to give it. The judge, Woodrow Seals, further concluded that the services Texas provided for writ writing were within the bounds prescribed by *Johnson v. Avery*. He was also complimentary of the system and the ability of the personnel to make progressive changes, such as hiring an additional lawyer, to meet current legal requirements.[97]

On the matter of solitary confinement the court also ruled for the defendants. It concluded that solitary confinement was the most severe form of punishment used in Texas prisons, but that as it was practiced by the TDC, it did not violate the Eighth Amendment. The ruling ended with praise for the TDC as an outstanding institution and Beto as a fair, kind, and just man, and an excellent administrator. The circuit court, considering an appeal, affirmed the district court on the solitary confinement ruling, but one of the judges intimated that it might review the confinement practices and that he was troubled by lightless cells, limited bedding, and minimal food. Beto then discontinued the bread and water diet.[98]

The two remaining cases were both titled *Cruz v. Beto* and both were resolved in favor of the plaintiffs. *Cruz v. Beto* (1972) was a civil rights action filed on May 21, 1970, claiming several charges, but especially the First Amendment right to free exercise of religious beliefs. Cruz was a member of the Buddhist faith but was not allowed to use the prison chapel or to correspond with his religious advisor in the Buddhist sect. The TDC encouraged inmates to attend the Catholic, Jewish, and Protestant religious services and gave good-time points for attending these orthodox religious services. The TDC also paid the salaries of chaplains. Because Cruz shared his Buddhist religious materials with other inmates he was placed in solitary confinement for two weeks. While he was in solitary confinement, he was not allowed access to newspapers, magazines, or other sources of news. The federal district court dismissed the case. Cruz, however, appealed and in 1972 the United States Supreme Court ruled that all religions must be given access to worship and religious observance.[99]

Even before the case had been filed, on November 15, 1969, Jalet had sent Windham a letter concerning a petition from Cruz in which he had requested a commutation of time. Windham replied that he would discuss the matter with Cruz on his next visit to the Ellis Unit. Jalet wrote on November 23 that Cruz wanted to be present at the board hearing. Windham replied that board policy did not permit prisoners to be present, but he would present the matter to the board and notify her of the decision. Jalet on January 4, 1970, requested that since Cruz could not be present, Jalet would like to appear before the board on his behalf. Windham advised the board that he had met with Cruz on numerous occasions, and did not believe that Jalet could offer any new information. The board denied her request and then at the January 12 meeting the board found that Cruz had not been denied any rights or privileges and denied his petition.[100] However, early in 1972, Cruz was released after serving ten years of his fifteen-year sentence. In March of that year following his release, Jalet, age sixty-one, married Cruz, age thirty-two. Therefore, after that date, Mrs. Jalet was properly referred to as Mrs. Cruz.

Another development that took place between the two *Cruz v. Beto* cases was a case brought by three inmates against Mrs. Jalet. In September 1971 the inmates charged that she conspired to cause a revolution among the inmates in the state prison and asked that she be barred from the prison. The case smacked of prisoners currying favor with the prison administrators, but it is important because it shows the growing hostility between Beto and Mrs. Cruz.

Beto agreed with the claimants and said that "the seeds of unrest exist in every penal institution, and are being compounded by a few lawyers—some financed by federal anti-poverty funds—who make prison administration more difficult by stirring up malcontents behind the walls." He did not object to prisoners receiving legal advice from outside the prison, but he firmly believed that a national movement, assisted by some lawyers, was underway which was aimed at breaking down prison authority. Beto admitted that Texas prisons had problems, but that a policy of direct "communication between him and the inmates, plus prompt, consistent and fair discipline is working well."[101]

Mrs. Cruz's distrust of Beto appeared in a letter she sent after she had been given a tour of the Goree Unit. She acknowledged the cordial treatment, but then stated that "whatever I saw was pleasing (though I imagine some areas of the prison not open to the public are not as pleasing)." Then during the trial Mrs. Cruz's lawyer, William Kilgarlin demeaningly suggested that Beto's primary function was that of a politician and lobbyist with the legislature as well as with the influential members of the community. Beto was called to testify and defended his administration of the penitentiary and stated that the media had instant access and complete cooperation from the TDC to check any reports of brutality. Beto in turn was critical of both Cruz and his wife. Beto testified that he had first met Cruz ten years earlier and found him to be insolent and a "nonconformist who looked at other people as being stupid." As for the future Mrs. Cruz, he said that her visits to prison were "very numerous compared to other lawyer-client relationships, and that she spent unusual periods alone in a room with Cruz and that the wardens complained that she was a disturbing influence on the prisoners."[102]

In September, Judge Carl O. Bue, found against the prisoners and in favor of Mrs. Cruz. There was insufficient evidence, and the judge noted that one plaintiff had changed his testimony saying that prison officials had pressured him into suing Mrs. Cruz. Addressing the increased filings in his court (eighteen percent were prisoner petitions) he recommended the creation of an ombudsman system to review the petitions to consider their merit before they reach the federal courts, thereby reducing the complaints that the courts were trying to run the prisons. He also praised Beto for instituting educational programs and employment while maintaining discipline.[103]

On October 14, 1971, one month after the three inmates had brought the case against Mrs. Jalet, Beto set the stage for *Cruz v. Beto* (1976). After reluctantly cooperating with Mrs. Jalet's mission for four years, he lost patience and denied her admission into any prison units on the grounds that her activities were disruptive and threatened prison security. Other legal advisors warned Beto of his ill-advised decision, so in November Beto stepped back and withdrew his restrictions against Jalet, but he transferred Cruz and some other of Jalet's clients to the Wynne Unit. Beto then limited her correspondence and visits to only the clients she was already representing. At the Wynne Unit the convicts were assigned to a cellblock and also placed on a "hoe squad" to take part in manual labor.[104] Jalet and her clients responded with a case, filed in 1971, the year Beto decided to retire from the TDC, charging Beto with harassment and constitutional rights violations, and asked for $750,000 in damages for the convicts and $50,000 for herself for embarrassment and humiliation.[105] At the March 21, 1972, meeting of the board, Beto asked the board to secure the services of Tom Phillips for his defense. The board approved Phillips or any other attorney and authorized the payment of attorney's fees. At the May meeting the board was notified that the defendants were represented by Phillips, Jennings, and Saunders.[106]

In 1976, U.S. District Judge Carl O. Bue, Jr., ruled against Beto because he could find no evidence of any illegal activity that undermined prison security. He instead found that "Beto's actions were prompted by his long-standing antagonism towards Mrs. Cruz's contact with TDC inmates; and they were taken primarily to discourage prisoner-plaintiffs from exercising certain constitutional rights. . . ."[107] He ordered Beto to pay $10,291 in damages to the twelve inmates and Mrs. Jalet Cruz. Even though ruling against Beto, the judge praised him for his "outstanding administration of Texas prisons" and considered this case "an aberrant episode."[108]

The state appealed, and in 1980 the appeals court upheld Bue's decision. Nancy M. Simonson from the Texas State Attorney General's Office wrote Beto saying "My one regret is that I was unable to obtain a reversal of the district court's decision to correct the unjustified blemish on your exemplary career." The state of Texas paid the damages, but Beto was required to pay legal fees amounting to $27,825 that the state, by law, was prohibited from paying.[109]

Retirement

In spite of the legal controversy, 1970 and 1971 had been a good years for Beto. The American Correctional Association recognized his contributions by electing him president during its centennial year and the University of Texas honored him with the Distinguished Alumnus award. Both honors provided him satisfaction. The entire ten years, he and his wife agreed, were the most exciting and rewarding years of their lives, so why would he consider retirement? His wife, Marilynn, remembered that a ten-year limit had been set when he took the position in 1962. Beto had long held that ten years was long enough for a person to implement his ideas and apply his creativity to a specific post. Retirement at the peak of the career, when he could leave under his own terms, seemed appropriate. The first official indication of retirement appeared in the board minutes of the November 8, 1971, meeting. The retirement would be effective August 31, 1972, as Marilynn observed, six months longer than he had promised.[110]

Other factors, although not considerations in his decision to retire, can be seen as supportive of his actions. Two prison airplane crashes, one in Colorado and an earlier one near Huntsville, had distressed him. The crashes took a total of nine lives. He had also met the service requirement of ten years to qualify for a state pension. And, without doubt, the lawsuits that demanded more and more time in courts provided an added incentive. In a private correspondence to Robert Heyne, the Commissioner of the Indiana Department of Correction, Beto candidly summoned up his view of the state of affairs: "I have long ago learned that prison people have no way of keeping citizens happy. Accordingly, I have continued to live by an old low German proverb which my aged predecessor [Concordia Austin's Henry Studtmann] gave me when I was a college president: 'Ich tue mein Pflicht, und wenn es ihnen nicht gefaellt, sie koennen mein arsch luecken." ("I do my duty and those who do not like it can kiss my ass.")[111]

To another friend Beto wrote: "Prison administrators (including myself) are fighting a losing battle. Things are going to get worse before they get any better."[112] He was a good poker player and knew when to fold 'em.[113] After serving as director under three governors (Price Daniel, John Connally, and Preston Smith) Beto's last meeting with the board was on July 10, 1972. He completed his tenure as director at the end of July and took a month's vacation.

When the word went out that Beto would retire, newspapers carried articles of praise and listed the many reforms he had initiated. Recognition dinners, luncheons, and receptions in his honor filled the following weeks. He also received many overtures from colleges and universities interested in hiring him as president. He turned them all down, including an attractive position at the Lyndon B. Johnson School of Public Affairs at University of Texas in Austin, and instead accepted a teaching position at Sam Houston State University.[114]

Chapter 7

SAM HOUSTON STATE UNIVERSITY
(1972–1991)

August 31, 1972, was Beto's last day as head of the Texas Department of Corrections; September 1, 1972, was his first day as Distinguished Professor of Corrections at Sam Houston State University's Institute of Contemporary Corrections and Behavioral Sciences.

Beto's new career was by no means a journey into the unknown. Although his occupational change required a different residence, it did not demand a change of communities. Six months prior to vacating his position with the TDC he had moved his family and possessions out of the director's mansion to Wit's End Ranch. He then became a commuter, driving the six miles to his prison office; six months later, when he joined the faculty at Sam Houston State University, his commute was lengthened by two blocks.

The remaining differences also were minor. While his previous focus had been on corrections, his new one was broader to include all aspects of criminal justice. At the TDC he had been the administrator with total responsibility; at SHSU he was a member of the faculty. In this case no one changed his name from "Walking George" to "Talking George," even though it would have been true. He now had the dignity of an elder statesman and a distinguished professor.

No orientation program was necessary for him as he assumed his faculty position because he had been a significant force in the creation and implementation of the program he joined. When he had been a member of the Prison Board in 1953 and made his visits to Huntsville, his teacher mentality led him to see that cooperation between the two state institutions, the penitentiary and the college, could result in a mutually beneficial collaboration. But there was no tradition of cooperation between the two. The original mission of the college was to prepare teachers for the elementary and secondary classrooms of the state and the selection of Huntsville, in 1879, as the home for the Normal Institute, had nothing to do with the existence of the penitentiary.

The Criminal Justice Program

There had been cooperative arrangements between the TDC and other universities for some time. Texas A&M University, for example, had provided assistance with plants and animals on prison farms and helped plan the construction of agricultural buildings. The University of Texas Medical School assisted with diagnosis of illnesses and specialized surgery. The potential for further expansion of the cooperative concept was illustrated by a dual position held by Rupert Koeninger. He was the chairman of the Sociology Department at Sam Houston State Teachers College as well as the Director of Classification with the state prison system. But instead of further developing the relationship, the college chose to adhere strictly to its initial mission of teacher education and the administrative officer told Koeninger to choose between the two institutions. He relinquished his position with the penitentiary.[1]

So, for approximately ten years, until Beto became head of corrections, the institutions went separate ways. This situation puzzled Beto, causing him to wonder:

> why, when a prison system and a university were in the same community, what with all the prison records, there was not more cooperative research being conducted, and utilization of the university for the education of guards. I talked with Dr. Lowman, who was then President of Sam Houston [State College]. While he expressed a genuine interest in a greater degree of cooperation, he was dying of cancer,

and his ability was limited. There was one member of the faculty, W. E. Lowry, who caught the vision of cooperation. During the interim between the Lowman administration and the Templeton administration, he kept the spark alive and cooperated with me. A member of the legislature from Conroe, David Cruse, [Crews] came to see me one day and indicated that he believed there should be a greater degree of cooperation. He asked me to write a resolution that could be passed in the Legislature mandating that cooperation, which I did.[2]

In 1963 Crews introduced the bill, House Resolution No. 469, into the Texas Legislature, instructing the administrations of both institutions to conduct a feasibility study of creating a broad criminal justice program including the study of criminology, penology, and juvenile delinquency. Crews hoped to make SHSC famous for its criminology program rather than as a school of cheerleaders. The bill further stipulated that the results of the study must be presented to the next session of the State Legislature.[3] No study was ever made or submitted. The following year, however, Arleigh Brantley Templeton became president of SHSC, and Beto found another willing and enthusiastic supporter of his vision. Years afterwards Beto mused: "I didn't know him [Templeton] prior to his presidency, but I talked with him after his appointment had been announced and told him that I believed there should be greater cooperation, and that Sam Houston ought to have an outstanding criminology school. Dr. Templeton told me, 'I'm for it, but only if it can be the best in the nation.'"[4]

Templeton and Beto aggressively began implementing the program without formal approval, focusing their energies on cooperative research, cooperative training, and education. This procedure set the tone for much of what followed, and is reminiscent of what Beto said at Springfield about forgiveness being easier to get than permission. Templeton confessed that some things they did may have been illegal, but nothing had been immoral.[5]

The first step was to secure the employment of a director. But because there was no academic home for the newly created Institute of Contemporary Corrections and the Behavioral Sciences, or funding for the position, Templeton placed the program in the Department of Sociology and tied the director's position to the chairmanship of that department. Then after consulting with colleagues and reading resumés, the two administrators offered the position to Dr. George Glen Killinger of Florida State University at Tallahassee. As professor of criminology with prior administrative experience, he seemed to be the ideal candidate. While interested, he was unsure about accepting the offer, fearing the facilities at the teachers college were inadequate. To reassure him and to offer additional inducements, Templeton, Beto, and several others met with Killinger at the New Orleans airport and he accepted the position.[6] Beto's second triumvirate, similar to his first with Ellis and Coffield, was in place.

Killinger, as Chairman of the Department of Sociology, set to work creating new courses to supplement those in sociology and to hire professors and assign them to courses. By the fall semester of 1965 nearly two hundred full-time students enrolled. During the summer of the next year, Beto's desire for institutional cooperation was realized when thirty-eight students earned internship credit for performing services in the prison system. Beto read the applications and helped Killinger match the student with an appropriate task.[7] In rapid succession, Killinger offered workshops on the Huntsville campus and extension courses in the major metropolitan areas of the state. A master's degree program was available in 1966 and a doctoral program in 1971. The previous year, 1970, Beto had delivered the commencement address and with "pardonable pride" enumerated the accomplishments of the criminology program in its five years of existence and reported that it was the best in the nation.[8]

But soon the program outgrew its university facilities, and the three, Beto, Templeton, and Killinger, decided to construct a separate Criminal Justice Center. The first hurdle was to obtain a construction site. Space on the university campus was inadequate so Beto called on the resources of the Houston Endowment for $100,000 for acquisition of a four-acre site adjoining the campus just across the hollow from the south wall of the Department of Corrections. Additional funds for construction were available from the federal government, but the federal administrators required matching funds. Beto, always alert for opportunities to provide meaningful labor for the inmates, proposed using prison labor as a substitute for matching funds. The practice of using prison labor for construction, however, had previously been limited exclusively to prison facilities and critics argued that the use of prison labor for any other purpose would set a precedent for other state agencies to make similar requests. The solution was to identify the new structure as a facility for the joint operation by both the university and the TDC.[9]

During the next five years, the inmates constructed virtually everything from the million bricks to the cabinets and then laid the bricks and installed the cabinets. The total cost of the building, 197,000 square feet in size, was a mere seven million dollars, while the construction cost, if built by an outside contractor, would have been approximately $20 million.[10] When Beto joined the Sam Houston faculty in 1972, the construction was in its early stages, and Beto found himself in the crowded facilities of the Woods Building. Eventually, in 1977, the building was completed and Beto could enjoy the luxury of the new center. The center not only included 106 offices and twenty-six classrooms, but also a courtroom, a crime laboratory, a 500-seat auditorium, and a hotel of ninety-eight rooms. The courtroom was used for mock trials, moot court competitions, and for actual trials when a case was moved on a change of venue.[11]

Shortly after the completion of the building, Killinger, his goal in overseeing the creation of a criminal justice program accomplished, retired from his position as director on June 30, 1977. Beto became the interim director and began the task of finding a replacement for Killinger. The new director was Dr. Victor G. Strecher. Strecher served for seven years until 1985, when he returned to full-time teaching. Beto again served as the interim dean and director of the Criminal Justice Center until Charles Friel was hired to serve as director in 1986. Beto, then seventy years old, returned to the classroom, but on a reduced schedule in which he taught one graduate course each semester.[12]

The twenty-fifth anniversary of the program was celebrated in 1990 and Beto, in his address, heralded the program as "the largest criminal justice education and training program in the English-speaking world." During those years the school had granted 5,200 baccalaureate degrees, 900 master's degrees, and ninety-nine doctorates. The Institute administered an extensive continuing education program to meet the needs of the criminal justice community in Texas and included a Police Academy, a Probation Training Academy, and a Correctional Training Academy. And finally it was the site of the College for New Judges as well as the certification program of the Texas Association for Court Administration.[13]

Beto made a special reference to the library and archives in the center, which included the personal libraries and papers of some of the nation's leading penologists. He added his hope that there would be no erosion of academic standards at the center. Beto did not mention that in 1979 the Houston Endowment provided funds for the creation of The Beto Chair in Criminal Justice. This grant made it possible to obtain some of the best scholars in the nation to serve a term of residency at the Center.[14]

Beto in the Classroom

Beto's teaching assignments reflected his academic status and professional background. Instead of being burdened with large lecture classes and numerous preparations he taught two advanced courses and one graduate seminar. The advanced courses were "Special Topics in Correctional Administration" and "Special Problems in Correctional Treatment and Custody" while the seminar was titled "Seminar in Corrections." On the first day of class each student received a lengthy syllabus containing an outline of the course, the assignments, and a bibliography. In all three courses the grade was based on the final exam, the quality of written work, and discussion in class.

On a typical morning Beto arrived at the Criminal Justice building at 6:00 AM and, because at that early hour the parking lot was empty, parked his pick-up truck closest to the entrance. He then made his way to the hotel to check the guest list and learn of any meetings scheduled, so that he might meet and visit with individuals during the day.[15] Beto was always dressed in a suit and tie.

To some of the newer students his daily apparel seemed incongruous with his mode of transport to the institute. He invariably drove his rusted-out and beat-up pick-up truck. Some of the bolder wits among the graduate students quipped that his pick-up looked like it was "rode hard and put up wet," while others offered the opinion it was held together with baling wire and chewing gum.

His seminars were generally limited to fifteen students, and he addressed them formally, without nicknames. Like any advanced course or graduate seminar at the institute, there was always a lot of chatter and bantering among the students prior to the beginning of class. But the moment Beto made his appearance, the room immediately fell silent. In keeping with Beto's wishes, the men removed hats from their heads. He would breeze in carrying only a thin file folder with no more than two or three pages containing a brief outline of the issues and questions he wanted to cover that day. Beto never stood behind a lectern. Rather, he calmly sat down at a desk, quickly looked at the class, casually lit an unfiltered Camel cigarette, opened his file folder, and after exhaling a cloud of smoke, began asking questions, such as:

A member of the Legislature calls you and asks you to transfer one of his constituents who holds the rank of major from a southern unit to one of the northern units at which there is no vacant slot for a major. Moreover, the employee has not requested a transfer through formal channels. How do you respond?

On Christmas morning, as you visit several prisons, one of the wardens proudly shows you an expensive hat and a pair of boots which the employees under his supervision have given him for Christmas. What kind of directive do you write the following day to all wardens in the system?

Three M Corporation, which has an interest in persuading the fifty states to use reflectorized rather than simple painted license plates, invites you to participate in an all-expense paid trip to their hunting and fishing lodge in Montana. Do you accept? Why or why not?

One of your associates develops an imaginative plan which would require $100,000 to implement. No money is available during the current fiscal year. What steps would you take to implement it immediately?

The warden of the unit responsible for discharging convicts advises you that a celebrated political figure is discharging his sentence and asks that he be released at 4:00 AM in order to avoid meeting reporters at the gate. Do you grant the request?[16]

His pedagogic style was purely Socratic. He was renowned among the institute's graduate students for employing a dialectic method of instruction that was characterized by questioning and gently prodding students to respond to a query with a clear, precise, and accurate answer. He was a master at parsing a student's reply to one of his questions by challenging them on the difference between a fact and an opinion, stimulating them to recognize and evaluate bias and rhetoric, motivating them to assess for themselves the strength of supposed cause and effect relationships, probing them to examine the accuracy and completeness of the information upon which their views were based, forcing them to compare and contrast different points of view, and having them, through his questioning, recognize logical fallacies and faulty reasoning. He expected much from his students, and everyone had a healthy fear of showing up to his seminars either late or unprepared.

While Beto obviously had his own views on many controversial issues, which he was not hesitant to express, he never used his status to indoctrinate students with his particular perspective. Beto had little use for sycophants and the final letter grade in his graduate seminars was not based on reciting his views. Rather, he expected graduate students to understand the socio-legal context of the issue under discussion, the proponent as well as the opponent arguments that attended the issue, and to respond to both positions. Although he was rigorous and demanded much of those who sat in his seminars, the male graduate students revered him, and the females adored him as a father figure.[17] Even though he was a Distinguished Professor, he was subjected to an evaluation, just like the other professors. The evaluation procedure included ratings by the chairperson and the students, activities supporting the university programs, and professional and scholarly activity. In 1988 he stood, on a scale from 1 to 7, precisely at 6.794.

Public Speeches

From the very beginning of his teaching and work at the institute, Beto applied his skills in public relations for the benefit of his new calling, or, as he said, "working the trade." His experience at the prison had resulted in public acclaim and he was known by some as the "grand old man of the cold gray walls."[18] As a recognized authority on criminal justice, he was able to cash in on his reputation by giving speeches throughout the state and winning recognition for the institute.

He was also asked to write articles for professional journals and textbooks on criminal justice for textbook publishers, but speaking, rather than writing, was his preferred medium. He admitted that he no longer had the discipline needed for writing.[19] So he spoke frequently and wherever he spoke, local newspapers invariably carried reports on his message. Beto never left any doubt about his views and his views were so strong that his students referred to them as "Beto's Biases." These views were frequently repeated and restated in speech after speech and can be summarized, although sadly stripped of Beto's rhetoric, under five categories.

1. Public Attitudes toward Crime and Law Enforcement.

Beto had little faith in the public's attitudes toward criminal justice. People did not want effective law enforcement. If law enforcement were strictly enforced then they would be apprehended for breaking the speed limit, their children would be jailed for evading the marijuana laws, and they and their friends would be arrested for white collar crimes. The amount of money stolen by bank robbers was small when compared to that purloined by bank employees. If forced to choose between the costs for that kind of effective enforcement and the costs of social disorder, the people would choose disorder. And in addition, to effectively eliminate social disorder, the citizens would be forced to accept social engineering, which like effective enforcement, was not the public's goal.

On the purpose of prisons, the public, however, was ambivalent. Should they be for punishment, retribution, rehabilitation, warehousing (quarantining), or reintegration into society? The public on any given day complained about the prisoners being coddled, and on the next would complain about prisoners being abused. Often, after the conviction of a person for committing a heinous crime, the public called for revenge. But by the time for execution arrived, the thirst for revenge had long been diminished. To prove his point Beto proposed placing the electric chair into a mobile unit so the execution could be conducted in the county where the sentence had been imposed (as was the law in the state prior to 1924) and in the presence of the jury that convicted him.[20] Beto maintained his own ambivalence toward capital punishment. While he was firmly in agreement with the concept of the death sentence, he opposed it in practice because it was not equally administered. Many other inmates had also committed murder, just like those on death row, but they had not been given the death sentence.

The inconsistent public attitudes resulted in a penal code that was unfair. There was a confusion between sins and felonies. Victimless crimes such as gambling, prostitution, and public drunkenness should be handled in the local communities. He also argued for probation for the first offence for marijuana dealers as well as marijuana users. Beto supported different treatments for first offenders as well as those who committed victimless crimes. In his view, the certainty of punishment was a better deterrent than the harshness of the punishment.

2. The Prison Population

A recurrent theme in his speeches was that the prison population was composed of "the flotsam and jetsam of society—the poor, the stupid, and the inept." Beto was not being ugly or flippant when he said this, just brutally honest. The profile of those who actually made it into prison support this characterization because 96 percent of the inmates were school dropouts, 60 percent came from broken homes, 18 percent were illiterate, 20 percent were mentally retarded, 1 percent actively psychotic, and 40 percent had no record of sustained prior employment. The average I.Q. was 80.

In Beto's view Texas sentenced too many people to jail. Pennsylvania and Illinois had populations similar in size to Texas, but imprisoned only about half as many people. Beto observed that "there must be something in Southern culture that believes in locking people up."

3. Treatment of Prisoners

Although prisoners are not normal people, imprisonment should be the last resort for people who are dangerous. Beto, nonetheless, agreed with penologist John Conrad that, under all circumstances, prisons must be lawful, safe for both the keeper and the kept, industrious, and hopeful. Ninety-six percent of the prisoners would be out on the street again, so Beto supported the concept of rehabilitation, or change in attitude and behavior, as one of the objectives of penal confinement. Yet he admitted that he did not know why people changed. Often it was the aging process. No one could be rehabilitated against his will. All that could be done was to create an environment that may be conducive to change.

He favored measures that gave prisoners hope. Juries often assessed excessive sentences, so programs such as parole and term reduction mitigated harsh sentences. Long sentences also did not constitute a deterrent. "We've had hell for a long time and the last time I looked, we still had sin." Sentences mandating life or twenty years of "flat time" prior to parole destroy hope. A policy permitting conjugal visits had the potential for administrative confusion, and Beto instead preferred furloughs.

Educational programs were essential, beginning with a program for the functional illiterates and dropouts and continuing on through college. This study included the liberal arts and humanities, which he believed did more to change attitudes than the vocational-technical courses. And because almost half had no record of sustained work, they should be involved with work that was as comparable to the free world as possible, including production and quality control.

Conditions conducive toward the development of good habits were important because many inmates had not lived disciplined lives. They should learn to bathe properly, to eat properly, and not to infringe on the rights of others.

4. Reform of the Criminal Justice System.

Additional funding by the taxpayer was not the answer to the prison problems. Greater imagination was. It did not cost much to prepare and serve food in a tasteful manner. Electronic devices in certain instances could be used instead of personnel on gun towers.

Greater utilization must be made of the alternatives to incarceration such as mental institutions, and also structured environments for low-functioning individuals. He opposed both mandatory sentencing and assigning that task to juries. Instead he favored the practice used in the federal courts in which the judge conducted a pre-sentencing investigation and then pronounced the sentence. The parole system should be expanded across the state and prisoners should be paroled ninety days prior to release. That would provide a transition to the free environment and the parole officer could help in finding a job and a place to live.

County and city jails were "the horrors of our age" and cried out for upgrading. On the other hand he supported the concept of regional detention centers. He also opposed the civil service system for law enforcement officials because it provided a haven for employee mediocrity.

Beto was skeptical of fads being proposed in the name of reform. He did not support halfway houses because they brought felons together rather than separating them. He preferred electric monitoring. He found boot camps objectionable because inherent in that approach was the verbal abuse that he tried to prevent the guards from using. Privatization of the prisons reminded him of the old convict lease system and its abuses. And finally, he opposed the ombudsman program because it gave authority without requiring commensurate responsibility.

5. Social Factors in Crime Prevention

The family was crucial in rearing children to be law-abiding. There were too many working mothers, and both the families and society were too permissive. Churches had become middle class institutions and no longer exerted an influence on all of society, especially in the lower economic and social levels. And religion should be part of the home. A year of public service for everyone at age eighteen was a good way of instilling discipline in a difficult stage in life and could compensate for the shortcomings of the family.[21]

Ruiz v. Estelle

Near the end of Beto's tenure as director of the TDC, on June 29, 1972, an inmate, David Ruiz, filed a handwritten petition with the court to protest the treatment he suffered when he had been placed in solitary confinement. The Ruiz petition was not the only one filed during Beto's administration, and there had been other prisoners claiming abridgement of their civil liberties. Judge William Wayne Justice, of the Federal District Court in Tyler, Texas, responded to these petitions in 1974 when he combined several of these petitions into a single class-action suit titled *Ruiz v. Estelle.* Although the petitions had been filed during the last days of the Beto administration, Beto was no longer the director and therefore was not named as the defendant. The control system, however, that he had designed and implemented, and which had been continued by his successor W. J. "Jim" Estelle, Jr., was sharply challenged by the court.[22]

Jim Estelle was Beto's hand-picked successor and assumed the office on September 1, 1972. Beto had first met Estelle at the American Correctional Association in 1970, two years before Beto retired. Estelle, then responsible for the Montana prison system, asked Beto to visit the state of his birth and speak to the prison staff at Deer Lodge. Estelle's budget restricted him from offering an honorarium, but he could compensate Beto for travel. Beto accepted the invitation and asked for a Montana flag and travel for himself and his mother to Hysham. Later in 1971 Beto and Estelle met again at another conference and following that meeting Beto asked Estelle to submit his resumé for the position of assistant director at TDC. In November, when Estelle flew to Houston for an interview, he learned that Beto planned to retire in eleven months. Coffield and the board members had accepted Beto's decision to retire, but requested Beto to find his own successor. Beto selected Estelle and the board concurred. After Estelle found a home for his family in Huntsville, he served under Beto for nine months, meeting people and learning the system. Estelle went on to serve as director for eleven years, until October 1983, throughout the duration of the *Ruiz* case.

The *Ruiz* case brought out varying responses. An administrator of the TDC whose views were representative of other prison personnel, said, "The *Ruiz* case virtually challenges everything we do. The work system, the discipline system, security system, health care and other treatment programs. Most of those [lawsuits] are frivolous. There are some issues in that case though that we recognized long ago before any civil rights action. For example, overcrowding. We'll be quite candid with you. We're overcrowded."[23]

The chief staff council associated with the American Civil Liberties Union, on the other hand, took a different position: "It's an efficient system in terms of moving bodies, but it's not inaccurate to say they run the biggest slave plantation in the country. They maintain order and security at the price of human individuals and human sensitivity. In the long run, their type of efficient system may be the most brutalizing system."[24]

In the four years between the initiation of the case in 1974 and the opening of the trial, attorneys for the Justice Department and William B. Turner, the attorney Judge Justice assigned to represent the plaintiffs, inspected the prison system, deposed prison officials, and interviewed the convicts. Although Judge Justice's court resided in Tyler, he transferred the case to Houston to accommodate the witnesses from Huntsville. The trial itself began on October 2, 1978.

In representing the TDC, the lead attorney for the Texas State Attorney General's Office, Ed Idar, Jr., was convinced that the case was in a hostile court and the inevitable result would be an "overbearing decision." So instead of adopting a compliant demeanor, he responded aggressively to every issue, except over-crowding, in the hope that the court's decision would be "overkill" and there would be grounds for appeal.[25] After 349 witnesses testi-fied, the trial concluded on September 20, 1979. Fourteen months later, on December 12, 1980, Justice presented his 256-page opin-ion, and in fulfillment of Idar's strategy, found fault with nearly every aspect of the TDC.

The state appealed to the United States Court of Appeals for the Fifth Circuit which, in May 1983, overturned almost one-half of Justice's orders, including the prohibition of housing more than one person in a cell. But the appeals court upheld the major ele-ments of Justice's orders such as the requirements to abolish the Building Tender program and the rights of inmates to associate more freely. Estelle, Attorney General John Hill, and the Prison Board all favored an appeal to the United States Supreme Court for additional relief, but when Hill resigned in order to run for governor, the new attorney general, Mark White, decided against further appeal.[26]

Estelle hoped that he would be permitted to implement the court order himself, but in 1980 the court instead appointed Vincent Nathan as the "Special Master" with the responsibility of overseeing the implementation of the court rulings. Estelle consid-ered Nathan an adversary instead of a facilitator and resigned on October 7, 1983, to avoid the stress inherent in such a relation-ship.[27] From then on there was a rapid succession of directors.

Following the resignation of Estelle, the Texas Department of Corrections never fully recovered from the leadership vacuum resulting from Beto's retirement and the court's intervention in the *Ruiz* case. D. V. "Red" McKaskle, a veteran of the TDC, served as interim director from October 1983 until May 1984. Raymond

Procunier, a seasoned penologist, served as director from March 1984 until June 1985 and was succeeded by O. Lane McCotter, a retired army colonel. McCotter, asked to resign by Governor William Clements in late 1986, was succeeded by James A. Lynaugh, an accountant by training. In 1989 the Texas Department of Corrections was merged with both the Board of Pardons and Paroles and the Texas Adult Probation Commission to form the Texas Department of Criminal Justice (TDCJ), and the Texas Department of Corrections became the Institutional Division of the TDCJ. Lynaugh became the first executive director of the newly formed department, and James A. "Andy" Collins was named director of the Institutional Division.[28]

Conditions in the prisons mirrored the disarray in leadership and the controls Ellis and Beto had assembled began to unravel. From 1983 to 1986, the statistics used to measure the health of the prison system highlighted the crisis. In 1984 alone, twenty-five murders were committed and by November of the next year Texas led the nation with twenty-seven. Gangs, such as the Aryan Brotherhood, the Texas Syndicate, and the Mandingo Warriors, formed on racial lines. Also in 1984 there were more than 1,000 assaults on guards and 404 stabbings. The prison system was forced to purchase disposable plastic utensils to replace the metal ones because the convicts were turning the metal dinnerware into shanks, or jailhouse knives. Beto was not unaware of these developments. It was public information and his students talked about it in class. Beto wrote a friend, "The killings and stabbings continue. I shall continue to send you clippings."[29]

John J. DiIulio, Jr., in his perceptive and balanced study, *Governing Prisons*, argued that Justice should not be singled out as the single cause for the demise of a remarkably good period in the Texas prison system. Other elements coincided with the ruling that also played into this decline. DiIulio found one element in the system itself, the Building Tender program, to blame. This program, which utilized prisoners to supervise and control other prisoners, was susceptible to abuse. It was cost effective because it reduced the number of correctional guards, and it worked under Beto's watch because of his close supervision and attention. DiIulio maintained that the Building Tender program was not a necessary ingredient of the control model, but a "weak crutch" that should have been purged by Ellis and Beto. Instead, Beto's successor attempted to preserve it and tied it to the valid mechanisms of the control system, so when it was removed, it took along too many effective procedures. And in the vacuum left by the Building Tender program, the "con-boss" system emerged in which prisoners exploited each other and formed gangs.[30]

According to DiIulio, another damaging development, which coincided with the court's action, was the decline of monolithic support from the Board of Corrections and the state legislature, both fiscally and publicly. Coffield, who had wielded his power in support of Ellis and Beto, had retired from the board in 1974, and Bill Heatly, the key to appropriations, retired from the legislature in 1982. The unity on the board was also lost, and issues that had been resolved at the Board meetings now became public quarrels. And finally there was turnover of directors in rapid succession during a time of a mushrooming prison population and court ordered changes. Three different directors in three years were unable to provide administrative continuity.[31] All this was happening when the prison population more than doubled from 16,000 in 1974 to 35,000 in 1984.

But DiIulio inevitably returned to the role Judge Justice played. He exonerated the judge by saying that there was nothing in the *Ruiz* case that made the proper management of a prison impossible, but he also added that there was nothing in the case that contributed to the better governance of the Texas prisons.[32] The question, however, is Beto's activity during this period, both publicly and privately.

Even though Beto was vocal in his views of the criminal justice system in general, he avoided making public statements about events at TDC. When he stepped down he said to Estelle, "Here are the keys. It's all yours."[33] Yet Beto was a public figure and with his opportunities of presenting speeches, could have railed against the developments. He, however, maintained a discreet public silence and did not lash out against Judge Justice or attempt to find a scapegoat. Beto respected Justice's dedication to his work and was instrumental in inviting Justice to speak at the 1984 Congress of the American Correctional Association meeting in San Antonio. Beto, in turn, was asked to introduce Justice and could have used the occasion to express his dissatisfaction. People were cognizant of developments and assumed some hard feelings existed between the two. Beto, aware of this assumption, said that anyone who believed it "betrays an ignorance of Judge Justice and of me." Justice was a representative of the judiciary and the judiciary was one of the branches in government. Anyone who occupied a position of authority in the government, whether Beto agreed or disagreed, had Beto's respect. "Judge Justice has served his sovereign with courage and faithfulness and for that he deserves respect. . . ." Nothing in the introduction even hinted at any existing ill-will. At the very most, Beto, in his reference to Justice being a member of one of the three branches of government, the judiciary, may have offered a veiled suggestion that Justice should limit himself to judicial decisions and not to legislate from the bench.[34]

Beto's public restraint on Justice's ruling or on developments at the TDC did not preclude making comments on the criminal justice system. A comparison between Beto's speeches delivered before 1980 and those after that date reveals subtle differences. Even though many of the themes remained the same, some new positions could be viewed as a growing disenchantment with developments. It is unknown whether they were conscious changes and covert protests against events or simply the result of additional study. One visible difference, for example, was over public opinion. While before 1980 Beto considered the public as vacillating on correctional issues, after 1980 he accused the public of being "invincibly ignorant," the implication being that corrections should be left to the professionals.

In other speeches he stated that the criminal justice system was a euphemism and not a system at all, and on other occasions that the criminal justice system had broken down. The "system" was too fragmented with excessive overlapping of jurisdictions. To be effective it was necessary to integrate policing, detention, prosecution, adjudication, probation, incarceration, and parole. As a result, "crime pays." The clever criminals, those who commit white-collar crimes and those who commit burglaries, are generally not caught. Only twenty percent of crimes led to arrest and less than one-half of the arrests led to conviction. Ninety percent of all cases were settled through plea-bargaining instead of a jury trial. Even if half of all cases went to juries, the court system could not handle the caseload either in personnel or facilities.

He also contrasted his own approach to corrections, which stressed discipline, safety, and education, with the new trend that he called "human warehousing." Warehousing, with its high construction and maintenance costs, discouraged taxpayers from expanding facilities so that fewer criminals would be sent to prison and those who were, received shorter sentences. Most of these human warehouses "will continue to be overtly—or covertly—convict-run."

Beto's final speech, presented less than a month before his death, was the clearest and most unified of his speeches. The occasion was an address to the School of Law of Valparaiso University, the school that had awarded his bachelor's degree and also granted him a Distinguished Alumnus Award. The title was "Prison Administration and the Eighth Amendment." In it he assembled his most telling arguments, and then concluded, "As I reflect on forty years involvement in the criminal justice system in one capacity or another, I cannot escape the conclusion that the system is no better than it was almost one-half century ago."[35] (See Appendix A)

In private Beto disapproved of Justice's actions because Beto believed that the courts were untrained and not competent in the matter of corrections.[36] And he did quietly involve himself with the TDC, especially in the selection of the directors. His endorsement of Estelle's administrative actions was well-known. Also, the interim director, McKaskle, had been a warden under Beto and had accompanied him on several consulting assignments. For the permanent position of director, Beto had supported Orson L. (Lane) McCotter. McCotter had attended Sam Houston as part of the military program in which the United States Army sent military police to SHSU to obtain advanced degrees in criminal justice. He had earned a master's degree and had been one of Beto's students.

He was later promoted to colonel and given the responsibility of bringing order to the military prison at Fort Leavenworth. McCotter, in 1984, asked Beto to inspect the facilities and Beto was pleased and impressed. He wrote, "Nowhere, in those visits [to other prisons] have I seen a penal institution which equals in excellency the Disciplinary Barracks at Ft. Leavenworth." McCotter, even though he had the support of Beto and Governor White, who consulted with Beto on prison matters, was not the Prison Board's choice and the board extended the position to Raymond Procurier who had experience with California prisons. McCotter, however, was hired as Procurier's assistant and then in 1985, when Procurier resigned, became the director.[37] Beto's influence on the TDC, therefore continued, and three of the four successors were closely tied to him.

But beyond the selection process, the nature and extent of the counsel Beto may have offered his successors is difficult to gauge. At least on one occasion he gave advice to McCotter. The increased size of the prison population and the paperwork associated with the *Ruiz* case required McCotter to spend more time behind the desk instead of walking the prisons. Initially McCotter attempted to run the prison in the bureaucratic administrative style of his predecessor. For Beto, delegating authority and acting like an executive was anathema, and he encouraged McCotter to become directly involved. Beto had an abiding dislike for the business management style because he wanted to know exactly what was going on and the only way to do it was to be there.[38] Beto was clearly frustrated with what he saw, and did not think the future held great promise. When asked what he thought was the major problem facing American prisons, he said:

> I don't believe the problem in American prisons today is primarily money. Money is part of the problem, but I think the basic problem is administrative. An administrator's common reaction to any criticism is, "If you just give us the money, we'll do the job." So, in recent years money has been pouring into prisons. Money does improve the salary situation and can attract better-qualified employees, but it doesn't require money to serve food attractively. It doesn't require money to

keep a prison clean. It doesn't require money to curb sex perversion. It doesn't require money to communicate with inmates or to establish rapport with them. Imagination, creativity, and faithfulness are required. I think we are approaching disaster in prison administration.[39]

John DiIulio, Princeton professor, even though he tried to be even-handed in his study of prisons, could not hide his admiration for Beto's ability. Tucked away in the small print of the Annotated Bibliography is a "what if" question. DiIulio calls it a "counterfactual question"; Beto called that kind of question a "future pluperfect question." What if Beto had not retired but had remained the director of the TDC? Would he have managed the court intervention differently? DiIulio believed that if Beto had stayed on he would have handled the *Ruiz* litigation, dismantled the Building Tender system "and made the TDC into a model prison bureaucracy."[40] Even so, making the successful adjustment was not only a matter of ability but also matter of attitude. The important question was "Who controls the prison?" Beto's philosophy, based on Ragen's motto, was "Either you control it or they do." And by "you" he meant a small group of professionals with loyal support in the Prison Board and in the state legislature. The new reality required the court's participation in the affairs of the prisons. The court never intended to place the inmates in control and both Justice and Beto agreed that the primary objective of a prison was the safety of the inmate.[41] Assuming Beto's willingness to include the court, DiIulio's point is valid.

But Beto was not the director and the control system that he had perfected ceased to exist, and while he could look back to ten successful years as director of TDC, he could not look back at a program that future generations could inherit. Even though most of the directors who followed him were his colleagues, they were unable or unwilling to adapt his system to function with the restraints the court placed on them.

Texas Constitutional Revision Commission

In 1972, the same year that Beto retired from the Department of Corrections, the citizens of Texas voted to re-examine the ninety-eight-year-old state constitution and consider ways in which it could be modernized and streamlined. One of its 212 amendments, for example, still allowed the governor to activate the militia to fight marauding bands of Indians.

The procedure for carrying out the will of the voters called for three steps. The first would be the selection of a committee of thirty-seven people. Anyone could nominate a candidate, but the actual selection was made by a handful of state officials. The committee would propose changes and these proposals were then forwarded to the second stage, the members of both houses of the legislature meeting in joint session. The final step was the ratification by the citizens of Texas. Beto was one of the committee of thirty-seven that met throughout 1973.

Beto was identified by the journalists as a "purist." The purists admired the United States Constitution for the way it set down the principles of government in broad, general terms, making it possible for the Congress to pass statutory law to provide the specifics. As a result, the United States Constitution contained relatively few amendments. The Texas Constitution, however, was more specific and included statutory law, so that when changes needed to be made, an amendment to the constitution was necessary. Beto and the purists worked to eliminate from the constitution such topics as the state highway fund and a ten percent *ad valorem* tax fund for college construction which, they believed, could more easily be handled by legislation. For example, the Texas Constitution stipulated that seventy-five percent of all taxes on gasoline are earmarked for highway construction. Beto wanted to free that revenue source so that it could be used for other projects such as mass transit programs or for programs of human value such as care of mentally retarded children. Beto was outvoted.[42]

He also spoke out frequently on other issues such as the line-item veto, which he opposed because it granted the governor too much power and could be used to coerce the legislators.

He favored the election of judges because they should be made answerable to the people and he opposed granting public funds for all kinds of religious reasons because it was philosophically wrong. As the former director of the Texas Department of Corrections, he urged the committee to exclude constitutional provisions on liquor and lotteries because that confused sins with felonies and he also supported restoring voting rights to ex-convicts after they had completed their sentences.

The committee often did not agree with his arguments, especially on keeping the constitution general, and he soon realized the futility of opposing groups who had certain vested interests. His impatience with lengthy meetings also surfaced and on one occasion he commented that in the latest round of oratory he had not heard anything new, and believed that the arguments had been presented more effectively the first time around. Privately he was disappointed and hoped that the legislators at the second step would correct the mistakes, but publicly he supported the results and identified the work as "a compromise between representatives of all colors of the Texas political spectrum."[43] All the efforts bore no fruit, however, and Texas continued under its antiquated 1876 constitution.

Consulting

The less structured teaching schedule that made it possible for Beto to participate in the meetings considering the constitution also enabled Beto to serve as a consultant and apply his philosophy to prison systems in other states. Beto quit the prison system on August 31, 1972, and almost immediately traveled to Mississippi for three days to advise them on their work program for inmates.[44]

But it was his work as consultant with the Alabama system that was his longest engagement and had the most significant results. The Alabama prison reform program also provides material for comparing two judicial approaches to reform, and at the same time, yields more than a little irony. While Texas had brought reforms to the prison system in the administrations of Ellis and Beto, the prisons in Alabama languished, underfunded, understaffed, and

barbarously inhumane. In 1971, the year before Ruiz filed his petition in Texas, an inmate in Alabama, N. H. Newman, an orderly in
the hospital, filed a complaint with Judge Frank M. Johnson, Jr.,
claiming that the medical treatment was inadequate and had
resulted in the death of several inmates. Judge Johnson requested
that the Office of the United States Attorney act as *amicus curiae,*
and with the help of the Federal Bureau of Investigation, verify the
charges. The advantage of this procedure was that it placed the
burden of investigation on the FBI rather than on the plaintiff's
attorneys. When Judge Justice was preparing the *Ruiz* case, Johnson informed Justice of this procedure and Justice followed it as
well.[45]

Thereafter, however, the two judges followed different paths.
When Justice issued an order, and the TDC resisted its implementation, Justice examined another matter and issued a separate order
on the second issue. One order followed another order until the
appeals court made its ruling. Johnson, on the other hand, issued a
single order dealing with the medical issue, and when it was
resisted, he pursued that same matter until it was resolved. But the
other problems remained, and after yet another case, Judge Johnson, in 1976, took charge of the prison system and established a
Human Rights Committee to advise him. The committee hired Beto
as their full-time consultant. After eighteen months, however, an
appellate court ruled that the district judge lacked authority to take
over the prison system, and dissolved the committee.

The problems with the Alabama prison system remained until
1979 when the new governor, Fob James, admitted that reform of
the system could wait no longer. In the meantime Johnson had been
assigned to the appellate court bench and Robert E. Varner was
chosen as his successor. Varner and Governor James agreed on the
necessity of reform, and with the support of Varner, James took
charge of the prison system. Beto met with the governor in 1979
and advised him to employ a prison director who had managerial
ability, a "compassionate heart," and someone who was familiar
with agriculture. The governor selected Robert Britton, a former
subordinate at the Texas Department of Corrections under Beto, as

the director. In 1983, a committee of five individuals, the Prison Implementation Committee, was formed to work with the governor on reforming the prisons and Beto was one of the two consultants. Ralph I. Knowles, Jr., one of the committee members, did not view Beto as a "friend to prisoners' rights" and questioned Beto's selection. Before long, however, Knowles came to appreciate Beto as "an extremely well-educated man who honestly cares and actively contemplates the human condition."[46]

Finally in 1989, thirteen years after the case was filed, the committee reported to the court that the objectives had been accomplished. The *Montgomery Adviser* reported that Beto had an "enormous impact on the Alabama criminal justice system."[47] The irony is that with Beto's help, Alabama was able to introduce extensive reforms in its system, at the same time that the Texas system, which Beto had nurtured, was being reformed with murders, stabbings, and related problems. Professor DiIulio, who spoke of Judge Justice in a clinical tone in his 1987 book on prisons, spoke more harshly in his book written in 1991. "In Texas," DiIulio wrote, "an intervening judge had clumsily revolutionized that state's prisons rather than attempt to preserve and build upon the good things that Beto had built there; but at the same moment in Alabama, the second of two more judicious judges called upon a Beto-tutored director and Beto himself to bring an equally massive and disruptive intervention to a safe landing."[48]

International Conferences and Travel

Beto's reputation as a penologist led to invitations at international conferences which gave credence to his reputation and at the same time provided him with opportunities to gain more experience and insights. Three of the invitations were as a United States delegate, chosen by the State Department, to the United Nations Congress on Prevention of Crime and Treatment of Offenders. In 1970 he attended the Fourth Congress held at Kyoto, Japan. Here he toured Japanese prisons. In 1975 he attended the Fifth Congress in Geneva, Switzerland. There the focus was on the increase in female crime and on international terrorism such as hijacking. And in 1985 Beto was a U.S. delegate to the Seventh Congress in Milan, Italy, with its concern on the control of narcotics and terrorism.[49]

In 1974 Beto toured the Army confinement facilities in Germany. The purpose was to find ways to improve programs at SHSU that were attended by Army personnel. Thirty-seven officers had earned masters degrees from SHSU.[50] Because Beto's son Mark was stationed in Europe, his other children, Dan and Beth, also rendezvoused there. Between his inspections of the facilities at such places as Berlin, Nuremburg, and Mannheim he accompanied his children to typical tourist sites including Heidelberg. With his knowledge of German and of European history Beto felt comfortable in the country and relished the German food, especially cheesecake. As a tour guide, trying to explain the significance of certain sites to his adult children, he was less than successful, contributing more to their amusement than to their edification.[51]

In 1976 he received a fellowship from the Department of Health Education and Welfare for travel to Egypt and Poland for seventeen days beginning on March 26, 1976. Working with William Flanagan of HEW, Beto was expected "to monitor rehabilitation research projects" in several areas including delinquency and drug addiction. It was an International Research Program of the Rehabilitation Services Administration. He visited physical rehabilitation institutions for blind, deaf, and paraplegic people.[52]

His last international travel came in 1990 with a trip to Japan. He was the recipient of a Takeuchi fellowship, which required him to tour prisons and correctional facilities and to deliver several lectures at the United Nations Far Eastern Institute. Beto had been in Japan on two earlier occasions and was not eager to go again. He was not as comfortable in Japan as he was in Europe. In Europe he could decipher the road signs and menus, but could not do the same in Japan. The trip, however, promised an opportunity to formalize the relationship between SHSU and the Ministry of Justice, and would, in turn, enable students as well as practitioners to travel to Texas and enroll in classes. He resolved his dilemma by asking Dan, also a recipient of a fellowship, to help with the presentations in order to reduce the length of the stay. During their visit, Dan was amused at the lengths Beto went in order to avoid the rice and raw fish of the Japanese diet. At every opportunity Beto headed for the underground shopping area next to the railroad station for a cup of coffee and some American food. Because of an unspecified illness, either physical or psychosomatic, Beto apologized to the hosts and made an early departure. Dan noticed Beto's almost instantaneous recovery the minute they boarded the plane.[53]

The Texas Youth Council (later Commission) 1975–1987

In 1973, Ron Jackson, newly appointed director of the Texas Youth Council, employed Beto as a consultant. The council traced its history back to 1949 when the legislature created the State Youth Development Council and made it responsible for the management of the delinquent youth of Texas. In 1957 the agency became the Texas Youth Council, and in 1983 the name was changed to its current title, the Texas Youth Commission. Its mission, however, remained the same and during Beto's term the TYC was responsible for any delinquent person between the ages of ten and twenty-one. The TYC was a parallel agency to the Board of Corrections, so Beto's experience on that board, in addition to his experience as administrator of corrections, made him an ideal consultant. A major difference between the two boards was the number of its wards. The TYC looked after approximately 1,500 offenders while the TDC had 15,000.

Beto's broad range of experience was helpful with all aspects of the TYC's operation but it was especially valuable at that time because in 1971, Judge Justice, one year prior to initiating *Ruiz v. Estelle,* implemented a class-action lawsuit, *Morales v. Turman,* against the Texas Youth Council, its officers, and staff. The plaintiffs were Alicia Morales and eleven children confined in the juvenile corrections facilities. At the time Justice initiated the suit, Beto was in his final year as the director of prisons and involved in his own cases. Two years later, however, Beto was in the academic world, and the council could draw on his experience and knowledge.

However, after Beto had served as a consultant for two years, Governor Dolph Briscoe appointed Beto to the council's board in

May 1975. Earlier in the year, the legislature had increased the number of board memberships to six, and Beto's appointment for a six-year term was to one of the new positions. Beto continued as a member of the board for the next twelve years, and during that time served two terms as the board's chairman.

As both consultant and board member, Beto served his entire tenure in the context of the *Morales* case. By the time Beto joined Jackson's board, the atmosphere in which the TYC responded to Judge Justice was less resistant to court intervention than it had been under the previous administration. The *Morales* case actually served as the catalyst for change and Jackson recognized the need for reform and sought to implement changes even as the case was working its way through the judicial system. Beto played an important role in the reform program by winning support from the legislature and in suggesting direction to the board. By the time the case concluded in 1988, most of the reforms, such as decentralization of facilities and guarantees of procedural due process, had been implemented, and the TYC was widely recognized for its dramatic reforms. In contrast to the TDC and the *Ruiz* case, the TYC was able to accomplish reforms on its own initiative and was never under the supervision of a court-appointed special master. Currently the agency operates sixteen correctional institutions and one of them, a halfway house at McAllen, is named the Beto House.[54]

The FBI Nomination

In the fall of 1977 Clarence Kelley announced he would retire as Director of the Federal Bureau of Investigation on January 1, 1978. President Jimmy Carter selected U.S. District Judge Frank Johnson to fill the vacancy. Johnson was the judge with whom Beto worked to implement reforms in Alabama's prison system. Johnson's candidacy for the position was short-lived, and in November he declined because of health problems.

In December, Rep. Robert Krueger, a Democratic congressman from New Braunfels (and a candidate for the Democratic nomination for the U.S. Senate), wrote U.S. Attorney General Griffin Bell and urged him to recommend to President Carter that Beto be nominated to fill the position of FBI Director. Krueger wrote, "Beto is a man of impeccable integrity, a proven and widely respected administrator and a man who is uniquely familiar with law enforcement and the nature of crime in this nation. His background in theology, in academia, in penal administration and in the study of crime and criminal justice leaves him with an accumulation of knowledge and experience that is indeed rare."[55]

But not everyone was convinced that Beto was the man for the job. Charles Sullivan, the Executive Director of CURE (Citizens United for the Rehabilitation of Errants), an organization that was lobbying for penal reform, community-based corrections, and abolition of the death penalty, was outraged. He wrote a letter to Attorney General Bell, saying: "CURE cannot fanthom [sic] how a person under court order for violation of constitutional rights could even be considered by the Carter Administration to be Director [of the FBI]."[56] In interviews with the press, Sullivan played up the fact that "Beto had been ordered to pay $38,086 to prisoners and their attorney [Jalet] after Houston federal judge Carl Bue, Jr., found that Beto had denied certain inmates access to an attorney."[57] Sullivan thought Beto exhibited "unreasonable impatience with inmate complaints and dissent."[58]

The harsh words from Sullivan very likely had no influence on the outcome of Beto's nomination. It is not known if Bell forwarded Krueger's suggestion to the White House. The position subsequently went to William Webster, a judge on the Eighth U. S. Circuit Court of Appeals.

Beto's Philosophy

Philosophically Beto was more of a problem-solver than an abstract thinker. Nevertheless, his attitudes and those of his closest associates fit into the conservative tradition, both politically and socially. He did not believe in the perfectibility of man but in the necessity of establishing limits or restraints and viewed life through the lens of Lutheran theology. "It's an evil world" was a frequent comment. He pointed out that Robinson Crusoe had no need for conventions when he was alone, but the minute Friday appeared, everything changed. Limits needed to be established and implemented for the benefit of all. But within the context of these safeguards, freedom was the overarching aspiration. Freedom took precedence over equality. Freedom provided the basis for achievement, and in an address to the honors students, he praised them for their accomplishments. The struggle for equality, however, led to mediocrity and the erosion of standards. "The quest for equality rather than excellence manifests itself in such phenomena as across the board rather than merit raises for teachers, open admissions to institutions of higher learning . . . and the debasing of standards for admission to the professions."[59]

Beto identified himself as a Democrat, but like many Southern Democrats, he was more conservative than the party brethren elsewhere in the country. Some staunch Texas Democrats considered themselves to be "Yellow Dog Democrats." They could never bring themselves to vote Republican. If they could not vote for a Democratic candidate, they preferred to cast their ballot for a yellow dog. Instead Beto identified himself as a "Red River Democrat." He generally voted for Democrats south of Red River, but for Republican candidates north of that stream.[60]

Although Beto endorsed President Lyndon Johnson's civil rights record, neither he nor many of his friends and associates admired Johnson. Beto considered him ruthless. But when it came to choosing between Johnson and Barry Goldwater in the 1964 election, even though Goldwater's conservative philosophy struck a responsive chord, Beto found Goldwater unrealistic. "It is unrealistic to believe that people who have lived under the specious benefits of the welfare state for over twenty years are willing to exercise the self-discipline necessary for the type of government which Mr. Goldwater desires." A conservative by nature, his political odyssey took him from a strong conservative Democrat in his early years to a ticket-splitter in his later years. Often he knew the candidate personally, and the candidate's character was more important than his party. Yet he was cautious about liberals and stated that the liberals "whether they be in the Church or in governmental politics; they have no principles."[61]

Socially he believed that a strong family provided the foundation for the formation of a law-abiding citizenry. Broken homes contributed to the chances of criminal activity, and he favored mandatory national service to replace some of the benefits lost with the declining family. Welfare programs, which further weakened the family, especially Aid to Dependent Children, created a setting that fostered new generations of children who would become "the public wards of tomorrow." His recipe for personal success instead called for a nuclear family that shared at least one meal each day, and a family life that was centered around a religious faith, the work ethic, and a focus on excellence. And a strong society, in turn, would be based on such virtues as hard work, keeping one's word, and reverence for God.[62]

Social Circles

Beto's social life in his years at Huntsville revolved around four groups. The first was informal and more active during his academic years than during his term at the TDC. Early on Saturday morning, or occasionally during the week, he patronized the Texan Cafe on the west side of the Walker Courthouse square. There he had breakfast, coffee, read the newspaper and visited with friends. Beto referred to these associates as "the wise men down at the Texan Cafe." Later he shifted his weekend schedule to the Holiday Inn.[63]

A second highly structured group, which met monthly, was "The Longfellow Literary and Inside Straight Society of Walker County." The purpose of the group was more on the inside straight and less on Longfellow's poetry. This group of poker enthusiasts usually met on Tuesday night generally at Judge Rogers' home. When Wit's End Ranch became his residence, Beto set up a table and hosted some of the meetings. The rules were strict. Starting time was at seven o'clock and the quitting time was ten. No drinking and no eating. Seating was assigned and each chair was an oak banker's chair with a brass nameplate on the back. Guests were often invited. At the end of the evening each player determined his winnings or losses. If the group went out afterwards for some food, the highest winner paid.[64]

They had nicknames for each other. Beto's was "the Pastor" or "Doc" and Judge Max Rogers was "Old Rover." Beto generally played well, but not always, as the following comment from Judge Rogers attests: "We had a called meeting . . . at my house last night and the Pastor did not fare as well as usual; . . . but playing the second best hand a lot last night left him something less than garrulous." Rogers was, without doubt, Beto's closest friend and confidant, and while the membership varied between the groups, Rogers is the one who was present in all of the groups.[65]

The third group, known as the "Rough Bunch," ostensibly had fine dining as its *raison d'etre*. It convened only once a month in Houston at different clubs such as the Coronado Club and the Inns of Court. There were approximately a dozen men in the group, including some men from the Longfellow Literary Society, such as Judge Rogers and Byron Frierson (Beto's TDC Assistant Director for Agriculture). Other members were prominent individuals from Houston including Joe Foy, vice chairman and later president of Houston Natural Gas Corporation, W. Ervin James, a judge on the 127th District Court, as well as leading journalists, bankers, lawyers and politicians. Each person took his turn in selecting the venue and serving as host. But it is difficult to imagine that in any meeting with such a group of influential men that the conversation was limited to the cuisine. The intellectual stimulation and the sharing of information took priority.

Beto found great solace in the company of these men, and looked forward to spending time playing poker and dining with congenial companions. The importance of these social groups in Beto's life after his resignation from TDC was made clear when Beto wrote to Judge Rogers and Joe Foy, "I have reached the point in my life where the friendship of good men has become increasingly meaningful to me."[66]

The last group activity was the traditional annual hunt on the Diamond H Ranch near Catarina, in South Texas. This group was the largest, usually twenty men. It was also the most diverse, varying from year to year and including people from out of state. Beto's brothers Walter and Louis for example, attended during the 1960s. Beto also prevailed on Coffield to invite his friends such as Billy

Bittle from Rockford and Frank Mason from Springfield, Illinois. Beto continued to participate in the hunt even after Coffield's death and attended the hunts well into the 1980s.[67]

At the end of the school year in May 1991, five years after he became professor emeritus, Beto took leave of the classroom completely, and in September he and his wife left Huntsville and returned to Austin, Mrs. Beto's early home. When Beto arrived in Austin, he was named Board Member Emeritus and Chief of Chaplaincy Services with the Texas Youth Commission, a position he held briefly until his sudden death later that year. Before his departure and in recognition of his contribution to the school, the university administration announced the decision to name the criminal justice center The George J. Beto Criminal Justice Center on August 26, 1991. The dedication was scheduled for early the next year, but death intervened, and he did not live to see that event.

Death and Legacy

Beto knew the biblical insight on the length of life for most humans as being three-score years and ten, and that there were few exceptions who exceeded the milestone. Already in 1979 he had made preparations for his death by applying for a grave site in the state cemetery. In an attempt to simplify later decisions for his wife, he also acquired a tombstone engraved with his and Marilynn's names.[68] While still at the Huntsville ranch, Beto, finally yielded to Marilynn's repeated urging and took the time to write his requests for his funeral. He took his copy of the *Lutheran Agenda,* the book containing all the orders of service, and circled the prayers he wanted read for the memorial service. He also specified that the casket should be closed at all times, and he requested a brief memorial service instead of a funeral. At the memorial service absolutely no personal reference was to be made about him. He finished his assignment in ten minutes.[69]

His death came suddenly approximately at 6:00 in the morning of December 4, 1991. Both he and Marilynn were early risers, and had a brief conversation. As George was selecting a shirt, Marilynn left the room on her way to the kitchen. After only a few steps in the hall she heard a slamming of the closet doors and found her husband kneeling at the bed with no sign of life. She telephoned 911 but the paramedics who responded tried CPR without effect. Cardiac arrest ended his life at the age of seventy-five, three score and fifteen.

Three days later, after brief services at the funeral home and the cemetery, the general public was invited to a memorial service at Redeemer Lutheran Church in Austin, which George and Marilynn had joined. Two days later a second memorial service was held at Faith Lutheran Church in Huntsville where they had been members for almost thirty years. In the *Agenda,* where he had circled the prayers he wanted read, he also had written a theme for both services: "A Christian's death is not a tragedy. It is cause to celebrate new life."[70]

Of the many memorials written about Beto, Victor G. Strecher, former Dean and Director of the Criminal Justice Center wrote one that showed great insight into the Beto style:

He was, of course, the classic man with an idea, but there are many men with ideas. What made the difference was that George Beto was a man of action with an idea. He could hitch an idea to the plow and make it produce. The plow, for him, was power—social, financial, and political power. Power was just one more tool, but one that came easily to George Beto's hand. He moved along the corridors of Austin and through the executive offices of Houston with facility, grace, and humor. He knew everybody and saw everybody regularly, Walking George did. He would just drop by to visit for a little while. He always had something to say that his momentary hosts considered worth hearing.

Within a month of my becoming Dean and Director of the Criminal Justice Center, George Beto began gently towing me through those corridors in Austin, into the offices of Lt. Governor Bill Hobby, Representative Heatly, Senator "Bull of the Brazos" Moore, the Legislative Budget Board, the Texas Supreme Court justices, and all the executive Criminal Justice boards and councils. He took me to testify before the Senate Finance Committee and various House committees on the needs of the Criminal Justice Center. I hear Senator Moore intone to

Senate Finance, "Oh, give it to them (the half-million dollar special appropriation), they spend it well," and that settled it. I was with him at the Democratic caucus to hear the gubernatorial candidates in Woodville, and at innumerable barbecues, ranging from the Texas Cattlemen's Association huge affair at the Moore brothers' place in Millet, to those of judges, district attorneys, sheriffs and wardens.

George Beto took me to see Mr. Johnson, Publisher of the *Houston Chronicle*, Philip Warner of his staff, later a member of our Board of Regents, and Miss Daisy, who was a key intermediary in our later obtaining the endowed chair which carries George Beto's name. Next came Mr. Creekmore, who presided over the Houston Endowment, which contributed the Beto Chair and has always generously supported graduate students in Criminal Justice. "Mean Joe" Green, President of the Rockwell Fund, would take us to the Inns of Court for an afternoon of sipping and greeting the notables of the bench and bar; he supported various needs of the Center, which could not be funded from state revenue.

George Beto, without ever making the point explicitly, taught me to visit these good people often, not merely when the Center needed something. It was the whole point of my tutorial of 1978–79. Dr. Beto was simply laying in stones for the future of one of his children, the Criminal Justice Center.[71]

George John Beto was the consummate educator equally adept as administrator or professor. Wealth and power were there for the furthering of education and the previous comment shows how he not only taught his successor the sources of wealth, but also for what purposes the wealth and power were to be used. Education was available for everyone, including those in prisons, and had an intrinsic value for every student, whether incarcerated or free. When Beto looked back into his life and accomplishments, he confessed that he was "unabashedly proud" of two contributions. The first was the formation of the Windham School District and the second was his role in creation of the SHSU Criminal Justice program.[72]

When he stated, "I have an immigrant child's belief in education," and he frequently did, he referred to the innumerable children from poor surroundings, who used education to raise their standard of living. And as they raised their own standard of living, they contributed to the nation. In a speech to the beneficiaries of an education, the graduates of SHSU, he first commended them for their accomplishments, but reminded them of their responsibilities to work in defense of democracy and a classless society. He compared what they were doing to the "great work" of Nehemiah when he rebuilt the city of Jerusalem. "Support education at all levels," Beto said, "And as you do this say, 'I am doing a great work.' You have had much given to you, by your parents and the state of Texas. Now give some back. Improve yourselves and society."[73]

This conviction in the universal value of education for the individual, brings us back to beginning of this study and Beto's speech at the ROTC in which he refers to his ancestors and concludes, "In spite of handicaps—ignorance of the language and culture of this land—they were able to carve out for themselves respectable places on the economic, social, religious, and political horizons of this country. For them, and for us, America, with all of its imperfections, remains the world's great hope."[74]

Epilogue

During the twentieth century there has been no more striking and picturesque personality in American penology than that of George John Beto. His personal force and unique accomplishments defined him in the public mind more strongly than any of his contemporaries in the United States. During his years as director of the Texas Department of Corrections he was one of the most conspicuous men in Texas, and the tradition of his administrative skills, at once both vigorous and economical, were so impressive that Texas had come to regard him as the apostle of prison reform. His calm and measured appeals and frank declaration of reason on behalf of criminal justice, especially in the midst of sometimes miserly and parochial legislative attitudes, revealed his genius, and his reputation for telling the truth was unassailable. Beto was remarkable for perseverance and great steadiness of purpose and self possession, and no one ever looked or talked with Beto but he heard something which made him look or listen again. Beto endeared himself to all who knew him by his probity, courteous demeanor, and engaging modesty. In his later years as a distinguished university professor, he rode upon the storms of penological controversy that were sweeping across American society. In opposing those who would thwart the advancement of humane penological interests and rational laws, he was alert, sagacious, and, to some extent, successful. When he died, Texas buried one of the most famous penologists of the twentieth century without pomp or ceremony, but the man and his contributions are remembered. In addition to the George J. Beto Criminal Justice Center at Sam Houston State University, a Texas Youth Commission halfway house facility in south Texas, the George J. Beto Academic Center at Concordia University Austin, and two prison units near Palestine, Texas, have been named in honor of Beto. Finally, and perhaps most fitting, the Texas Corrections Association has named its most prestigious award, given annually in recognition of outstanding contributions made in the field of corrections, the George J. Beto Hall of Honor Award.

Appendix A

"PRISON ADMINISTRATION AND THE EIGHTH AMENDMENT"

[On November 9, 1991, less than one month before his death, Beto delivered this address at the Valparaiso University School of Law in Valparaiso, Indiana. This speech was part of a series of lectures given in celebration of the bicentennial of the Bill of Rights. This speech was Beto's last formal speaking engagement.]

Thirty Years of Criticism

The past three decades have witnessed a consistent criticism of America's prisons. In the 1960s, then Chief Justice Warren Burger, speaking before an annual meeting of the American Bar Association in Dallas, Texas, delivered a landmark speech on America's prisons. He was highly critical of penal practices and concluded with the observation "there must be a better way." In 1971, President Richard M. Nixon convened the first White House Conference on Corrections. In his opening remarks he referred to America's prisons as "colleges of crime." The once highly influential National Council on Crime and Delinquency ran an advertisement in popular magazines showing a young lad holding a smoking handgun, apparently as he was committing a crime. The picture carried the caption "Prisons do teach a trade."

The volume of prison litigation which began in the 1960s has continued to the present, when over thirty state prisons are either totally or partially under court order. Through the years Eighth Amendment cases under categories of solitary confinement or punitive segregation, inadequate medical care, the totality of conditions, and physical abuse have been brought against prison administrators, and in many cases the suits have been won in whole or in part by the plaintiffs. The publicity attendant upon these suits did not heighten the esteem in which prisons are held by the general public. On the contrary, the publicity regarding alleged or actual Eighth Amendment violations tended to confirm the public's attitude toward prisons.

Why do They Lose?

It seems to me that the reasons prisons lose so many cases stems from four fundamental causes, which are as follows: poor cases; inferior counsel; failure to anticipate change; and excessive reliance on "expert witnesses."

Poor Cases

I believe that the state or prisons and prison administrators frequently go into court with poor cases. They would be better advised not to litigate the issues raised. The facts frequently do not support the position held by the defense. A case in point is *Jordan v. Fitzharris,* a case originating in California and involving punitive segregation. Some years after the case was litigated, I read the facts and was appalled—appalled that a state presumably as enlightened as California would tolerate solitary confinement conditions so indefensible. For instance, there was no regular inspection of the occupants of the cells, nor any record kept of inspections made. Excrement was splattered on the walls day after day, occupant after occupant. California litigated the case from the district court level to the circuit level and on to the United States Supreme Court.

In the early days of the abandonment of the "hands off" doctrine prison administrators and assistant attorneys general would have been well advised to settle such cases.

Inferior Counsel

Secondly, it is my firmly held opinion that the state or prison administrators are usually represented by inferior counsel. This opinion is based in part on my experiences as a reluctant litigant in court and as an expert witness in at least eight jurisdictions.

Penal institutions and prison administrators are usually represented by an itinerant assistant attorney general while the plaintiff or plaintiffs are represented by highly competent civil rights lawyers. A case in point is *Gideon v. Wainwright.* During the course of this litigation Louie Wainwright, then Florida's correction director, was represented by three different assistant attorneys general, while Gideon's attorney was the able Abe Fortas. His personal competency, coupled with the resources of his firm, made the outcome of the case almost inevitable.

There was a period when I thought that my opinion of the state's defense of prison cases was peculiar to me. However, in late 1974 I read a speech which Justice Powell delivered at a meeting of judges of the old federal Fifth Circuit Court of Appeals in New Orleans in May 1974. In that address he referred to the surprises which were his when he came to the United States Supreme Court. One of his major surprises was "the quality of briefs and oral arguments." He continued that "As a general observation, it is safe to say—especially where important issues of constitutional law or criminal procedure are involved—that law enforcement is frequently out-gunned and out-matched. There is little doubt that the marked trend of the law toward expanded rights of defendants, a trend so noticeable over the past two decades, has been influenced in part by the imbalance of the representation before the Court. Again, certainly the public interest would be better served if the contesting sides, in the great cases at least, were more evenly matched.

Failure to Anticipate Change

Too, it seems to me cases are often lost by the state in prison cases because of a failure on the part of administrators to anticipate change. *Trop v. Dulles* refers to the "emerging standards of decency" which characterize a "maturing society." Some prison practices, while possibly constitutional, should be abandoned when viewed against the standards of decency developing in a maturing society. A prudent administrator anticipates and resists the "we have always done it that way" precept.

Excessive Reliance on Expert Witnesses

Finally, I would assert that there is too great a reliance on the part of judges on expert witnesses. Too few judges follow the example of Judge Pettine in Rhode Island and Judge Kane in Colorado, whose personal inspection of the conditions resulted—especially in the case of Judge Kane—in a singularly creative order.

Criticism Justified

It would be foolish to deny that most of the criticism of America's prisons is justified. Abject and stultifying idleness characterizes America's prisons. In spite of the example set by the industrial program in the Federal Bureau of Prisons, in spite of Chief Justice Burger's frequent call to make factories of our prisons, idleness rather than some constructive work activity prevails.

Another area frequently criticized is that of the county jails. Back when the American Bar Association's Commission on Correctional Facilities and Services was still in existence, I can recall the late Karl Menniger crying and crying in vain for some attention to be paid to conditions in the county jails of this nation, referring to them as the "horror of our age." It appears ironic that we know how many whooping cranes there are in the United States each day, but no one in this highly computerized age knows on a given day how many human beings—made in the image of God—are confined in our county jails.

Most prisons and jails are either overtly or covertly convict-run. Several years ago there appeared on television Truman Capote's drama, *The Glass Cage.* Fiction though it was, the drama accurately portrayed the reality of a prisoner-run institution.

The average tenure for a director or commissioner of corrections in the United States is currently approximately three and one-half years. Operating in states with the cabinet form of government, they serve at the pleasure of the chief executive. Their tenure is too short to allow them any time for long-range planning or, even less so, for the implementation of planning.

In 1970, on the occasion of the centennial of the American Congress of Corrections, the highly articulate Norval Morris delivered an address titled "The Snail's Pace of Prison Reform." In his address, Morris attributed the lack of appreciable reform and constructive change in American corrections to a lack of leadership. He correctly asserted that "corrections has attracted too many second class minds, vacillating and timorous souls."

My experience in corrections covers a period of forty years. During that time I have known and observed the men and women active in corrections. I can count on the fingers of two hands those who do not fit Norval Morris' description. The leadership has been reactive rather than proactive. There weren't many James Bennetts, Garret Heyns, Sanger Powers, Joe Ragens, or Frank Lees.

The Defense

There is, however, some defense to be mustered in the face of the criticism. We tend to forget the short history of prisons. Originally these were places of temporary detention, places of confinement prior to execution or banishment. Prisons, as we know them today, are essentially an American innovation, founded by Quakers and developed eventually throughout the United States as an alternative to cruel and unusual practices.

Another defensive element is the ambivalence of the public. The American public in its invincible ignorance regarding the criminal justice system has never made up its mind as to why we have prisons. Do they exist for retribution, restraint, rehabilitation, or reintegration into society? Until society develops meaningful responses to those alternatives, prisons will remain the jungles they are.

Finally, we need to consider the prisoner profile. Contrary to the public conception of the violent, truculent, and dangerous criminal, the average prisoner is poor, stupid, inept, and amoral. In state prisons roughly ninety-six percent are school dropouts; twenty percent are illiterate; forty percent had no prior record of sustained employment; twenty percent are mentally retarded; and fifty percent are under the age of twenty-five. More important, ninety-eight percent will walk the streets again.

Conrad's Observation

At a meeting in Indianapolis a decade ago, John Conrad made a statement I often wish had originated with me. He asserted that "Prisons must be lawful, safe, industrious, and hopeful." Recently I asked John Conrad to give me a one-sentence definition of each of these terms. His response to my request was as follows: "The lawful prison is one in which it is the first goal of policy to prevent unlawful actions and conduct by the staff and prisoners. The safe prison is one in which enlightened architecture, and the training and supervision of staff for the maintenance of personal safety combine to achieve personal security for both prisoners and staff. The industrious prison keeps all prisoners occupied at full-time constructive work, in training, prison industries, or maintenance of the facility. In the hopeful prison appropriate educational, training, and medical services will be provided so that each prisoner can reasonably expect that his or her condition will be better than before incarceration."

If a prison is to be lawful, safe, industrious, and hopeful, the administration must unequivocally endorse these concepts. Too, if an administrator is to provide a lawful, safe, industrious, and hopeful prison, he must have some latitude in effecting and maintaining control.

The Rehabilitation Environment

Historically, we have considered rehabilitation or change in attitude and behavior one of the objectives of penal confinement.
Unfortunately, there is no single program employed by prison
administrators which can guarantee a positive change in behavior
and attitude.

It is almost axiomatic that no one can be rehabilitated against
his will. I believe, however, that a climate, or environment, can be
created which may be conducive to behavioral change. That environment embraces the components of discipline, work, and education. I make that recommendation on the basis of the character of
the prison population.

Most of the prisoners come from undisciplined environments.
They have never been exposed to internally or externally imposed
discipline. In a properly controlled prison environment they can be
exposed to the discipline which leads to a productive and reasonably happy life. An habituation to that discipline may continue
after release.

Discipline is related to Conrad's concept of safety. While no
one denies the state's right to incarcerate a citizen, it must also be
vigorously maintained that the state has an overriding obligation to
protect a prisoner, to guarantee his safety during his incarceration.

A second component is work. Almost fifty percent of the prison
population has no prior sustained record of employment. A work
program, comparable to that in the free world, with production
and quality controls, should represent the irreducible minimum in
a prison industry program.

And finally, education. If the ninety-six percent of the prisoners
are school dropouts, I submit there is a compelling state interest in
the creation and maintenance of a compulsory school program. If
Thomas Jefferson was correct in maintaining that a democratic
society can survive only with an enlightened electorate—and I
believe he was right—the state's interest in maintaining a prison
educational program beginning with literacy schooling and continuing to baccalaureate and graduate degrees becomes even more
compelling. Also, there is considerable empirical evidence that in a

controlled prison environment more can be accomplished in a shorter time than in extramural education programs.

John J. DiIulio, in his work titled *Governing Prisons,* writes "order, amenity, and service are the three ends of good prison government." What kind of people can achieve these ends? He continues: "First, successful prison directors and institutional managers are not here today, gone tomorrow. They are in office long enough to learn the job, make plans, and implement them. Second, they are highly 'hands-on' and pro-active. They pay close attention to details and do not wait for problems to arise but attempt to anticipate them. While they trust their subordinates to do their share of the paperwork, they keep themselves focused on the prisons and what is actually happening inside of them. At the same time, they recognize the need for outside support. In short, they are strangers neither to the cellblocks nor to the aisles of the state legislature. Third, they act consciously to project an image of themselves that is appealing to a wide range of people both inside and outside of the organization. Fourth, they are dedicated and fiercely loyal to the department and see themselves as keepers engaged in a noble and challenging (if mostly thankless) profession."

Conclusion

As I reflect on forty years' involvement in the criminal justice system in one capacity or another, I cannot escape the conclusion that the system is no better than it was almost one-half century ago.

In their book *The Politics of Crime and Conflict,* Gurr, Grabowsky, and Hula write that "A modicum of social order is rare in complex societies. Where it is found, it is more likely to be the result of long-term social engineering, consistently applied, than the workings of natural forces. The processes of 'social engineering' are manipulative and often repressive, a circumstance that raises a fundamental question: Are the costs of social disorder more bearable than the costs of order? The question has no empirical answer."

I would submit that the American people have answered in the affirmative.

Appendix B

CHI= Concordia Historical Institute
BFA= Beto Family Archives
SHSU= Beto Collection, Newton Gresham Library, Sam Houston State University
CSA= Concordia Seminary Archives, Fort Wayne, Indiana

Letter to the editor, *Lena Weekly Star,* August 1931, BFA.

"Circular Letter #1" to a group of his close friends from the St. Louis Seminary, undated, circa fall 1939, BFA.

"Circular Letter #2" to a group of his close friends from the St. Louis Seminary, undated, circa fall 1939, BFA.

Letter to Hartwig Schwehn, October 22, 1939, BFA.

"Circular Letter #3" to a group of his close friends from the St. Louis Seminary, January 26, 1940, BFA.

"The Marburg Colloquy of 1529: A Textual Study." Master's thesis, University of Texas, 1944. Published in *Concordia Theological Monthly* (February 1945).

"Personal and Professional Qualifications of the Housemaster: An Introductory Study." *Lutheran Education* 83, no. 6 (February 1948), 361–64. A statement of Beto's philosophy concerning caring for the spiritual and physical needs of boys in boarding schools.

Portals of Prayer: No. 104. St. Louis: Concordia Publishing House, 1951. A compilation of daily devotions by numerous Lutherans, including the following by Beto: "Receive the Word" (p. 9); "Simple Language" (p. 10); "Perfect Love" (p. 11); "Pray Persistently" (p. 12); "With the Lord in Glory" (p. 13); "We Cannot Come Down" (p. 14); "The Truth that Frees" (p. 15); and "Morning Prayer" and "Evening Prayer" (p. 56).

"Lutheran Concordia College." *The Handbook of Texas* 2. Walter Prescott Webb, ed. Austin: Texas State Historical Association, 1952.

"New Senior College." *The Lutheran Witness* 71, no. 4 (February 19, 1952), 10. Report on the work of the Synodical Convention with respect to establishing a Lutheran senior college in Chicago.

"Send Them Away, Lord!" *The Lutheran Witness* 71, no. 6 (March 18, 1952), 8. Editorial on the pressing need to expand and reorganize Lutheran colleges and seminaries in order to meet the demand for filling vacancies in the overseas missionary program.

"The Future of the Christian Day School." *Lutheran Education* 89, no. 3 (November, 1953), 125–31. Text on his commencement address delivered at Concordia Teachers College, Seward, Nebraska, June 1953.

Portals of Prayer: No. 120 (St. Louis, Missouri: Concordia Publishing House, 1953), 38–54. A booklet of daily devotions.

Letter to Alfred O. Fuerbringer (President, Concordia Seminary, St. Louis), June 3, 1954, SHSU.

"Arguments Found in the Literature for the Continued Existence of the Protestant Church-Related Liberal Arts College." Ph.D. diss., University of Texas, 1955.

"Changing Times and the World of Teaching." *Lutheran Education* 19, no. 3 (November, 1955), 147–48.

Letter to Allan Shivers (Governor of Texas), May 14, 1956, CHI.

Letter to Oscar Byron Ellis, October 15, 1959, SHSU.

Letter to Walter Wolbrecht, April 19, 1960, CSA.

Letter to the French Embassy, Washington, D.C., May 16, 1960, CHI.

Letter to H. H. Coffield, May 16, 1960, SHSU.

"Memo Book, 6 July–10 August 1960," BFA.

"Eating High on the Hog." *Austin American Statesman,* July 26, 1960, 9. A report on his inspections of prisons in West Germany.

"Churches in Europe Appear no Longer a Vibrant Force. *Austin American Statesman,* August 14, 1960. Final report on his inspection of European prisons.

"What Makes Education Christian?" *Lutheran Education* 96, no. 1 (September 1960), 5–14.

Letter to Gilbert W. Hermes, February 23, 1961, CHI.

Letter to Eugene McElvaney, February 24, 1961, CHI

Letter to O. B. Ellis, March 24, 1961, SHSU.

Letter to Eugene McElvaney, May 5, 1961, SHSU.

Letter to Joseph Ragen, May 9, 1961, SHSU.

Letters to C. N. Avery, Jr., June 21 and October 18, 1961, CHI.

Letter to Wallace C. Thompson, August 2, 1961, SHSU.

Letter to Mrs. O. B. Ellis, November 15, 1961, SHSU.

"The Faculty Views the Field," undated manuscript, CHI.

The Faculty Views the Field. St. Louis: Missouri Synod, 1961.

Letter to Austin MacCormick, December 6, 1961, SHSU.

Letter to William Steffen, December 11, 1961, SHSU.

Letter to H. H. Coffield, December 12, 1961, SHSU.

Letter to Merton Lundquist, February 13, 1962, SHSU.

Letter to Dr. Carl Rosenquist (Professor of Sociology, University of Texas at Austin), February 19, 1962, SHSU.

Letter to W. F. Wolbrecht, July 11, 1962, SHSU.

Report and Recommendations of the Illinois Youth Commission. Springfield, IL: Governor's Survey Committee, 1962.

Letter to O. B. Ellis, August 15, 1962, SHSU.

Letter to Herman Engalman, November 12, 1962, SHSU.

Letter to Philip L. Wahlberg, November 15, 1962, SHSU.

Letter to Hermann Sasse, December 14, 1962, SHSU.

Letter to Roosevelt Martin, January 21, 1963, SHSU.

Letter to E. J. Riske, February 8, 1963, SHSU.

Letter to Philip L. Wahlberg, February 11, 1963, SHSU.

Letter to Ernest L. Sample, February 14, 1963, SHSU.

"Christian Character: An Antidote for Moral Decay." *Christianity and Contemporary Moral Issues: Messages from the Seventh Annual Christian Life Workshop, Southwestern Baptist Theological Seminary, Fort Worth, Texas,* March 11–12, 1963. Dallas: Christian Life Commission, 1963.

"Introduction." *Annual Report of the Texas Department of Corrections* (1963).

"The Case for Prisons." *Texas Police Journal* (August 1964), 1–5.

"A Return to Values." *Dallas Morning News,* March 22, 1965. Editorial on crime and the decline in American values.

Letter to Joseph Ragen, May 29, 1965, SHSU.

Letter to Otto Kerner, August 19, 1965, SHSU.

Letter to Bill Todd, December 15, 1965, SHSU.

Letter to Harold M. Olsen, August 24, 1966, SHSU.

Speech at Texas Agricultural Workers Association Conference, November 9, 1966, SHSU.

Letter to Hartwig Schwehn, December 22, 1966, SHSU.

"Probing Prison Problems." *The Lutheran Witness* (March 1968), 11–13. This article was later reprinted in the January 1997 issue of *Texas Probation.*

"The Real Culprits." *The Baptist Student* 47, no. 7 (April 1968), 15–17. The rise in crime and prison populations is due to the rural-urban population shift, broken homes, and apathetic Christian churches.

Letter to Richard Daley, August 30, 1968, SHSU.

The Texas Prison System: Assets and Liabilities. Huntsville: Texas Department of Corrections, 1969.

Letter to Robert P. Heyne, February 16, 1970, SHSU.

"From the President." *American Journal of Corrections* 32, no. 5 (September–October 1970), 5. The future of probation and parole, pre-sentence investigation, prison productivity, and community-based corrections.

"Continue Work, So Much to be Done." *American Journal of Corrections* 32, no. 6 (November–December 1970), 4–7. Text of his presidential address before the Centennial Congress, Monday, October 12, 1970, in Cincinnati, Ohio.

"Foreword." *Causes, Preventive Measures, and Methods of Controlling Riots and Disturbances in Correctional Institutions* (Washington, D.C.: American Correctional Association, 1970), iii.

"What Are Prisons For?" *Lutheran Standard* 11, no. 3 (February 2, 1971), 6–7.

Speech at National Governors' Conference, September 13, 1971, SHSU.

Letter to John A. Gronouski, February 26, 1972, SHSU.

Speech at State Interim Drug Study Committee, April 10, 1972, SHSU.

Letter to Herbert H. Friese, May 15, 1972, SHSU.

"The Prison System Needs Work." *The Texas Star (Houston Chronicle)* 2, no. 15 (August 20, 1972). Guest commentary published in the newspaper's Sunday magazine, which had a circulation of more than four million.

Letter to J. J. Pickle, September 22, 1972, SHSU.

Letter to Don King, February 27, 1973, SHSU.

Letter to Kurt W. Biel, October 9, 1973, SHSU.

"Public Consensus Needed in the War on Crime." *Dallas Times Herald*, October 28, 1973. Editorial.

Letter to Judge Max Rogers and Joe Foy, January 29, 1974, SHSU.

"I Was in Prison: Christian Challenge." Speech to "The Christian and the Criminal Workshop," February 27, 1974, SHSU.

Letter to Herbert H. Freise, May 10, 1974, SHSU.

Letter to Maurice H. Sigler, September 12, 1974, SHSU.

"Problems in Development of an Undergraduate Criminal Justice Curriculum." *Federal Probation* 38, no. 4 (December 1974). Co-authored with Robert Marsh.

Letter to Otto Kerner, March 10, 1975, CHI.

Letter to Walter H. Ellwanger, July 15, 1975, SHSU.

"Lessons in State Agency-University Cooperation." *State Government-University Relations in the South.* Atlanta, GA: Southern Regional Education Board, 1975, 17–20. Text of a paper delivered at a conference on the academic community as a backup force to state government, May 5–6, 1975, in Atlanta, Georgia.

Letter to C. A. Hardt, May 14, 1976, BFA.

Letter to Laurie Caplane, April 18, 1977, SHSU.

"Introductory Essay." *Crime, Law, and Social Science.* Jerome Michael and Mortimer J. Adler. New York: Harcourt Brace, 1979. Co-authored with Bruce Jackson.

Speech at ROTC Commissioning Ceremonies, Sam Houston State University, May 8, 1981, BFA.

Honors Convocation Speech, Sam Houston State University, April 15, 1982, SHSU.

"Par Excellence." *Houston Chronicle,* August 27, 1982. Editorial excerpted from an address delivered to an honors convocation at the Institute of Contemporary Corrections and the Behavior Sciences, Sam Houston State University, Huntsville, Texas.

"The Texas Correctional System." *Proceedings of the Annual Meeting of the Philosophical Society of Texas* 46 (1983), 45–50. Text of an address delivered before the annual meeting of the Philosophical Society of Texas at Galveston, December 3–4, 1982.

Speech at Judge Max Rogers' Retirement Ceremonies, November 10, 1983, BFA; SHSU.

Letter to Orson L. McCotter, April 9, 1984, SHSU.

"Introduction of the Honorable William Wayne Justice" at the 114th Congress of the American Correctional Association, San Antonio, Texas, August 20, 1984, SHSU.

Letter to Wayne K. Patterson, November 5, 1984, SHSU.

"Mother's Funeral Sermon," September 29, 1985, BFA; CHI; SHSU.

Letter to August R. Sueflow (Director, Concordia Historical Institute, St. Louis), 21 November 21, 1985, SHSU.

Karl Menninger Lecture, Washburn University, Topeka, Kansas, November 20, 1986, SHSU.

"The Criminal Justice System Has Broken Down, Crime Pays, and the American People Don't Want Effective Law Enforcement." *Congressional Record—Senate* (April 29, 1987), S5740–5742. Text of the address Beto delivered at Washburn University when he was there as a Karl Menninger Lecturer. The text is substantially similar to the address given and the text published in 1983 by the Philosophical Society of Texas titled "The Texas Correctional System."

Commencement Address, Sam Houston State University, May 9, 1987, SHSU.

"Don't Privatize Prisons." *Houston Chronicle.* May 10, 1987. Editorial.

Letter to Eric C. Stumpf, November 21, 1987, SHSU.

"Is Ignorance Invincible?" *The Police Journal* 67, no. 2 (Fall–Winter 1987), 11–15. Discussion about the future of corrections.

Letter to W. C. Mullan, November 28, 1988, SHSU.

"Speech." *Texas Journal of Corrections* (July–August 1990), 18–19. Speech delivered on the twenty-fifth anniversary of the College of Criminal Justice, Sam Houston State University, Huntsville, Texas.

The Best of "Portal of Prayer" (St. Louis: Concordia Publish House, 1990). Includes the following daily devotions by Beto: "He Will Come Again" (p. 344); "Making the Most of Christmas" (p. 353); and "The Keepers of Christmas" (p. 384).

"Prison Administration and the Eighth Amendment." Speech at Valparaiso University School of Law, November 9, 1991, SHSU.

"Probing Prison Problems." *Texas Probation* 12, no. 1 (January 1997), 6–8. Reprint from *The Lutheran Witness,* where the article first appeared in the March 1968 issue.

"Response of George J. Beto on Recollections of His Life at the Seminary in St. Louis, 1935–1939," undated, CHI.

"My Future Occupation," undated manuscript, BFA.

"Heatly Funeral Sermon," undated, SHSU.

Speech at Texas A&M University, "The Texas Prison System Rehabilitation Program," n.d, SHSU.

Notes

Notes to Chapter 1

1. George Beto, Speech at ROTC Commissioning Ceremonies, Sam Houston State University, May 8, 1981, Beto Family Archives (Hereafter BFA).

2. BFA. Sidwell Map, Maine Township, Niles Historical Society. The word synod (pronounced SIN-ud) can be used to describe a gathering of clergymen or a group of congregations banded together by common beliefs. In the United States, Lutherans often used ethnic or geographical terms to identify these groups such as the Danish Synod or the Buffalo Synod. The synod to which George Beto belonged was formed in 1847 as *Die Evangelische-lutherische Synode von Missouri, Ohio, and Andere Staaten.* It is currently known as the Lutheran Church-Missouri Synod and that is the name that will be used throughout this study.

3. Werner Krause, "Biographical Record for Louis Henry Beto," Service Bulletin 3A (St. Louis: Concordia Historical Institute, 1990).

4. Howard Witsma to David M. Horton, June 9, 2002, in Horton's possession.

5. The traditional procedure used by vacant parishes when obtaining a pastor was to either send a "call" to a pastor in another parish or to request the church officials for a newly graduated seminarian. A call for a Lutheran pastor or parish teacher was much more than a job offer. Although the voter's assembly of a congregation issued a call, the decision to send it to a particular person was considered to be a "divine call" and the work of the Holy Spirit. The recipient of a call then compared all aspects of his current position with the conditions described in the call documents. After prayers for guidance, the pastor decided where his service was needed the most and either accepted or returned the call. Pastors already at work in a parish were not obligated to accept a call, but could return the call without giving any reason. Those parishes that could not entice a pastor to accept their call often were the ones who turned to the young graduates. The officials of the church then assigned the seminarians to the empty parishes and an official call and ordination followed. The practice still exists today in the Missouri Synod.

6. "Hysham Named for Texas Trail Herder," *Great Falls Tribune,* October 26, 1958. The young couple leased a small, four-room wooden clapboard house with a single coal-burning cast iron stove that served the dual purpose of heating the house and cooking their food. Kerosene lanterns provided light and hot water for bathing and laundry was brought in from an outside kettle. A privy stood behind the house. From time to time Louis supplemented his meager allowance from the Lutheran Church by working as a field laborer and by waiting on customers in the Hysham general store. Margaret contributed to reducing their household expenses by baking bread and sewing their clothes. After the potato harvest, Margaret also gleaned potatoes from the fields in the vicinity. Margaret Beto, "Grandma Beto" oral history tape, 1958, BFA.

7. Margaret Beto.

8. George Beto to Dr. August Sueflow, November 21, 1985, Sam Houston State University, Newton Gresham Library, Beto Collection (Hereafter SHSU). Contrary to his later claim, Beto was not the first white child born in the Montana Territory. Interview with Louis Henry Beto, Jr., June 22–23, 1998, in possession of Horton; George Beto, "Mother's Funeral Sermon," September 29, 1985, BFA, SHSU. On January 19, 1970, Beto's birthday, he and his mother toured Hysham. Beto had been invited to speak at Missoula and he asked his mother to meet him in Denver and travel along with him. When Beto saw the house where he was born, and the stark, wintry landscape (which reminded him of the movie, *Dr. Zhivago*) he remarked to his mother that if "I was dad I would have turned right around and gone back to Chicago."

9. William Kupsky to Louis Beto, November 17, 1916, BFA. Katherina Maria Sophia Zersen, "A Pioneer Pastor's Wife," oral history tape, 1965, BFA. The transcript bears a cover page in George Beto's handwriting that reads, "This woman's husband was my father's predecessor in North Dakota." Martha Gross, "Emmanuel Lutheran Church," *A Century of Sowers, a Harvest of Heritage* (New Rockford, ND: New Rockford Transcript, 1983),162; Ellwyn B. Robinson, *History of North Dakota* (Lincoln: University of Nebraska Press, 1966), 286–88. The German Russian tradition included a strong support for the church, but not for schools and education.

10. Louis Seidel.to Louis Beto, November 17, 1919, BFA.

11. Margaret E. Scholtz to David M. Horton, March 2, 1998, in possession of Horton.

12. Anon., *History of Stephenson County* (Mount Morris, IL: Kable Printing Company, 1972), 227.

13. Ibid., 229. By 1940 the club had ninety-one full dues-paying members, and there were 4,232 registered greens fees collected on over 6,500 rounds of golf played. Non-members paid fifty cents for eighteen

holes or seventy-five cents for all-day play. Dues and green fees were reinvested in the course's development and in the construction of a clubhouse where the men socialized and their wives held bridge club meetings. "Annual Meeting of Lena Golf Club Held," *Lena Weekly Star,* 1940, clipping, BFA. In the 1930s and early 1940s Louis earned a reputation as "a clever and consistent player" who took the championship three times and was runner-up four times. "L. H. Beto Wins Club Championship at Lena Golf Club," *Lena Weekly Star,* 1937, clipping, BFA.

14. Beto, "Mother's Funeral Sermon."

15. Interview with Louis Henry Beto, Jr.

16. Ibid.

17. Ibid.

18. Later in life, during his years as a professor at Concordia Lutheran College, in Austin, Texas, Beto often quoted the phrase to his classes, "Reading maketh the full man." On one occasion a student responded, "Full of what?"

19. George Beto, "My Future Occupation," BFA.

20. Margaret E. Scholtz letter.

21. Ibid.

22. Ibid.

23. Ibid.

24. Margaret Beto; "Memoirs from Grandpa," scrapbook, BFA.

25. Interview with Louis Henry Beto, Jr. On the second day of Horton's visit with Louis at his home in Danville, Kentucky, Louis unabashedly admitted to being present during many of George's pranks, but insisted that he went along only to assist his big brother, who was the sole mastermind!

26. Ibid.

27. Ibid.

28. Margaret E. Scholtz letter.

29. Interview with Louis Henry Beto, Jr.

30. Martin Duchow to David M. Horton, February 25, 1998, in possession of Horton. *Catalogue of Concordia College,* 1930–31 (Milwaukee, WI: Concordia College, 1930).

31. Interview with Louis Henry Beto, Jr.

32. George Witsma, Jr., to George Beto, October 21, 1931, BFA. Witsma studied briefly at the St. Louis Seminary before becoming a broker. George Beto to C. A. Hardt, May 14, 1976, BFA.

33. "George J. Beto: Hard Work Paved the Path to Presidency," *Austin American Statesman,* January 2, 1949.

34. "Editor's Observation," *Lena Weekly Star,* August 1931, clipping, BFA.

35. George Beto to the editor of the *Lena Weekly Star,* August 1931, clipping, BFA.

36. Interview with Louis Henry Beto, Jr.; Margaret E. Scholtz letter. After George graduated from Concordia College in 1935 he returned to Lena and spent the summer working on the farms in the area. Perhaps as a way to memorably mark his passage from preparatory school to the seminary, George decided to hitchhike to Niagara Falls and back. To accompany him on the adventure he invited Curtis Taylor, his best childhood friend. They both notified their respective employers that they would be leaving for a few weeks. A wealthy retired farmer who spent a good part of his day parked on one of the two wooden church pews in front of Ansel Duth's pool hall, heard about their adventure and gave each young man $100 for the trip. That amount was a significant sum of money at that time, but he had known both George and Curtis for many years and liked them. He was concerned that the trip would divert funds they would need when they returned to school.

37. George Beto to Eric C. Stumpf, November 21, 1987, SHSU. Stumpf was doing research on the life and times of students who graduated from Concordia Seminary, St. Louis, Missouri, during the period 1930–1940.

38. George Witsma, Jr., letter.

39. Today Valparaiso University is one of the largest Lutheran-affiliated institutions of higher education in the United States, with 250 faculty and 4,000 students.

40. George Beto, circular letter #1, ca. Fall 1939, BFA.

41. Ibid.

42. Henry Studtmann to John Fritz, "Application for Supply," July 28, 1939, BFA.

43. John Fritz to George Beto, August 2, 1939, BFA. Henry Studtmann to George Beto, August 11, 1939, BFA.

44. Walter Penk email message to George Nielsen, November 7, 2004.

Notes to Chapter 2

1. *Synodical Handbook,* Section 6.39.

2. Richard Dinda, *Concordia Connections* (Winter, 1992), 1. Marilynn Beto to David M. Horton, March 8, 1998, in possession of Horton. Mrs. Beto's ancestor, Johann Knippa, migrated with Pastor Kilian.

3. George Beto, circular letter #1, ca., Fall 1939, Beto Family Archives (hereafter BFA).

4. Roddy Braun to David M. Horton, July 30, 1998, in possession of Horton.

5. Henry Studtmann to George J. Beton [*sic*], August 11, 1939, BFA.

6. Interview with Fred Viehweg, July 2, 1998, in possession of David M. Horton.

7. Interview with Charles Wukasch, July 7, 1998, in possession of David M. Horton. Other awards included a cement necktie and a crocheted bath tub.

8. Interview with Paul Bohot, July 21, 1998, in possession of David M. Horton. See Jeremiah 8: 22.

9. Interview with Ray F. Martens, March 4, 1998, in possession of David M. Horton.

10. Interview with Richard Dinda, July 1, 1998, in possession of David M. Horton.

11. Interview with James Linderman, July 8, 1998, in possession of David M. Horton

12. George Beto to Hartwig Schwehn, October 22, 1939, BFA.

13. The following incident illustrates a congenial yet rebellious spirit in the school. On one occasion the administration requested the students to add the room number to their return address so the distribution of returning mail would be simplified. The request was presented in a student body meeting but during the debate the atmosphere became negative. After all, voluntary cooperation with yet another procedure just did not seem the way to go. But one of the Houston students, well known as a recalcitrant, rose and stated that he did not see anything wrong with adding the cell number to the envelope. The students cheered and the motion passed.

14. Interview with Ted Zoch, August 20, 1998, in possession of David M. Horton.

15. Braun interview. The dormitory rooms in Kilian Hall had been planned for two occupants. There were two closets in each room and each closet contained a Murphy bed. These beds were swung out at night and returned to the closet each morning. There were also two desks, two chairs, and a lavatory. The showers and toilet facilities were shared in Room 210. Later, as enrollment increased, a cot and a desk were added to each room to accommodate a total of three students. The housemaster assigned students to their rooms, so that there was an upperclassman in each room and two lower classmen. The upperclassman, or room buck, was given responsibility for the room and was expected to teach the entering students the rules of the school, how to make a bed properly, and how to sweep the floor. The upperclassmen had hazing or shagging privileges whereby the lower classman was given tasks to do such as shining shoes and cleaning the room. The nature or reasonableness of the tasks reflected on the character and image of the room buck and maintaining a reputation had much to do with keeping the system from becoming oppressive. On occasion Beto threatened to prohibit shagging if the system became abusive.

16. Dinda interview.

17. Viehweg interview.

18. Ibid. Zoch interview.

19. Interview with Robert Wilkins, July 23, 1998, in possession of David M. Horton.

20. George Beto, "Personal and Professional Qualifications of the Housemaster," *Lutheran Education* (February 1948), 362.

21. George Beto, circular letter #2, ca., Fall 1939, BFA.

22. George Beto, circular letter #3, January 26, 1940, BFA.

23. E. J. Mathews to George Beto, October 3, 1939, BFA.

24. Permanent Record Card, George Beto, Office of the Registrar, University of Texas at Austin, BFA.

25. Beto circular letter #3.

26. The thesis was published in the *Concordia Theological Monthly* (February 1945), 73–94.

27. Permanent Record Card.

28. The only football game he ever attended he did so under protest so that he could receive an Alumnus of the Year Award from the University of Texas. He left prior to the second half and when the press asked him for the reason for his premature departure he said that "the University of Texas, which prides itself as being a top ranked academic institution has no more reason to have a first class football team, than the University of Texas Medical School has a reason to include a department of witchcraft." Milton Riemer, interview with David M. Horton, March 6, 1998, in possession of Horton. See also the cartoon published in the *Concordia Record* (February 15, 1957), 2. The caption reads as follows: Student: (playing volleyball) "Why don't you get some exercise with us, Prof?" Dr. Beto: (with hands on hips) "No, I'll get my exercise being a pallbearer for my friends who exercise."

29. Donald Weisenhorn, "George Beto," *The Mandate* (Huntsville, TX: Sam Houston State University, College of Criminal Justice, Winter 1992), 2. Beto chose German as the second language to meet the Ph.D. requirement. He knew the language well and maintained his skill by reading the German edition of *Portals of Prayer*, a daily devotional booklet.

30. Beto circular letter #3.

31. "Brief News Items," *Concordia Informer*, June 1940.

32. "College Movie Nears Completion," *Concordia Enterprize* [*sic*], November 14, 1941; "Concordia Color Film Now Available to All," *Concordia Informer*, November 1943.

33. "School Film is Ready," *Concordia Informer*, March 1943. The production cost of the film was approximately $75, which supporters of Concordia paid for in full.

34. "Minutes of the Board of Control," Lutheran Concordia College (Austin), January 29, 1941.

35. *Reports and Memorials for the Twenty-third Delegate Synod* (Fort Wayne, IN, June 18–28, 1941).

36. F. H. Stelzer to George Beto, March 25, 1942, BFA.

37. W. H. Bewie to George Beto, March 5, 1942; Martens interview.

38. Interview with Charles Wukasch, August 27, 1998, in possession of David M. Horton.

39. The stores were located on Congress Avenue, West 6th Street, and Guadalupe.

40. Marilynn Beto to David M. Horton, April 19, 1999, in possession of author.

41. Marilynn Beto to David M. Horton, March 8, 1998, in possession of author. Marilynn's close friends provided music for the service. Lois Zabel played the piano and Mildred Kieschnick sang "Because" and "The Lord's Prayer."

42. Beto considered naming his youngest daughter Beersheba so he could say his children ranged from Dan to Beersheba. See Judges 20:1

43. Each congregation set aside a Sunday in the autumn months dedicated to raising money for foreign missions. If possible the congregation secured the services of a foreign missionary on furlough who preached mornings and afternoons in both English and German. If a foreign missionary was not available, the congregation secured the services of a guest preacher, the more dramatic the better. An apocryphal story maintains that Beto preached a mission sermon with the text from I Corinthians 16:1: "Now concerning the collection."

44. Marilynn Beto letter, March 8, 1998. Beto's son Mark remembers finding a scrap of paper used as a bookmark in his father's Bible on which was written, "But if any provide not for his own, and especially for those of his own house, he has denied the faith, and is worse than an infidel" (1 Timothy 5:8). Mark Beto to David M. Horton, June 18, 2002, in possession of the author.

45. In 1942, for example, Concordia received 251 pounds of bacon, 168 pounds of chicken, and 168¾ dozen eggs. Ray F. Martens, ed., *Concordia of Texas* (Austin: Concordia Lutheran College of Texas, 1977), 47–50. When storage and preservation of the food became a problem, the servings were not limited. Beto had little patience with students who complained about the food. Interview with Martin Eifert, January 15, 2003, in possession of George R. Nielsen. The food was served family style, with six students assigned to each table. At the head was a senior flanked by two juniors. At the bottom were the freshmen and sophomores. With everyone standing behind their chairs, the seniors took turns opening the meal by tapping a glass for attention and then praying. The freshmen or sophomores darted to the kitchen to procure the bowls of food, which they immediately handed to the seniors, who, after taking their portions

first, passed the food along the table in descending order of seniority. If the procedure could be executed quickly, there was always the possibility of obtaining seconds from the kitchen. In the center of the table stood two containers, one with peanut butter and the other with syrup. These items were available for sandwiches to any student whose appetite had not been satisfied. At some point during the course of the meal the senior who led the prayer would tap his glass and then announce to all the diners which food items had been donated and then he would offer a thank you to the person or group that made the donation.

46. Linderman interview. Beto was a long-standing member of the Austin Kiwanis Club. The group of four hundred members elected him president for a term beginning in 1950. "Rev. George Beto Elected President of Kiwanis Club," *Austin American Statesman*, October 25, 1949.

47. Martens interview; *Reports and Memorials for the Twenty-fifth Delegate Synod* (Chicago), 1947; *Concordia Informer*, March 1950.

48. Dinda interview.

49. "Minutes of the Board of Control," Concordia Lutheran College (Austin), July 25, 1945.

50. *Concordia Informer*, November 1945.

51. "Flapjack Geography Helps Austin Get Concordia," *Austin American Statesman*, July 26, 1970.

52. Dinda interview.

53. Bohot interview.

54. Zoch interview.

55. Linderman interview.

56. *Concordia Enterprize* [*sic*], December 18, 1947.

57. *Concordia Informer*, November 1957.

58. The grant was largely in stocks, which Beto, applying his expanding knowledge of the stock market, held a bit longer, thereby increasing the value of the gift.

59. Viehweg interview.

60. Florence Reiboldt to George Beto, April 30,1945, SHSU.

61. "George J. Beto: Hard Work Paved the Path to Presidency," *Austin American Statesman*, January 2, 1949.

62. Ibid.

63. Dinda interview.

64. "Beto Takes over President's Residence," *Concordia Enterprize* [*sic*], 1949. To prevent information from leaking to the Lutheran constituency, Beto preferred a non-Lutheran secretary. Rather than respond to an argumentative letter with further argument, he often replied with the brief statement, "You may very well be right."

65. *Reports and Memorials for the Twenty-sixth Delegate Synod* (Milwaukee), 1950.

66. Hispanic students had been enrolled in the late 1940s without incident. The Austin busses did not insist on actual racial segregation. Nevertheless, on the back of each seat a sign was stenciled saying "Colored Seat from the Rear." When a group of Concordia students boarded the bus on Congress Avenue or Barton Springs, they invariably headed for the back of the bus and the U-shaped seating so they could talk as a group. As teenagers, rather than civil rights activists, they took a gleeful satisfaction out of forcing the black passengers to sit in the front next to the white riders.

67. George R. Nielsen. Another juror, obviously not an independent thinker, constantly chimed "accordin' to y'all."

68. *Austin American Statesman,* November 12, 1950.

69. Immanuel College had been founded in 1903 by the Synodical Conference, an alliance of the Missouri, Wisconsin, and Slovak synods.

70. Interview with Henry Sorrell, August 27, 1998, in possession of David M. Horton.

71. Ibid.

72. Ibid.

73. Ibid.

74. Ibid. On numerous occasions Sorrell assisted the Federal Bureau of Investigations with surveillance and investigations in the Baltimore area.

75. "Synod O.K.'s Co-Education at Concordia," *Concordia Informer,* July 1953.

76. "Faculty Slates First Curriculum Changes," *The Record,* March 1954.

77. Zoch interview.

78. Jo Ann Farr Petersen to David M. Horton, September 22, 1998, in possession of Horton.

79. Dana Pickett to David M. Horton, September 14, 1998, in possession of Horton.

80. John Oppliger to George Beto, May 7, 1954, Concordia Historical Institute.

81. George Beto to Alfred O. Fuerbringer, June 3, 1954, SHSU.

82. "Concordia to Honor Its Dr. Beto," *Austin American Statesman,* January 14, 1959.

83. "Concordia Honors Beto on Tenth Year of Presidency," *The Record,* January 1959.

84. *Austin American Statesman,* January 14, 1959.

Notes to Chapter 3

1. H. P. N. Gammel, *The Laws of Texas,* 1822–1897 (Austin: Gammel Book Company, 1898), (1854), 1524; (1860), 1504; (1868), 42–44;

(1871), 90, 916–18; (1876), 2; (1879), 1347–48; (1881), 130–32; (1883), 422–23. *Texas Almanac,* 1857 ed., s.v. "State Penitentiary Statistics." Production of textiles has continued into the twenty-first century. George Washington Cable, "The Convict Lease System in the Southern States," *Century Magazine* (1884), 593–95. See also "The Texas State Penitentiary," *Proceedings of the Annual Congress of the National Prison Association* (1874), 236–38; and J. S. Duncan, "Richard Bennett Hubbard and State Resumption of the Penitentiary, 1876–1878," *Texana* (1974), 47–55.

2. Benjamin E. McCulloch, "The Texas Penal System," *Proceedings of the Annual Congress of the National Prison Association* (1889), 248; "Messages of Governor Ireland: January 13, 1885," *Collections of the Archive and History Department of the Texas State Library: Executive Series; Governors' Messages, Coke to Ross, 1874–1891* (Austin: Archives and History Department, Texas State Library, 1916), 535. For a short history of the Harlem Farm see *The New Handbook of Texas,* 1996 ed., s.v., "Jester State Prison Farm," by Stephen L. Hardin; "What Some Wardens Say," *Journal of Prison Discipline and Philanthropy* (1898), 19–20. See also, Charles C. Campbell, *Hell Exploded: An Exposition of Barbarous Cruelty and Prison Horrors* (Austin: n.p., ca., 1900); J. S. Calvin, *Buried Alive, or; A Term in the Texas State Prison, 1898–1902* (Paris, Texas: n.p., 1905); John Shotwell, *A Victim of Revenge, or Fourteen Years in Hell* (San Antonio: E.J. Jackson, 1909); Andrew L. George, *The Texas Convict: Sketches of the Penitentiary Convict Farms and Railroads, Together with Poems* (n.p.,1895); Charles A. Favor, *Twenty-Two Months in the Texas Penitentiary* (Corsicana, TX: Democrat Print, 1900); and T. D. Hennessey, *The Life of A. J. Walker, an Innocent Convict* (Iola, TX: Iola Enterprise Print, ca., 1903).

3. "Minutes of the Texas Prison Board" (November 1943), 635, 647–650, Texas State Archives.

4. Austin MacCormick, "Behind Those Prison Riots," *Reader's Digest* (December 1953), 97.

5. During his lifetime MacCormick surveyed every prison and adult reformatory institution in the United States, and was instrumental in helping set the agenda for the reformation of the prison systems in Alabama, Arkansas, Louisiana, Mississippi, North Carolina, and Texas. MacCormick died on October 24, 1979. See Roberts J. Wright, "Austin H. MacCormick: A Memorial Statement," *Corrections Today* (January–February 1980), 60–61; "Austin H. MacCormick," *Current Biography* (July 1951), 48–51; "Personalities and Projects," *Survey* (April 1951), 180–81; R. M. Yoder, "Trouble Shooter of the Big House," *Saturday Evening Post* (May 12, 1951), 19–21.

6. "Time Hangs Heavy: Hard Work Blessing to 6,000 Inmates of Prisons," *Austin American Statesman,* January 17, 1949.

7. "State Prison Guard's Job Offers Few Attractions," *Austin American Statesman,* January 18, 1949.

8. "Minutes of the Texas Prison Board," (March 1944–July 1945), 677.

9. Ibid., (January–November 1947), 706.

10. "Texas Prison System Praised," *Houston Chronicle,* October 25, 1954.

11. Ibid.

12. "Minutes of the Texas Prison Board" (1947), 725.

13. Ibid.

14. Cleveland was given consistently as Ellis' place of birth in the *Memphis Commercial Appeal. The New Handbook of Texas* cites Oneonta.

15. "Ellis Expected to Accept Call to Run Texas Prisons," *Memphis Commercial Appeal,* November 25, 1947.

16. "Minutes of the Texas Prison Board" (1947), 725.

17. Ibid., (1948), 737.

18. Ibid., 729–30, 734; "Ellis New Head of Texas Prisons," *Houston Post,* November 26, 1947; "Windsor of Tyler," *Dallas Morning News,* January 30, 1953.

19. Oscar Byron Ellis, *Annual Report,* General Letter #38, insert in "Minutes of the Texas Prison Board" (December 31, 1948).

20. "Public Meetings," *Prison World* (July–August 1948), 18.

21. Charlie Evans, "Behind the Bars: A Progress Report on Texas' Dramatic Prison Reform," *Texas Parade* (February 1954), 37–40.

22. Oscar Byron Ellis, *Annual Report to the Texas Prison Board* (1949).

23. "Prison Reform Project Begun," *Austin American Statesman,* March 8, 1949.

24. "Prison Board Hires Ellis' Tennessee Aide as New Assistant," *Dallas Morning News,* May 3, 1949.

25. "State Prison Board Requesting Appropriation Boost," *Austin American Statesman,* September 6, 1950.

26. "Minutes of the Texas Prison Board" (1951), 988.

27. Ibid., 1102.

Notes to Chapter 4

1. John [no name] to George Beto, October 3, 1991, Concordia Historical Institute (hereafter CHI).

2. Beto's support for the Republican Eisenhower was matched by his mother's support for a Democrat when she voted for Paul Simon in his 1970 race for the U.S. Senate. Simon was a preacher's boy, so she not only gave him her vote, but also sent some money. George Beto, "Mother's Funeral Sermon," September 29, 1985, CHI.

3. George Beto to Allan Shivers, May 14, 1956, CHI. In 1957 Yarborough became a U. S. Senator, and was instrumental in placing the liberal William Wayne Justice on the federal bench.

4. Gaynor Kendall and Nobel Prentice to George Beto, July 30, 1958, CHI.

5. R. Craig Copeland, "The Evolution of the Texas Department of Corrections" (master's thesis, Sam Houston State University, 1980), 222.

6. Interview with Dan Beto, January 13, 2003, in possession of George R. Nielsen.

7. Interview with Dan Beto, April 19, 1998, in possession of David M. Horton.

8. Ibid.

9. George Beto to Richard Daley, August 30, 1968, Sam Houston State University, Newton Gresham Library, Beto Collection (hereafter SHSU); John J. DiIulio, Jr., *Governing Prisons: A Comparative Study of Correctional Management* (New York: The Free Press, 1987), 113.

10. George Beto to C. N. Avery, Jr., October 18, 1961, CHI. Coffield was called the worst guest and the best host, because as the host he was solicitous, but as a guest he arrived late and departed early.

11. Lewis Nordyke, "Pete Coffield: A Friend of Good Boys and Convicts," *Texas Parade* (June, 1959); "Pete Coffield: He and Columbus Took a Chance," *The Dallas Morning News,* January 2, 1966; Jimmy Banks, "His Work is His Relaxation," *Texas Star,* June 25, 1972. In his will, Coffield added a provision that gave his friends a twenty-year right to use the Diamond H Ranch for their pleasure. Beto, less than a month before his death, received an invitation for the annual hunt scheduled for November 15–17, 1991. Coffield Estate to George Beto, October 11, 1991, CHI.

12. "Minutes of the Texas Prison Board" (1953), 1306; "Unguarded Prison Farm Turns Out Better Men," *The Dallas Morning News,* February 11, 1953.

13. "Former Tennessean Revolutionizes Texas Prison System," *Nashville Tennessean,* February 21, 1954.

14. George Beto, "Heatly Funeral Sermon," SHSU; George Beto to Harold M. Olsen, August 24, 1966, SHSU; "'Bear' Holds Legislators in His Teeth," *Austin American-Statesman,* February 1, 1981; "Heatly Works Hard, Guards His Power," *The Dallas Morning News,* May 2, 1971; "Duke of Paducah Bids Adieu to House," March 28, 1982, The *Dallas Morning News*; "Bill Heatly: Folks Swear by Him or at Him," clipping, Texas State Archives.

15. "Minutes of the Texas Prison Board" (1954), 2010, 2028; "Texas Prison Methods Are Lauded by Oklahoma Solons," *Houston Chronicle,* December 9, 1954.

16. "Minutes of the Texas Prison Board" (1954), 1991.

17. Ibid., 1206.

18. Ibid., 2011.

19. Ibid., 2007–2011; Charlie Evans, "Behind the Prison Bars: Progress Report on Texas Prison Reform," *Texas Parade,* February 1954.

20. "Minutes of the Texas Prison Board" (1957), 2323.

21. "Crowded State Prison System Has New Name, Old Problems," *The Dallas Morning News,* September 1, 1957; "Dr. Beto Learned Early of Prison System's Needs," *Houston Post,* March 2, 1958.

22. David M. Horton and Ryan K. Turner, *Lone Star Justice* (Austin: Eakin Press, 1999), 303–307.

23. Ibid., 274–78.

24. "Minutes of the Texas Prison Board" (1956), 2163.

25. Robert Crichton, *The Great Impostor* (New York: Random House, 1959); George Beto to O. B. Ellis, October 15, 1959, SHSU.

26. Copeland, 133; *Life* (January 28, 1952); "Minutes of the Texas Prison Board" (1955), 2087; (1956), 2138. The Federal Bureau of Investigation later discovered Demara masquerading as a Russian diplomat at the United Nations.

27. "Minutes of the Texas Prison Board" (1955), 2053–2058; "Third Meal Denied for Rebel Band," *The Dallas Morning News,* April 15, 1955.

28. "O. B. Ellis, Son Injured in Accident," *Austin American Statesman,* February 1, 1957; "Ellis, Son Said Doing All Right," *Austin American Statesman,* February 2 1957.

29. "Minutes of the Texas Prison Board" (1957), 2320; "State Prison Farm Strike is Resolved," *Austin American Statesman,* August 26, 1957.

30. Interview with Dan Beto, January 13, 2002; George Beto to Mrs. O. B. Ellis, November 15, 1961, SHSU.

31. "Minutes of the Texas Prison Board" (1953), 1343; "Dr. Beto Learned Early of Prison System's Needs," *Houston Post,* March 2, 1958.

32. "Minutes of the Texas Prison Board" (1958), 2420.

33. "Minutes of the Texas Prison Board" (1953), 1389–1392; (1955), 2032; (1957), 2286; Interview with Charles Wukasch, July 7, 1998, in possession of David M. Horton.

34. "Medal Given to Dr. Beto," *Austin American Statesman,* October 4, 1957; "Austin Minister Wins Texas Heritage Medal," *Houston Chronicle,* October 4, 1957. An appreciation luncheon honoring Beto was held at the Austin Club on October 30. Governor Shivers was the master of ceremonies and the luminaries feasted on Chukar Partridge Veronique (Texas-raised, of course!).

35. "Prison Inmates Use 'Time' to Earn School Diploma," *Austin American Statesman,* February 1, 1957; "Dr. Beto Aids Prisoners to Continue Education," July 21, 1957.

36. "39 Convicts Graduated," *Austin American Statesman,* September 26, 1957.

37. George Beto to Gilbert W. Hermes, February 23, 1961, CHI.

38. Price Daniel to George Beto, August 25, 1958, SHSU.

39. "Nominations for the Office of President of Concordia Theological Seminary," *The Lutheran Witness,* (February 24, 1959), 94; "Concordia to Name President," *Illinois State Journal,* April 9, 1959; "Dr. Beto Takes Job at Illinois Seminary," *Austin American Statesman,* May 27, 1959.

40. "Concordia Tabs Texan as President," *Illinois State Journal,* April 11, 1959.

41. Beto Family Roundtable, September 19, 1998, in possession of David M. Horton.

42. "Texan Accepts Concordia Presidency," *Illinois State Journal,* May 27, 1959.

43. "Minutes of the Board of Control" (Austin), September 22, 1953.

44. "Morris Dunbar, the Amiable Yardman," *The Record,* (December 1955).

45. Interview with Walter Dube, May 14, 1998, in possession of David M. Horton; Interview with Marilynn Beto, January 12, 2003, in possession of George R. Nielsen; *Concordia Informer,* July 1959.

46. "Minutes of the Texas Prison Board" (1959), 2553; "Dr. Beto Resigns," *The Echo,* June 1959.

Notes to Chapter 5

1. Erich H. Heintzen, *Prairie School of the Prophets: The Anatomy of a Seminary 1846–1976* (St. Louis: Concordia Publishing House, 1989), 78.

2. "Dr. Beto's Coming Here Has Great Possibilities," *Illinois State Register,* September 25, 1959.

3. The name refers to the *Book of Concord,* a work containing the Confessions of the Lutheran Church.

4. Heintzen, 17, 30, 56.

5. Ibid., 56, 150, 183.

6. Interview with Walter Dube, June 23, 1998, in possession of David M. Horton.

7. The total number was comprised of four years of high school, two of junior college, two of senior college, three of seminary, and one year of vicarage. George Beto, "New Senior College," *The Lutheran Witness* (February 19, 1952); *Reports and Memorials: Forty-Fourth Regular Convention, The Lutheran Church-Missouri Synod* (1959), 45.

8. Heintzen, 195–96.

9. "Beto Looks Over Site of Concordia's New Dormitory Project," *Illinois State Journal*, July 21, 1959.

10. Heintzen, 196. The selection process began with congregations nominating candidates for the position. From that list, representatives from the school's Board of Control, the Board of Higher Education, and the synodical president's office made the selection.

11. "Testimonial Dinner Given in Honor of Dr. Beto," *Rotary Review* (Springfield, Illinois), September 25, 1959.

12. Interview with Curtis E. Huber, September 14, 1998, in possession of David M. Horton.

13. Interview with Ray Martens, March 4, 1998, in possession of David M. Horton.

14. Heintzen, 204.

15. *Reports and Memorials: Forty-Fourth Regular Convention, The Lutheran Church-Missouri Synod* (1962), 7.

16. Martens interview.

17. "Campus Sets Long Range Plans," *Sem Quill*, December 12, 1961.

18. *Reports and Memorials,* 7; "Concordia Breaks Ground for $550,000 Library," *Illinois State Register*, April 6, 1960.

19. Richard Dickinson, *Roses and Thorns: The Centennial Edition of Black Lutheran Mission and Ministry in the Lutheran Church-Missouri Synod* (St. Louis: Concordia Publishing House, 1977), 157; George Beto to Walter H. Ellwanger, July 15, 1975, Sam Houston State University, Newton Gresham Library, Beto Collection (hereafter SHSU).

20. David Zersen to David M. Horton, September 10, 1998, in possession of Horton.

21. George Beto, "From the Desk," *Sem Quill,* October 10, 1961; November 7, 1961.

22. *The Springfielder* (Summer 1961), 2.

23. Roddy Braun to David M. Horton, July 20, 1998, in possession of Horton.

24. Dube interview; interview with Richard Dinda, July 1, 1998, in possession of David M. Horton.

25. To illustrate Beto's lack of interest in theological issues, he gave his copy of C. F. W. Walther's *Law and Gospel* to a student with the comment, "Take this. I never found much use for it." Zersen letter.

26. *The Springfielder* (April, 1960), 1.

27. George Beto to Hermann Sasse, December 14, 1962, SHSU. Beto's reference may have been to a joint meeting held November 27–29, 1961, at which he presented a paper with traditional views, and suggested that "activism" be curtailed and an emphasis "molding the minds of . . . students" be maintained. George Beto, "The Faculty Views the Field," 1961, Concordia Seminary Library, St. Louis, Missouri.

28. George Beto to C. N. Avery, Jr., June 12, 1961, Concordia Historical Institute (hereafter CHI).

29. *The Springfielder* (Summer 1961), 2.

30. George Beto to Kurt W. Biel, October 9, 1973, CHI. J. A. O. "Jack" Preus, the synodical president and leader of the conservatives, had been a member of the Springfield faculty during Beto's presidency, and received Beto's endorsement for succeeding him as president of the seminary. From the time the two first met, well before Beto's move to Springfield, they had respected and admired each other. On one occasion Preus had visited Beto when Beto was still at Concordia Austin, and Beto escorted him on a tour of the Texas prison system. Samuel Goltermann e-mail message to George R. Nielsen.

31. "Response of George J. Beto on Recollections of His Life at the Seminary in St. Louis, 1935–1939," CHI.

32. "Minutes of the Texas Prison Board" (1953), 2396–2397.

33. George Beto to O. B. Ellis, March 24, 1961, CHI.

34. James B. Jacobs, Stateville: *The Penitentiary in Mass Society* (Chicago: The University of Chicago Press, 1977), 29. Jacobs' book was at the top of Beto's required reading list for his course "Special Topics in Correctional Administration" at Sam Houston State University.

35. George Beto to Orson L. McCotter, April 9, 1984, SHSU.

36. Gladys A. Erickson, *Warden Ragen of Joliet* (New York: E. P. Dutton, 1975), 185; Jacobs, 43, 47.

37. Erickson, 62, 242.

38. Jacobs, 48, 51.

39. George Beto to O. B. Ellis, August 15, 1961, SHSU. In writing to Ellis, Beto referred to Ragen as "our mutual friend."

40. *St. Louis Post-Dispatch,* May 27, 1965.

41. George Beto to Joseph Ragen, May 29, 1965, SHSU.

42. *Chicago Tribune,* August 28, 1965.

43. *Illinois State Register,* March 7, 1961.

44. Huber interview; J. A. O. Preus to Otto Kerner, (n.d.), CHI; George Beto to McElvaney, February 24, 1961, CHI; May 5, 1961, SHSU. Coffield also persuaded Vice-President Lyndon B. Johnson to support Beto, and later encouraged Beto to send a note of thanks for the record, even if Johnson's efforts had had little effect. H. H. Coffield to George Beto, May 25, 1961, CHI.

45. George Beto to O. B. Ellis, March 24, 1961; Beto to McElvaney, May 5, 1961; Beto to Joseph Ragen, May 9, 1961, SHSU. Some local Democrats had supported the nomination of a Springfield attorney, and there was some consternation among the party faithful over the newcomer receiving the nomination. Martens interview; *Illinois State Register,* March 7, 1961.

46. Beto was sensitive to potential criticism about his role on the board. In his letter to Ellis he wrote, "What with these Parole hearings and my normal travel on behalf of the seminary, I don't want to incur any unnecessary criticism by being away more than is necessary." George Beto to O. B. Ellis, August 15, 1961.

47. The report was broken into two parts: recommendations regarding the Correctional Services Division (which Beto wrote), and recommendations regarding the Division of Community Service (which he did not write, but signed off on).

48. *Report and Recommendations of the Illinois Youth Commission. Governor's Survey Committee on the Youth Commission* (Springfield, Illinois: 1962).

49. William E. Barnhart and Eugene F. Schlickman, *Kerner: The Conflict of Intangible Results* (Urbana: University of Illinois Press, 1999). Beto invited Kerner to the Diamond H Ranch near Catarina, Texas, for the 1965 hunt. Beto added that "the accommodations [are] nothing short of luxurious, the game plentiful, and the fellowship relaxing." George Beto to Otto Kerner, August 19, 1965, SHSU.

50. George Beto to Maurice H. Sigler, September 12, 1974, CHI.

51. Ibid.; George Beto to Otto Kerner, March 10, 1975, CHI.

52. Barnhart and Schlickman, 87.

53. On April 19, 1960 Beto wrote the BHE requesting $1,957 for the trip. He justified it by saying that it would refresh his knowledge of the Reformation course he taught at the seminary. The BHE granted him $1,657, and he received $1,000 from the Lutheran Brotherhood, a fraternal insurance company for Lutherans. George Beto to Walter Wolbrecht, April 19, 1960, Concordia Seminary Archives, Fort Wayne, Indiana (hereafter Concordia Fort Wayne); A. M. Ahlschwede to George Beto, May 16, 1960; R. H. Gerberding to George Beto, May 31, 1960, Concordia Fort Wayne.

54. George Beto to the French Embassy, Washington, D.C., May 16, 1960, CHI; Joseph E. Ragen, to E. R. Cass, June 10, 1960, Concordia Seminary Archives, Fort Wayne. Also helpful was the award for his six years of service on the Texas Board of Corrections. The award had been authorized by Gov. Price Daniel, but because Beto had already moved to Illinois it was presented to Beto by the lieutenant governor of Illinois, John W. Chapman, on September 2, 1960, three days after his installation as president of Concordia Seminary, Springfield, Illinois.

55. George Beto, "Eating High on the Hog," *Austin American Statesman,* July 26, 1960; "Churches in Europe Appear No Longer Vibrant," *Austin American Statesman,* August 14, 1960.

56. George Beto, "Memo Book," SHSU.

57. George Beto to H. H. Coffield, May 16, 1960, SHSU; Beto, "Memo Book."

58. The members of the Texas Board of Corrections swiftly passed a resolution honoring Ellis, saying "he was director of the Texas Prison System from January 1, 1948, until his death on November 12, 1961. He was instrumental in transforming the penal system of Texas from one of the worst in the nation to one of the best. His services were characterized by extreme faithfulness, vision, devotion to duty, and personal sacrifice." After the resolution was adopted by the board, James Windham stated that "it would be a fine tribute to the outstanding work of Ellis in modernizing the Texas Department of Corrections to name the [prison] farm acquired from the Smither family in his memory." The vote of the board was unanimous in favor of renaming the Smither State Penal Farm the Ellis Unit. "Minutes of the Texas Board of Correction" (1961), 2972.

59. "Board is in no Hurry to Fill Prison Position," *Houston Post,* November 13, 1961.

60. H. H. Coffield telegram to George Beto, November 20, 1961.

61. "Concordia's Dr. Beto is Offered Texas Prison System Position," *Illinois State Journal,* November 21, 1961.

62. Austin MacCormick to George Beto, December 4, 1961, SHSU.

63. Marvin Vance to George Beto, November 21, 1961, SHSU.

64. "Beto to Remain at Concordia," *Springfield News.* Also displeased was J. L. McCurdy, Chief of Police of Houston. He did not believe convicts needed a preacher or professor, and he preferred Jack Heard, one of Ellis' assistants. Craig R. Copeland, "The Evolution of the Texas Department of Corrections" (master's thesis, Sam Houston State University, 1980), 219–20.

65. George Beto to Austin MacCormick, December 6, 1961, SHSU.

66. George Beto to William Steffen, December 11, 1961, SHSU.

67. George Beto telegram to H. H. Coffield, December 12, 1961, SHSU.

68. H. H. Coffield to George Beto, December 13, 1961, SHSU.

69. "Minutes of the Texas Board of Correction" (1962), 3010.

70. Ibid., 3004; "Dr. Beto Accepts Texas Prison Job." *Houston Post,* February 10, 1962.

71. George Beto to Dr. Carl Rosenquist, February 19, 1962, SHSU.

72. During the previous special session of the legislature an attempt was made to increase the salary to $22,500. Governor Price Daniel supported the increase and recommended it to the legislature, but they failed to approve it. "Lutheran Minister Named Prison Head," *The Dallas Morning News,* February 10, 1962; "Beto Head of Prisons in Texas," *Houston Post,* February 10, 1962; "No Extra Pay for Prison Head," *Houston Chronicle,* February 21, 1962.

73. "Prison Chief Veteran of Humanitarian Work," *Illinois State Journal,* February 21, 1962.

74. "Dr. Beto Takes Over As Prison Director," *Huntsville Item*, clipping, Beto Family Archives.
75. George Beto to Merton Lundquist, February 13, 1962, SHSU.
76. Zersen letter.
77. Heintzen, 190.

Notes to Chapter 6

1. *The New Handbook of Texas*, 1996 ed., s.v. "Huntsville, Texas," by Charles L. Dwyer and Gerald L. Holder.
2. Marilynn Beto, "Our Ten Years with the Texas Prisons (1962–1972)," 1–4, Beto Family Archives (hereafter BFA).
3. Ibid., 5. Mrs. Beto played an extensive role in training the inmates who worked in the director's house how to cook and read recipes. She also gave them devotional material and spoke of spiritual matters. One of the successes of her concern was J. D. "Sonny" Wells, a multi-offender who, when paroled, went to work for the *Forward Times*, a black newspaper in Houston, and eventually opened a halfway house for offenders released on parole. When Wells married, Beto conducted the ceremony and Marilynn hosted the reception in the director's house. Beth McDonnell and Mark Beto to authors, August 27, 2003.
4. "Beto Honored at Dinner Here," *Houston Chronicle*, April 13, 1963; Jack Kyle to David M. Horton, September 26, 1998, in possession of Horton.
5. Craig R. Copeland, "The Evolution of the Texas Department of Corrections" (master's thesis, Sam Houston State University, 1980), 229.
6. "Dr. Beto's Prison Plan," *Texas Magazine* (*Houston Chronicle*), May 6, 1962; "November Profile: Doctor George Beto," *Texas Public Employee* (November 1962), 8; Rachel Conrad Wahlberg, "Texas Prison Boss," *The Lutheran* (March 13, 1963), 16–19. Ferguson's warden, a Beto appointee, failed to adequately control the prison, and the men sat down in the fields. After a meeting with other wardens, Beto placed them in charge and returned to Huntsville. Interview with D. V. "Red" McKaskle, September 27, 2004, in possession of George Nielsen.
7. "Inmates Chose Biblical Option," *Houston Post*, July 28, 1974; "Doctor in the Big House," *Houston Post*, October 10, 1971.
8. Interview with Marilynn Beto, April 21, 1998, in possession of David M. Horton.
9. Kyle letter; Marilynn Beto, "Our Ten Years."
10. Marilynn Beto, "Our Ten Years;" Copeland, 231.
11. Marilynn Beto, "Our Ten Years."
12. Mark Beto to David M. Horton, March 27, 2000, in possession of Horton.

13. "The Man Is Back On Job as TDC Chief," *Houston Post,* November 6, 1964.

14. Kyle letter. Through the purchase of adjacent properties, the size of the farm eventually was increased to one hundred acres.

15. Marilynn Beto, "Life at Wit's End Ranch, and the Big Fish Story," BFA.

16. "Penal Chief, Dr. Beto, Hurt In Farm Tractor Accident," *Houston Post,* September 23, 1964; "Power Mower Rips His Stomach Open," *Houston Post,* November 9, 1964.

17. Marilynn Beto, "Our Ten Years."

18. October 6, 1986, SHSU; "McElroy's Pub," *Houston Chronicle,* December 28, 1994.

19. Both Richard J. V. Johnson, publisher of the *Houston Chronicle* and Everett Colliers, the editor, were Beto's personal friends. Interview with McKaskle.

20. Mark Beto e-mail message to Nielsen, December 2, 2003; Ray Schkade e-mail message to Nielsen, December 21, 2003; Lester Bayer e-mail message to Nielsen, January 5, 2004.

21. George Beto, "Speech at Judge Rogers' Retirement Ceremonies," November 10,1983, BFA; "Visiting Judge Likes People, He Declares," *Houston Post,* September 24, 1959.

22. George Beto to Herman Engelman, November 12, 1962, Sam Houston State University, Newton Gresham Library, Beto Collection (hereafter SHSU); George Beto to Philip Wahlberg, November 15, 1962, SHSU; Roosevelt Martin to George Beto, January 16, 1963, SHSU; George Beto to Roosevelt Martin, January 21, 1963, SHSU.

23. Ernest L. Sample to George Beto, February 11,1963, SHSU; George Beto to Ernest L. Sample, February 14, 1963, SHSU; "Minutes of the Texas Board of Corrections" (1966), 3696.

24. "Prison Changes," *Dallas Times Herald,* October 26, 1972. Marilynn Beto recalls one incident that Beto found particularly moving, and never forgot. While walking from his holding cell to the death chamber that housed the electric chair, one condemned inmate sang "Swing Low, Sweet Chariot."

25. George Beto to Herman Engelman, November 12, 1962.

26. "Electric Chair Idle in 1965," *Houston Post,* January 6,1966; "Discipline Swift, Sure, and Life Placid," *San Antonio Light,* February 6, 1972; "Beto Talks to Inmates in Final Hours on Job," *Houston Post,* July 31, 1972. Because of the moratorium Texas placed on executions, Beto's fourteenth and last execution took place on July 30, 1964. After that time, and as he became more secure, he spelled out his position.

27. Copeland, "Department of Corrections," 232.

28. The thirteen separate units facilitated the classification and segregation of prisoners. The Walls Unit, located in Huntsville, had been completely renovated by Ellis in 1957. It housed 2,000 inmates, largely first offenders and inmates who had been promoted after proving themselves on the farm units. Labor at the industries at the Walls was considered preferable to work on the farms. This unit was also the place of departure for all inmates who were released, either through expiration of sentence or parole. All central administrative offices were located here with the exception of agriculture. The Walls also included the Segregation Unit (later called Disciplinary Unit), or the Shamrock, with space for as many as four hundred inmates who did not adjust to the working units. Harlem (est. 1885 and after 1967 changed to Jester) was located in Fort Bend County. The unit also included 5,400 acres of land and the brick plant. Goree (1900), four miles south of Huntsville, was for women. It housed 400 inmates and the garment factory. A new cellblock was under construction in 1962 for 264 inmates. Clemens (1901) was in Brazoria County and was geared for first offenders under the age of twenty-five. It was agricultural and included 8,000 acres of land. As late as 1964 there were no single cells, only tanks, and the sewage system did not meet standards. Ramsey (1908), Brazoria County, consisted of 15,800 acres of Brazos River bottomland. It was a maximum security facility for 1,700 inmates who were multi-recidivists. It was largely agricultural with a cotton gin and a grain dryer. Like the Clemens unit, there were no single cells, only tanks. And its sewage system also did not meets standards. Central (1908), located near Sugar Land, was for first-offenders and had 5,000 acres of land, the meat-processing plant, a canning plant, a feed mill, and a cotton gin. Eastham (1917), in Houston County near Weldon, was surrounded by 13,000 acres of Trinity River bottomland and held 1,700 recidivist inmates. Like Ramsey it was a maximum security facility. It was an agricultural operation for both crops and animals. Retrieve (1918) was located on 7,000 acres of fertile soil on the Brazos River near Angleton and boasted the highest yield per acre. It was used for multi-recidivists and held an average population of 450. In 1964 there were no single cells, only tanks but its new sewage system met standards. Darrington (1918), on 7,000 acres in Brazoria County, twenty-four miles south of Houston, held five hundred recidivists who were considered a better element. It produced agriculture products, including rice. Wynne (1937) was three miles north of Huntsville and designed for 1,400 of the physically and mentally handicapped of all ages. It also contained a treatment center, opened in 1959 for four hundred mentally ill patients. Its land was limited in size, so the focus was on a dairy herd, swine, and production of vegetables. Ferguson, located in Madison County near Midway, which was dedicated in

June 1962, three months into Beto's administration, was an Ellis project. Using prison labor and prison-produced bricks, the cost of the unit was $3,000 per bed, compared to $9,000 at federal institutions of similar dimensions. The total cost was $4.5 million, less than a third of what the cost would have been if it had been done under contract. It was a medium security unit for first offenders between the ages of seventeen and twenty-one. It had been planned for 1,100 inmates and was built with single cells and single beds. The focus was on education and vocational training. Ellis (formerly the Smither Unit), located eighteen miles north of Huntsville on the Trinity River was under construction when Beto took office and would be completed in 1963. It was the maximum security unit for older recidivists and high escape risks and held 1,700 inmates. It had 8,000 acres of farm land, a cotton gin, chapel, and shop. The Diagnostic Unit, also under construction when Beto became director, would be completed in 1964. It was located about one mile north of Huntsville, had a capacity for 500 inmates and was the facility where the staff tested the mental, physical (including dental exam and vaccinations), and educational aptitudes of inmates. All new inmates spent the first four to six weeks at the facility. David M. Horton and Ryan K. Turner, *Lone Star Justice* (Austin: Eakin Press, 1999), 227–42; *Annual Reports of the Texas Prison Board*.

29. "Crime Does Pay," *Texas Magazine*, January 30, 1966.

30. Marilynn Beto, "Our Ten Years."

31. Copeland, 241; Kyle letter; "Beto Talks to Inmates in Final Hours on Job," *Houston Post*, July 31, 1972; "New Prison Head Firm Man of God," *Fort Worth Star Telegram*, March 11, 1962.

32. Marilynn Beto, "Our Ten Years." By 1970, "wholly black or wholly white units" no longer existed, although there was some segregation on a voluntary basis. The prison population was forty percent black, forty percent white, and twenty percent Latin American. Beto to Ronnie Dugger, December 15, 1970, SHSU

33. Kyle letter; George Beto to W. F. Wolbrecht, July 11, 1962, SHSU.

34. "Frierson Fed the Prisoners," *Houston Post*, July 9, 1972; "Vast Cattle Operation Impressive," *San Angelo Standard-Times*, October 26, 1970; George Beto to Don King, February 27, 1973, SHSU. When the market price for high quality horses became prohibitive and Frierson turned to cheaper mounts, some guards who used the horses for field operations resigned. The solution was to breed their own. *The Western Horseman* magazine reported that crossing the Tennessee Walker with the Quarter Horse resulted in a "well-gaited" animal for field operations.

35. *Annual Report of the Texas Department of Corrections* (1966).

36. "Prison System Operates Smoothly on Small Budget," *Houston Chronicle*, July 8, 1970.

37. McKaskle Interview; Funeral Sermon for B. W. Frierson, November 9, 1983. In possession of George R. Nielsen; Dan Beto e-mail message to Nielsen, October 24, 2004.

38. "Minutes of the Texas Board of Corrections" (1963), 3184–3185; *Annual Report of the Texas Department of Corrections* (1966).

39. "Prison Industries Progress more than was Foreseen," *Houston Post*, September 6, 1964.

40. "The Texas Prison Industrial Complex: A Growing Threat to Free Enterprise?" *Texas Business & Industry* (September 1969), 10–18.

41. Anon., "The Administration of Dr. George J. (Walking George) Beto," n. d., SHSU

42. *Annual Report of the Texas Department of Corrections* (1966).

43. George Beto, "The Case for Prisons," *Texas Police Journal* (August 1964), 3–4.

44. "State Prison Director Says He Doesn't See Crime Rise," *Dallas Morning News*, February 7, 1969.

45. "Minutes of the Texas Board of Corrections" (1966), 3657; (1965), 3453.

46. *Annual Report of the Texas Department of Corrections* (1963); "Prison Appreciation Day Tour Draws 350," *Huntsville Pictorial*, May 24, 1962.

47. George Beto, "Introduction," *Annual Report of the Texas Department of Corrections* (1963).

48. George Beto, "The Texas Prison System Rehabilitation Program," Speech at Texas A&M University, SHSU; "Tribute is Paid Dr. Beto on Texas Prison Reform," *Houston Post*, April 13, 1962; "Beto To Give Lecture On Rehabilitation Job," *Austin American Statesman*, April 19,1962; "Beto Describes Fred Cruz as Nonconformist," *Houston Chronicle*, May 26, 1972.

49. "Minutes of the Texas Board of Corrections" (1965), 3547–3548.

50. "Minutes of the Texas Board of Corrections" (1968), 4252; (1969), 4655.

51. "A Curriculum for Windham School District," Texas State Archives.

52. *Annual Report of the Texas Department of Corrections* (1966).

53. "Minutes of the Texas Board of Corrections" (1970), 4969. Beto had been interested in a program in which SHSU offered courses leading to degrees. Dr. Templeton refused, and said that as long as he was the president of Sam Houston, no inmate would "earn a degree from Sam" and stand beside one of his free students to receive a diploma. He remained true to his word. Jack Kyle interview, February 24, 2003, in possession of George R. Nielsen.

54. Clemens Bartollas, *Introduction to Corrections* (New York: Harper and Row, 1981), 308.

55. "Prison System is Helping Juveniles," *Houston Post,* April 13, 1962; "TDC Program One of Best for Training Prisoners," *Houston Chronicle,* July 7, 1970.

56. "Firm, But A Friend, Dr. Beto's Prison Plan," *Texas Magazine* (Houston Chronicle), May 6, 1962.

57. "Prison 'Rip Van Winkles' Oriented Now," *Austin American Statesman,* July 30, 1963.

58. "Minutes of the Texas Board of Corrections" (1969), 4687; "Houston Is Trial Site for Prison Work-Release Plan," *Houston Post,* August 17, 1969.

59. Bartollas, 308.

60. George Beto to E. J. Riske, February 8, 1963, SHSU.

61. Ibid.; George Beto to Mrs. Philip L. Wahlberg, February 11, 1963, SHSU.

62. Untitled document, n.d., n.a. SHSU.

63. George Beto, "I Was in Prison: Christian Challenge," Speech to The Christian and the Criminal Workshop, February 27, 1974, SHSU.

64. "Chaplains at TDC Honor Dr. Beto," *Huntsville Item,* August 23, 1972.

65. "Minutes of the Texas Board of Corrections" (1963), 3227–28, 3253.

66. "Crime Does Pay," *Texas Magazine* (*Houston Chronicle*), January 30, 1966.

67. George Beto, Speech before the State Interim Drug Study Committee, April 10, 1972, SHSU.

68. "Prison Guards' Salary Is Immoral, Beto Says," *Houston Post,* February 5, 1963.

69. "Minutes of the Texas Board of Corrections" (1964), 3304; George Beto. "The Case for Prisons." *Texas Police Journal* (August 1964).

70. "Minutes of the Texas Board of Corrections" (1964), 3341.

71. "Minutes of the Texas Board of Corrections" (1965), 3417.

72. "Minutes of the Texas Board of Corrections" (1964), 3280, 3395.

73. "Minutes of the Texas Board of Corrections" (1969), 4569.

74. "Minutes of the Texas Board of Corrections" (1963), 3215–16; (1964), 3304.

75. Kyle letter. Other sources identify Bobby McGown as the first black employee. McKaskle interview.

76. On the Windam School District staff there were eleven blacks and one Hispanic compared to eighty-two whites. A. P. Manning to George Beto, February 2, 1971, SHSU.

77. "Discipline Swift, Sure, and Life Placid," *San Antonio Light,* February 9, 1972.

78. "Regional Prisoners," *Austin American Statesman,* July 20, 1970.

79. "Work Hard, but Fair," *San Antonio Light,* February 7, 1972.

80. George Beto, Speech to Texas Agricultural Workers Association Conference, November 9, 1966.

81. "Murder Can Net You Up to 10 Years in Texas," *Daily Times* (Laredo), February 23, 1972.

82. "13,000 Inmates Call Him 'The Man,'" *Lutheran Layman,* October 1, 1965.

83. "Minutes of the Texas Board of Corrections" (1968), 4177. Beto identified Jackson as "the only liberal I ever knew whom I could trust;" Donald Weisenhorn, interview with George R. Nielsen, January 14, 2003.

84. John J. DiIulio, Jr., *No Escape: The Future of American Corrections* (New York: Basic Books, 1991), 28.

85. Ibid.; "Minutes of the Texas Board of Corrections" (1969), 4669–70, 4786.

86. "Beto Outlines TDC Policies," *Houston Post,* May 26, 1972.

87. "The Inmate: A Texan Tells of Two Bitter Years," *San Antonio Express,* January 12, 1972.

88. Steve J. Martin and Sheldon Ekland-Olson, *Texas Prisons: The Walls Came Tumbling Down* (Austin: Texas Monthly Press, 1987), 27.

89. "Governors Hear Beto's View," *Houston Post,* August 14, 1971.

90. "Beto Believes Prisons Will Soon be Obsolete," *Houston Chronicle,* July 15, 1970; George Beto, Speech given at an unnamed Southern university "next to one of the great metropolitan areas," n.d., SHSU; George Beto, Speech at the National Governors' Conference, September 13, 1971, SHSU.

91. George Beto, "Continue Work, So Much To Be Done," *American Journal of Corrections* (November–December 1970), 4–7.

92. George Beto to Richard Daley, August 30, 1968, SHSU.

93. "Minutes of the Texas Board of Corrections" (1964), 3299.

94. "Minutes of the Texas Board of Corrections" (1966), 3733.

95. Martin and Eckland-Olson, 30–31.

96. "Minutes of the Texas Board of Corrections" (1969), 4669–70, 4786.

97. "Minutes of the Texas Board of Corrections" (1971), 5199–5200.

98. Martin and Ekland-Olson, 35; "Minutes of the Texas Board of Corrections" (1970), 5061–62.

99. Rolando V. del Carmen, Susan E. Ritter, and Betsy A. Witt, *Briefs of Leading Cases in Corrections* (Cincinnati: Anderson Publishing Co., 1993), 91–92.

100. "Minutes of the Texas Board of Corrections" (1970), 4796–97.

101. The American Bar Associations Young Lawyers section this year evaluated the Texas prisons as best in the nation; "When They Complain, the Top Man Listens," *Dallas Morning News,* September 19, 1971.

102. "Beto Outlines TDC Policies," *Houston Post*, May 26, 1972; "Beto Describes Fred Cruz as Nonconformist," *Houston Chronicle*, May 26, 1972.

103. "Mrs. Cruz Exonerated on Conspiracy Charge," *Houston Chronicle*, September 19, 1972.

104. Martin and Ekland-Olson, 50–51.

105. "Lawyer Sues Prisons Director; Claims Damages to Self, Felons," *Houston Post*, December 1, 1971.

106. "Minutes of the Texas Board of Corrections" (1971), 5559–5600.

107. Martin and Ekland-Olson, 52.

108. "Former Prison Boss Ordered to Pay Inmates," *Houston Chronicle*, March 20, 1976; "Decision Delayed on Beto Judgment Appeal," *Houston Post*, March 20, 1976.

109. Nancy M. Simonson to George Beto, December 15, 1980, SHSU; "Beto Loses Civil Suit to Inmates," *Houston Chronicle*, March 20, 1976. Martin reports that the costs were actually paid by TDC, which evaded the law by posting a bond for $50,000 and then forfeiting $40,704.53. See Martin and Ekland-Olson, 256.

110. "Creativity at Peak, Prison Chief to Quit," *Daily Advocate* (Victoria), October 3, 1971; Marilynn Beto, "Our Ten Years"; "Beto Recalls TDC," *The Houstonian* (Sam Houston State University), November 1984.

111. George Beto to Robert P. Heyne, February 16,1970, SHSU.

112. George Beto to Herbert H. Friese, May 15, 1972, SHSU.

113. Kyle letter.

114. George Beto to John A. Gronouski, February 26, 1972, SHSU. When Beto made plans to change his residence to Wit's End Ranch, he decided to include an outbuilding accessible from the house through the carport, which was identified as his "museum." In it he displayed his plaques, badges, saddles, letters, and other awards extended to him. In the center of the room stood a poker table for those occasions when he hosted his friends. Dan Beto e-mail message to Nielsen, October 11, 2004.

Notes to Chapter 7

1. George Beto, "Lessons in State Agency-University Cooperation," *State Government-University Relations in the South: Proceedings of a Conference on the Academic Community as a Backup Force to State Government* (Atlanta, GA: Southern Regional Education Board, 1975), 17–20; George Beto, "Speech Delivered on the Twenty-fifth Anniversary of the College of Criminal Justice," *Texas Journal of Corrections* (1990), 18–19.

2. Craig R. Copeland, "The Evolution of the Texas Department of Corrections" (master's thesis, Sam Houston State University, 1980), 256–57.

3. Beto, "Speech Delivered on the Twenty-fifth Anniversary," Sam Houston State University, Newton Gresham Library, Beto Collection (Hereafter SHSU). Sam Houston State University awarded Crews the Defenso Pacem Award in 2003.

4. Copeland, 257.

5. Arleigh Templeton, Speech delivered at the dedication of the George Beto Criminal Justice Center, SHSU; "Goodbye, George," *Huntsville Item,* September 1, 1991. In 1965 the school's name was changed to Sam Houston State College and in 1969 to Sam Houston State University.

6. "University and Prison Unite," *Houston Chronicle,* August 7, 1977; Beto, "Speech Delivered on the Twenty-fifth Anniversary."

7. Mitchel Roth, *Fulfilling a Mandate: A History of the Criminal Justice Center at Sam Houston State University* (Huntsville, TX: Sam Houston State University Press, 1997), 15, 18.

8. "Goodbye, George," *Huntsville Item*; Roth, 26.

9. Roth, 35.

10. Ibid., 36, 41.

11. Ibid., 36.

12. Ibid., 89; *Huntsville Item,* August 24, 198.

13. Beto, "Speech Delivered at the Twenty-fifth Anniversary."

14. "Chair Established at Sam Houston in Honor of Beto," *Houston Chronicle,* July 17, 1979.

15. Jack Kyle to David M. Horton, January 15, 2000, in possession of Horton.

16. David M. Horton, Syllabi and notes, 1976–1978.

17. Students were amused by his aphorisms, and lists of "Betoisms" circulated around the campus. The following selection is drawn from these lists: "He's like a catfish: all mouth and no brains"; "Man's inhumanity to man is as old as mankind itself"; "That's like pulling hen's teeth"; "No more morals than a billy goat"; "As right as rain"; "As popular as sin"; "He speaks from a well of ignorance"; "It has fallen on evil days"; "Like nailing Jello to a tree"; "Like vultures over a rotting carcass"; "Repent of the errors of his ways"; "You don't have to be able to lay an egg to be able to criticize an omelet"; "Experience is a great teacher, but the tuition is so high"; "I'm not a prophet nor the seventh son of a prophet"; and "Never confuse change with progress."

18. "Death Penalty," *Houston Post,* July 7, 1976.

19. Roger F. Noreen to George Beto, April 24, 1973, SHSU; George Beto to Laurie Caplane, April 18, 1977, SHSU. Beto's caution with signing

a book contract may have been influenced by his attempt at writing one while he was at TDC. In 1963 he agreed to write a 26,000-word manuscript for Concordia Publishing House as one volume in a series titled "The Christian Man in the World." Seven years later, after extensive correspondence between author and editor, and numerous drafts, Beto found the result less than what he hoped for and the manuscript was never published. The original drafts of the manuscript are in the possession of the Beto family.

20. Beth Beto O'Donnell to the authors, August 27, 2003, in possession of authors.

21. George Beto to J. J. Pickle, September 22,1972, SHSU; "Dr. Beto Claims Real Purposes of Prisons Undefined," *The Battalion* (College Station), September 21, 1972; "Beto, Ex-Texas Prison Chief, Attacks Penal Code as 'Unfair'," *Houston Chronicle*, September 22, 1972; "Beto Urges Quick Penal Reform," *Dallas Times Herald*, March 7, 1973; "Beto Speaks of Constitution, Prisons," *Eastfield Era*, November 19, 1973; "Acts 'Illegal, Unethical'; Beto Quits Prison Reform; Brooks 'Terse,'" *Huntsville Item*, August 25, 1974; "County Jails Medieval, Says Beto," *Austin American Statesman*, October 22, 1975; "Death Penalty," *Houston Post*, July 7, 1976; "Ex-Prison Official Says Apathy Hurts," *Commercial Appeal* (Memphis), November 29, 1980; George Beto, "Continue Work, So Much to be Done," (Presidential Address), *American Journal of Corrections* (November–December 1970), 4–7.

22. Frank R. Kemerer, *William Wayne Justice* (Austin: University of Texas Press, 1991), 357–61. Beto, "Continue Work."

23. "Texas System of Corrections Praised, Sued," *Chattanooga Times,* February 4, 1979.

24. Ibid.; Bruce Jackson in "Texas Prisons Go on Trial," argues that the zeal of the Civil Rights Division of the Department of Justice was based on its desire to validate the new correctional standards published by the Justice Department. *The Nation* (October 24, 1978), 437–39.

25. W. J. "Jim" Estelle, Jr., interview, July 23, 2000, in possession of David M. Horton.

26. Ibid.; Dick J. Reavis, "How They Ruined Our Prisons," *Texas Monthly* (May 1985), 242.

27. *Dallas Times Herald,* September 27, 1984; Estelle interview with Horton.

28. For more on the prison system see David M. Horton and Ryan K. Turner, *Lone Star Justice* (Austin: Eakin Press, 1999), 237–38.

29. George Beto to Wayne K. Patterson, November 5, 1984, SHSU; John J. DiIulio, Jr., *Governing Prisons: A Comparative Study of Correctional Management* (New York: The Free Press, 1987), 205, 215–16; Reavis, 152–246.

30. DiIulio, 211.

31. Ibid., 113–16.

32. Ibid., 219, 229. For other views see Steve J. Martin and Sheldon Ekland-Olson, *Texas Prisons: The Walls Came Tumbling Down* (Austin: Texas Monthly Press, 1987), and Ben M. Crouch and James W. Marquart, *An Appeal to Justice: Litigated Reform of Texas Prisons* (Austin: University of Texas Press, 1981).

33. William P. Barrett, "Life," *Houston City Magazine*, April 1982, 53–84.

34. George Beto, "Introduction of the Honorable William Wayne Justice," 114th Congress of the American Correctional Association, San Antonio, Texas, August 20, 1984, SHSU.

35. "Ex-TDC Head Says Cost of Prisons Will Force Shorter Sentences," *Houston Chronicle*, May 15, 1981; "Ex-TDC Director: No-Parole Laws Stupid," *San Antonio Express News*, February 8, 1989; "A Clash of Philosophies," *Dallas Morning News*, May 21, 1981; "Ex-Director of Prisons Lashes Out," *Fort Worth Star Telegram*, February 17, 1982; "Beto Says He Was Wrong About Crime," *Huntsville Item*, February 18, 1982; Lonnie Grigs, "Dr. George Beto," *Joint Endeavor*, September 1982; The Philosophical Society of Texas, *Proceedings of the Annual Meeting, Galveston, Texas, December 3 and 4, 1982* (Austin, TX: The Philosophical Society, 1983), 45–50; George Beto, Karl Menninger Lecture, Washburn University, Topeka, Kansas, November 20, 1986; George J. Beto, "Prison Administration and the Eighth Amendment," Speech at School of Law, Valparaiso, Indiana, November 9, 1991.

36. Donald Weisenhorn interview, January 29, 2003, in possession of George R. Nielsen. In the *Lutheran Standard* (February 2, 1971), Beto wrote cynically, "Groups of judges, meeting in conferences in Maryland and Nevada, spent some token time in state penal institutions and emerged as stridently vocal and highly critical penal experts."

37. George Beto to Orson L. McCotter, April 9, 1984, SHSU.

38. DiIulio, *Governing Prisons*, 227; Beto "Lessons in State Agency-University Cooperation." Beto even objected to Gov. Clements' attempts to apply the business style to corrections and said that "management by objectives is hot air in a halo. It may work for General Motors but when you are delivering social services, it's not so easy." Beto conceded it was difficult to speak against Clements' business ideal. "Being against it is like being against righteousness." "Clements Managerial View Labeled 'Hot Air in a Halo,'" *Houston Chronicle*, April 18, 1980.

39. Clemens Bartollas, *Introduction to Corrections* (New York: Harper and Row, 1981), 309.

40. DiIulio, *Governing Prisons*, 332.

41. Martin and Ekland-Olson, 170.

42. George Beto, "I was in Prison: Christian Challenge," Speech at The Christian and the Criminal Workshop, February 27, 1974, SHSU.

43. "Beto 'Pleased' With Proposed New Document," *Huntsville Item,* October 31, 1973; "New Document Not Ideal," *Eastfield Era,* November 19, 1973.

44. "Beto Plans Trip, Check on Prison," *Houston Post,* October 12, 1972; "Beto Recommends Some Changes in Mississippi Prisons," *Democrat* (Marlin), October 26, 1972; "Former Texas Prison Head Gets $100 A Day as Consultant on Mississippi Penal System," *Globe Times* (Amarillo), October 27, 1972. He then traveled to Colorado to advise them as well.

45. John P. Conrad, "From Barbarism toward Decency: Alabama's Long Road to Prison Reform," *Journal of Research in Crime and Delinquency* (November 1989), 311; Kemerer, 360.

46. "State Penologist Asked to Serve in Alabama," *Dallas Morning News,* February 1, 1976; "Prison Consultant to Advise James," *Montgomery Advertiser,* February 20, 1979; "James Meets Prison Expert," February 21, 1979; Ralph Knowles, Jr., "Monitoring Committee on Prisons in Alabama Folds; Court Gives Up Jurisdiction," *Journal of the National Prison Project* (Summer 1989), 5.

47. "U.S. Judge Relinquishes Control of Alabama Prison System," *New York Times,* January 15, 1989.

48. John J.DiIulio, Jr., *No Escape: The Future of American Corrections* (New York: Basic Books, 1991), 170–72.

49. "Beto Returns to SHSU Following U.N. Congress," *Houstonian* (Huntsville), September 26, 1975.

50. "Dr. Beto to Study Confinement in Germany," *Houston Chronicle,* May 5, 1974.

51. Beto Family Roundtable, September 19, 1998, in possession of David M. Horton.

52. Andrew Adams to George Beto, February 13, 1976, SHSU. In later speeches when Beto talked about the importance of the family in society, he referred to the low crime rate in Egypt, which had poverty, but strong families.

53. Beto Family Roundtable; "Beto Studies Japanese Prison System," *Bryan-College Station Eagle,* June 19, 1990.

54. Ron Jackson interview with George Nielsen, January 6, 2004; Kemerer, 149, 160, 168–75; "Texas Youth Commission," *The Handbook of Texas Online*; "Governor Appoints Beto to Texas Youth Council," *Houston Post,* May 6, 1975.

55. "Beto Pushed for FBI Position," *Houston Post,* December 13, 1977.

56. "Ex-Prison Director Nominated for top FBI Post," *Dallas Times Herald,* December 13, 1977.

57. Ibid.

58. "FBI Director Suggestion Criticized" *Houston Post,* December 14, 1977.

59. George Beto, Speech at Honors Convocation, Sam Houston State University, April 15, 1982, SHSU.

60. George Beto, "A Gift of Memories from Grandpa"; George Beto to Wallace C. Thompson, August 2, 1961, SHSU; George Beto to W. C. Mullan, November 28, 1988, SHSU.

61. George Beto to Herbert Freise, May 10, 1974, SHSU; Beto commented that Bruce Jackson was "the only liberal I ever knew whom I could trust." Don Wisenhorn interview.

62. *Lutheran Witness,* March 1968, 12.

63. Jack Kyle interview, February 24, 2003, in possession of George R. Nielsen.

64. Beto Family Roundtable.

65. Max Rogers to Billy Bittle, n.d., SHSU. In 1966 Beto kept a record of poker gains and losses for the entire year and in that year ended with a net gain of $3.85. George Beto to Hartwig Schwehn, December 22, 1966, SHSU.

66. George Beto to Judge Max Rogers and Joe Foy, January 29, 1974, SHSU.

67. George Beto to Bill Todd, December 15, 1965, SHSU; Estate of H. H. Coffield to George Beto, October 11, 1991, Concordia Historical Institute.

68. Dan Richard Beto interview, April 19, 1998, in possession of David M. Horton; *Victoria Advocate,* September 16, 1979.

69. Marilynn Beto, December 4, 1991, "The Day George Died," BFA; Paul Bohot interview, July 21, 1998, in possession of David M. Horton. Daughter Lynn Vann had preceded George in death as the result of an automobile accident in Houston in 1978. Her age was thirty-two.

70. Bohot interview; "George J. Beto Dies at Age 75," *Huntsville Item,* December 4, 1991.

71. *The Mandate* (College of Criminal Justice Sam Houston State University), Winter, 1992.

72. Beto, "Speech Delivered on the Twenty-fifth Anniversary." D. V. "Red" Kaskle considers Beto's efforts for the education for the TDC staff as a major contribution. Interview with D. V. "Red" McKaskle, September 27, 2004, in possession of George R. Nielsen.

73. "Beto to SHSU Graduates: Defend Democracy," *Huntsville Item,* May 10, 1987; George Beto, "Commencement Address," Sam Houston State University, May 9, 1987, SHSU.

74. George Beto, Speech at ROTC Commissioning Ceremonies, Sam Houston State University, May 8, 1981, BFA.

Selected Bibliography

Archives and Manuscript Collections

Beto Family Archives, Austin, Texas.
—Personal papers in possession of the family.
Concordia Historical Institute, St. Louis, Missouri.
—George J. Beto Files.
—Reports and Memorials of Synodical Conventions.
Concordia Seminary, Archives, Fort Wayne, Indiana.
—George J. Beto Files.
Concordia University, Archives, Austin, Texas.
—Minutes of the Board of Control.
Sam Houston State University, Newton Gresham Library, Huntsville, Texas.
—The George John Beto Papers fill six four-drawer file cabinets. The collection has been indexed by Professor Donald Weisenhorn.
Texas State Library, Archives, Austin, Texas.
—*Annual Reports of the Texas Prison Board* (1949–1963).
—*Annual Reports of the Texas Department of Corrections* (1963–1973).
—Biographical and Historical Files.
—Minutes of the Texas Prison Board.
—Minutes of the Texas Board of Correction.

Interviews

Beto, Dan Richard. Interview with David M. Horton, April 19, 1998.
———. Interview with George R. Nielsen, January 13, 2003.
Beto Family Roundtable with David M. Horton, September 19, 1998.
Beto, Marilynn. Interview with David M. Horton, April 21, 1998.
———. Interview with George R. Nielsen, January 12, 2003
Beto, Jr., Louis Henry. Interview with David M. Horton, June 22–23, 1998.
Bohot, Paul. Interview with David M. Horton. July 21, 1998.
Dinda, Richard. Interview with David M. Horton, July 1, 1998.

Eifert, Martin. Interview with George R. Nielsen, January 15, 2003.
Estelle, W. J. "Jim." Interview with David M. Horton, July 23, 2000.
Goltermann, Samuel, Telephone Interview with George R. Nielsen, December 9, 2002.
Huber, Curtis E. Interview with David Horton, September 14, 1998.
Kyle, Jack. Interview with David M. Horton, September 21, 1998.
————.Telephone Interview with George R. Nielsen, February 24, 2003.
Linderman, James. Interview with David M. Horton, July 8, 1998.
McKaskle, D. V. "Red."Interview with George R. Nielsen, September 27, 2004.
Martens, Ray. Interview with David M. Horton, March 4, 1998.
Riemer, Milton. Interview with David M. Horton, March 6, 1998.
Sorrell, Henry. Telephone Interview with David M. Horton. August 27, 1998.
Viehweg, Fred. Interview with David M. Horton, July 2, 1998.
Weisenhorn, Donald. Telephone Interview with George R. Nielsen, January 14, 2003; January 29, 2003.
Wilkins, Robert. Telephone Interview with David M. Horton, July 23, 1998.
Wright, Robert J. Interview with David M. Horton, August 27, 1998.
Wukasch, Charles. Interview with David M. Horton, July 7, 1998.
Zoch, Ted. Interview with David M. Horton, August 20, 1998.

Newspapers

Amarillo, Texas. *Globe Times.*
Austin, Texas. *Austin American Statesman.*
Bryan, Texas. *Bryan-College Station Eagle*
Dallas, Texas. *Dallas Morning News.*
— *Dallas Times Herald.*
Fort Worth, Texas. *Forth Worth Star Telegram.*
Great Falls, Montana. *Great Falls Tribune.*
Houston, Texas. *Houston Chronicle.*
— *Houston Post.*
Huntsville, Texas. *Huntsville Item.*
Lena, Illinois. *Lena Weekly Star.*
Marlin, Texas. *Democrat.*
Memphis, Tennessee. *Commercial Appeal.*
Mesquite, Texas. *Eastfield Era.*
Montgomery, Alabama. *Montgomery Advertiser*
Nashville, Tennessee. *Nashville Tennessean.*
New York, New York. *The New York Times.*
Laredo, Texas. *Daily Times.*

San Angelo, Texas. *San Angelo Standard-Times.*
San Antonio, Texas. *San Antonio Express.*
—*San Antonio Light.*
Springfield, Illinois. *Illinois State Journal.*
—*Illinois State Register.*
Taylor, Texas. *Daily Press.*
Victoria, Texas. *Daily Advocate.*

Journals, Reports, Student Publications, and Film

A Lamp Unto Thy Feet (CBS Television, 1970)
Battalion (College Station, Texas)
Concordia Enterprize (Austin, Texas).
Concordia Informer (Austin, Texas).
[Concordia] *The Record* (Austin, Texas).
[Concordia] *Sem Quill* (Springfield, Illinois)
[Concordia] *The Springfielder* (Springfield, Illinois).
Echo (Inmate newspaper. Huntsville, Texas).
Houstonian (Huntsville, Texas).
Huntsville Pictorial.
Reports and Recommendations of the Illinois Youth Commission. Springfield: Governor's Committee on the Youth Commission, 1962.
Rotary Review (Springfield, Illinois).
St. Louis, Missouri. *The Lutheran Layman.*
—*The Lutheran Witness*
Texas Journal of Corrections.
Texas Magazine (Houston Chronicle).
Texas Police Journal.

Books and Theses

Anon. *History of Stevenson County.* Mount Morris, IL: Kable Printing Company, 1972.
Barnhart, William E., and Eugene F. Schlickman. *Kerner: The Conflict of Intangible Results.* Urbana: University of Illinois Press, 1999.
Bartollas, Clemens, *Introduction to Corrections.* New York: Harper and Row, 1981.
Copeland, R. Craig. "The Evolution of the Texas Department of Corrections." Master's thesis, Sam Houston State University, 1980.
Crichton, Robert. *The Great Impostor.* New York: Random House, 1959.
Crouch, Ben M., and James W. Marquart. *An Appeal to Justice: Litigated Reform of Texas Prisons.* Austin: University of Texas Press, 1981.

Del Carmen, Rolando V., Susan E. Ritter, and Betsy A. Witt. *Briefs of Leading Cases in Corrections.* Cincinnati: Anderson, 1993.

Dickinson, Richard. *Roses and Thorns: The Centennial Edition of Black Lutheran Mission and Ministry in the Lutheran Church-Missouri Synod.* St. Louis: Concordia, Publishing House, 1977.

DiIulio, John J., Jr., *Governing Prisons: A Comparative Study of Correctional Management.* New York: Free Press, 1987.

————. *No Escape: The Future of American Corrections.* New York: Basic Books, 1991.

Erickson, Gladys A. *Warden Ragen of Joliet.* New York: Dutton, 1957.

Heintzen, Erich H. *Prairie School of the Prophets: The Anatomy of a Seminary, 1846–1976.* St. Louis: Concordia Publishing House, 1989.

Horton, David M., and Ryan K. Turner. *Lone Star Justice.* Austin: Eakin Press, 1999.

Jacobs, James B. *Stateville: The Penitentiary in Mass Society.* Chicago: University of Chicago Press, 1977.

Martens, Ray, ed. *Concordia of Texas.* Austin: Concordia Lutheran College of Texas, 1977.

Martin, Steve J., and Sheldon Ekland-Olson. *Texas Prisons: The Walls Came Tumbling Down.* Austin: Texas Monthly Press, 1987.

Robinson, Ellwyn B. *History of North Dakota.* Lincoln: University of Nebraska, 1966.

Roth, Mitchel. *Fulfilling a Mandate: A History of the Criminal Justice Center at Sam Houston State University.* Huntsville: Sam Houston Press, 1997.

Articles

Banks, Jimmy. "His Work is His Relaxation," *Texas Star* (June 25, 1972).

Barrett, William P. "Life." *Houston City Magazine* (April 1982).

Conrad, John P. "From Barbarism Toward Decency: Alabama's Long Road to Prison Reform," *Journal of Research in Crime and Delinquency* (November 1989).

"Austin H. MacCormick." *Current Biography* (July 1951).

Duncan, J. S. "Richard Bennett Hubbard and State Resumption of the Penitentiary, 1876–1878." *Texana* (1974).

Evans, Charlie. "Behind the Prison Bars: A Progress Report on Texas' Dramatic Prison Reform." *Texas Parade,* (February 1954).

Giggs, Lonnie, and Walter Walker. "Dr. George Beto: An Interview." *Joint Endeavor* (August–September 1982).

Jackson, Bruce. "Texas Prisons Go on Trial." *The Nation* (October 24, 1978).

Knowles, Ralph L., Jr. "Monitoring Committee on Prisons in Alabama Folds, Gives Up Jurisdiction." *Journal of the National Prison Project* (Summer 1989).

Krause, Werner. "Biographical Record for Louis Henry Beto." *Service Bulletin 3A.* (St. Louis: Concordia Historical Institute. February 19, 1990).

MacCormick, Austin. "Behind Those Prison Riots." *Reader's Digest* (December 1953).

"November Profile: Dr. George Beto." *Texas Public Employee* (November 1962).

Nordyke, Lewis. "Pete Coffield: A Friend of Good Boys and Convicts." *Texas Parade* (June 1959).

Reavis, Dick J. "How They Ruined Our Prisons." *Texas Monthly* (May 1985).

"The Texas Prison Industrial Complex: A Growing Threat to Free Enterprise?" *Texas Business and Industry* (September 1969).

Wahlberg, Rachel Conrad, "Texas Prison Boss." *The Lutheran* (March 13, 1963).

Weisenhorn, Donald. "George Beto." *The Mandate* (Winter 1992).

Wright, Robert J. "Austin MacCormick: A Memorial Statement." *Corrections Today* (January–February 1980)

Yoder, R. M. "Trouble Shooter of the Big House," *Saturday Evening Post* (May 12, 1951).

Index